Cutting and the Pedagogy of Self-Disclosure

Also by Jeffrey Berman

Joseph Conrad: Writing as Rescue
The Talking Cure: Literary Representations of Psychoanalysis
Narcissism and the Novel
Diaries to an English Professor
Surviving Literary Suicide
Risky Writing: Self-Disclosure and Self-Transformation in the Classroom
Empathic Teaching: Education for Life
Dying to Teach: A Memoir of Love, Loss, and Learning

CUTTING

and the Pedagogy of Self-Disclosure

JEFFREY BERMAN
PATRICIA HATCH WALLACE

University of Massachusetts Press / Amherst

LC 2007032768
ISBN 978-1-55849-615-6 (paper); 614-9 (library cloth)

Designed by Sally Nichols
Set in Electra
Printed and bound by The Maple-Vail Book Manufacturing Group, Inc.

Library of Congress Cataloging-in-Publication Data
Berman, Jeffrey, 1945–
    Cutting and the pedagogy of self-disclosure / Jeffrey Berman,
Patricia Hatch Wallace.
        p. ; cm.
    Includes bibliographical references and index.
    ISBN 978-1-55849-615-6 (pbk. : alk. paper)—ISBN 978-1-55849-614-9 (library
cloth : alk. paper)
1. Self-injurious behavior.   2. College students—Mental health.
3. College students' writings.   4. Mental illness in literature.
5. Self-disclosure.   I. Wallace, Patricia Hatch, 1970–   II. Title.
    [DNLM: 1. Self-Injurious Behavior—psychology.
2. Self-Injurious Behavior—therapy.   3. Self Disclosure.
4. Students.   5. Universities.   6. Writing.   WM 165 B516c 2007]
    RC569.5.S48B47 2007
    616.85'82—dc22   2007032768

CONTENTS

ACKNOWLEDGMENTS

Jeff's greatest debt of thanks is to his coauthor, Patricia Hatch Wallace, who was the inspiration behind this book. Part 1 of *Cutting and the Pedagogy of Self-Disclosure* is based largely on Patty's 2004 master's thesis at the University at Albany, "Contagion in Cutting." It was a joy to watch Patty develop from an outstanding master's student to a scholar of distinction, unafraid to challenge some of the long-standing clinical assumptions behind self-injurious behavior. "One repays a teacher badly if one remains only a pupil," Nietzsche observed wryly; Patty has long ceased being a student! She was also unafraid to use her real name, a decision that was not easy for her to make. As she observes in the Conclusion of Part 1, "self-disclosure of this magnitude is scary," but she was willing to use her own name to help others understand their own reasons for cutting. Jeff is also indebted to "Maryann," "Paige," and their classmates at the University at Albany. These students include Stephen Arena, Idalia Avila, Stefanie Bizan, Peter Bouleris, Julia Brandel, Kelly Burgess, Andrew Carnevale, Nicole Chernyakhovsky, Danielle Cothren, Vanessa D'Arcy, Kimberly Elia, Chelsea Facci, Tom Fitzgerald, Amelia Gagliano, Theresa Galgano, David Grimes, Emily Guckemas, Kristen Hagan, Erin Hale, Derek Halpern, Katelyn Holden, Jeremy Hosier, Stacey Husband, Alex Hyde, Marcy Isabella, Roy Kilkeary, Sara Kluberdanz, Travis Landry, Victoria Lawton, Natalie Lesser, Christian Louie, Stephanie Mazzotta, Kevin Meadows, Erin Medlar, Caitlin Monahan, Ariel Munoz, Angela Muscolino, Jay Peck, Lexie Pray, Lindsay Ragozzino, Charles Rezoagli, Erin Schambach, Elizabeth Schroeder, Laura Seestadt, Lauren Selmon, Erika Snyder, Randi Strauss, Crystal Sweet, Meredith Torres, Olivia Urcia, Lynn Weiss, and Dan Wiessner. Their willingness to write about their own cutting experiences and share their responses to classmates' essays on cutting made possible Part 2 of this book. They were exemplary in their empathic understanding of and respect for each other. Special thanks to Desma DeGraw. No one made a "cutting" criticism during class discussions.

Cutting and the Pedagogy of Self-Disclosure is Jeff's fifth book published by the University of Massachusetts Press, and he is grateful to everyone associated with the Press: Bruce Wilcox, Director; Clark Dougan, Senior Editor; Carol Betsch, Managing Editor; and Anne S. Gibbons, copy editor par excellence. Jeff is also grateful to Deborah Britzman, Distinguished Research Professor at York University; Marvin Krims, M.D., Lecturer in Psychiatry at Harvard Medical School; and Mark Bracher, Professor of English at Kent State University.

Patty wishes to thank Jeff Berman, an outstanding teacher, adviser, and person, for his wisdom, guidance, and patience during this long book-writing process. She could not have done it without him, and probably *would* not have done it without him! She is grateful for the extrinsic motivation Jeff provided, and for the kindness he has shown to her and to all of his students.

Patty also wishes to thank her husband Brett, her friend Sam Kastrinakis for the cookies that weren't, and everyone who was supportive of, understanding of, and happy for her.

INTRODUCTION

"Why Would I Have Ever Cut Myself?"
Patricia Hatch Wallace
Journal on *Surviving Literary Suicide*

English 581
July 28, 2003

I saw the reading list for this course in the summer catalog. It intrigued me, as did the course description. I was taking a spring semester class at the time, and I asked a woman who sat next to me if she had ever taken Jeffrey Berman for anything. She said she had, and that he was excellent. I decided to register for this course, and I promptly set out finding the books. I shop a lot on Half.com for textbooks and novels, and honestly expected to find the books I needed available for purchase—except yours. Why did I think that? Maybe because I had in mind a "local author" and I wasn't sure your book was being used nationwide. Well, I was wrong, as I am sure you know. I was able to get your book on Half.com, and it was the first one I received. I began reading it almost right away with great interest. First, the subject matter seemed very interesting to me. I was finishing up a course on Joan Didion and Ernest Hemingway, so I read chapter 4 ["Ernest Hemingway's Suicideophobia"] first. I immediately liked your prose style, and the very conversational tone of your writing. I thought to myself, I am going to love this class.

I didn't read the rest of Surviving Literary Suicide *until I saw our course syllabus. While part of me was relieved that we didn't have to read the whole book, the other part of me knew I would read it anyway. Chapter 1 is very eye-opening to say the least. The statistics on suicidal thinking make a lot of sense. I am a high school teacher, and it helps me to have these figures reinforced, so I am more alert to the very real possibility/probability that some of my own students are considering suicide as an option. It also brings to mind my own very painful adolescence, and the times I cut my arms and wrists. No, I never cut deeply enough to kill myself. It wasn't until many years afterward, while reading* Reviving Ophelia *and working in a residen-*

tial school with very troubled kids and girls who cut themselves, that I began to understand my own self-destructive behaviors. As a teenager, I was so hurt inside that I needed to manifest that pain on the outside as well, where it made sense and I could actually see my pain. How difficult it is for me to even think about that—recall it—share it with you. My own husband does not know I was a cutter. My parents refused to see it. I have distanced myself so much from the me of 17 years ago, it seems like I am thinking about a different person. But, upon scrutiny of the inside of my left forearm, halfway between my wrist and elbow, there is a very clear scar in the shape of a heart. How this has escaped the notice of people for so long I don't know—maybe they are just too polite or embarrassed to say anything. After all, I am a teacher, I am finishing my second master's degree, and I live a "normal" life—why would I have ever cut myself? Good question.

I don't know anyone who has committed suicide. I contemplated it many times in my youth, but, being the eternal optimist, I always thought, hey, I'll just wait and see if things get better. If not, I can always kill myself later! I wonder about Sylvia Plath, and what made her fail at so many attempts. Was she really trying? Did part of her have the will to live—enough to thwart her attempt? And in chapter 2 of Surviving Literary Suicide ["Romanticizing Suicide in Kate Chopin's Awakening"], thinking about Edna—did she have other options? Maybe she could have just gone on with her life the way it was. It didn't seem so bad. It's so easy as an outsider, and someone who has become a very positive person, to say, "Why would anyone do that?" But, this book has really helped to open my eyes and consider the individual circumstances of both real and fictional people, and I know that in both cases, the idea of suicide is very real.

Finally, I will mention chapter 8 ["Conclusion: Returning from the Dead"] of your book. It helped me think a lot about these diaries and what we use them for. I know I am able to put so much on paper that I could never say aloud—to anyone. Funny, I barely know you, but I can put my life in my diaries to you—my cutting history—and it's OK. It seems many of the students you have written about in the chapter felt the same way. Diaries gave them (and me) a safe haven, an almost anonymous place to be *real. I also was very disturbed about Mary, and your description on page 260 of what she went through. I have heard you talk in class about some people's opinions that your "Literary Suicide" class was dangerous. I guess for people like Mary, anything can be a danger. Is it your fault? Of course not. Is it the class's fault? Of course not. Was it Mary's fault? I don't know. But Mary had some serious problems before taking your class, which might be the reason she was drawn to the title of it anyway. I always think in situations like that one about the cartoon Tom and Jerry. My brother and I used to watch that cartoon every day, sometimes many times in a day. However, we never tried to hit each other with irons, burn each other with matches, hit each other with a broom, etc. Why? Because we could differentiate between make-believe and reality. Maybe some people can't—or maybe for them, the two are one.*

Thank you for an excellent course.

We begin with Patty's final reader-response diary written for Jeff Berman's graduate English class the Age of Freud at the University at Albany, State University of New York. Her entry on *Surviving Literary Suicide* was the first time that she wrote about the troubled period in her life when she cut herself. The entry is a striking example of what Jeff calls "risky writing," personal writing containing painful or shameful feelings that expose the writer's vulnerability.

Patty's diary reveals many of the ambiguities of cutting, including its complex relationship to suicide. She is aware of the high incidence of suicidal thinking, especially among young people. As Kay Redfield Jamison notes in *Night Falls Fast*:

> Suicide in the young, which has at least tripled over the past forty-five years, is, without argument, one of our most serious public health problems. Suicide is the third leading cause of death in young people in the United States and the second for college students. The 1995 National College Health Risk Behavior Survey, conducted by the Centers for Disease Control and Prevention, found that one in ten college students had seriously considered suicide during the year prior to the survey; most had gone so far as to draw up a plan.
>
> The figures for high school students surveyed in 1997 are even more worrying. One in five high school students said he or she had seriously

considered suicide during the preceding year, and most of them had drawn up a suicide plan. Nearly one student in ten actually attempted suicide during the twelve-month period. One out of three of the suicide attempts was serious enough to require medical attention. (21–22)

Patty's knowledge of the high incidence of suicidal thinking, along with her experiences as a high school teacher, elicits memories of her own unhappy youth, when she cut her arms and wrists and thought about ending her life. Depression underlies nearly all suicide attempts and suicide completions, and it is a major reason people cut themselves. Self-mutilation may take many forms, including self-cutting, self-burning, and skin-pulling. Whatever its form, symptomatology is "overdetermined"— that is, symptoms reveal multiple causes and interpretations. Cutting is often considered a self-destructive action, yet paradoxically, people who cut themselves generally do not wish to die but to find relief from unbearable psychological pain. Many people who cut themselves feel psychically numb; cutting themselves and seeing drops of blood remind them that they are still alive. In the memoir *Girl, Interrupted* about her year-and-a-half institutionalization at McLean Hospital, Susanna Kaysen includes her psychiatrist's clinical case notes about her state of depersonalization: "She felt that she wasn't a real person, nothing but skin. She talked about wanting to cut herself to see whether she would bleed to prove to herself that she was a real person. She mentioned that she would like to see an X-ray of herself to see if she has any bones or anything inside" (105). The pain that a cutter feels is thus, in a grim way, welcome—which is one of the reasons that it is so difficult for a cutter to give up this behavior. And so cutting may be viewed as both self-destructive and self-preservative for those who dwell in a nightmarish world of death-in-life. As Caroline Kettlewell observes in her memoir, *Skin Game* : "I kept cutting, because it worked. When I cut, I felt better for a while. When I cut, my life no longer overwhelmed me. I felt too keenly the threat of chaos, of how things can get away from you in a thousand ways. Bodies expand, grades plummet, pets die, paint peels, ice caps melt, genocide erupts. Entropy keeps eating at the ramparts, and I cut to try to shore them up. I cut to lay down a line between before and after, between self and other, chaos and clarity. I cut as an affirmation of hope, saying, *I have drawn the line and I am still on this side of it*" (176; emphasis in original).

Apart from the psychological meanings of self-mutilation, cutting is literally inscribing one's body, writing both on and about the body. Those who cut themselves are suffering writers, the suffering both a cause and an effect of their fleshly writing. To the extent that cutting produces pain, blood, and scars, it is also about self-victimization, self-crucifixion, and self-exposure. Insofar as most cutters are female, narratives of cutting are predominantly women's writing, like stories of eating disorders.

Self-Mutilation: An Ancient and Modern Phenomenon

Self-mutilation is a peculiarly modern phenomenon, but its roots can be traced to antiquity. Anthropologist Erving Goffman points out that the "Greeks, who were apparently strong on visual aids, originated the term *stigma* to refer to bodily signs designed to expose something unusual and bad about the moral status of the signifier. The signs were cut or burnt into the body and advertised that the bearer was a slave, a criminal, or a traitor—a blemished person, ritually polluted, to be avoided, especially in public places" (1). Psychiatrist Armando Favazza, whose book *Bodies under Siege: Self-Mutilation in Culture and Psychiatry* is cited by nearly every researcher in the field, points out that mutilation scenes may be found throughout literature, including in Sophocles' *Oedipus Rex*, Ovid's *Metamorphoses*, Catullus's poem about the self-emasculation of Attis, and Shakespeare's *Titus Andronicus* (18).

There are several references in the Old and New Testament to cutting, including Leviticus 19:28, Jeremiah 16:6, and Mark 5:5. I Kings 18:28 refers to men who "cried aloud, and cut themselves after their manner with knives and lancets, till the blood gushed out upon them," a ritual that, as Mollie Robins suggests, may have "something to do with the shedding of blood as an atonement for wrong doings" (PSYART, 5 October 2003). Self-mutilation is common in the Old Testament among those who worship false gods, such as Baal, but it is less common in the New Testament, where it is associated with devil-worship. Sharon Klayman Farber writes that despite several biblical injunctions against cutting, Jesus is said to have favored "self-castration, self-enucleation, and self-amputation" (66). She cites a well-known passage from Matthew 18:8–9 that has served as the religious justification for many cutters: "Wherefore if thy hand or thy foot offend thee, cut them off, and cast them from thee: it is better for thee to enter into life halt or maimed, rather than having two hands or two feet to be cast into everlasting fire."

The most famous nineteenth-century cutter was Vincent Van Gogh, who sliced off part of his ear lobe and sent it to a prostitute. His motivation for doing so remains unclear. The French photographer and painter Dora Maar, who had a nine-year relationship with Pablo Picasso, was a cutter. According to the online encyclopedia Wikipedia, Picasso was "attracted by her beauty and self-mutilation (cutting her fingers and the table—he got her bloody gloves and exhibited them on a shelf in his apartment)."

Self-mutilation appears in several adult and teenage films. In Ingmar Bergman's *Cries and Whispers*, Ingrid Thulin, reflecting on her lifeless marriage, utters the words "It's but a tissue of lies" and inserts a shard of glass into her vagina in a grisly act of self-cutting. She then lies on her bed, looking at her husband as she smears vaginal blood on her face. In *The Piano Teacher*, based on the novel by Nobel laureate Elfriede Jelinek, Isabelle Huppert cuts herself. Jelinek compares the act of cutting to a bride's loss of virginity. "From an intricate package, she carefully unwraps a razor blade. She always takes it everywhere. The blade smiles like a bridegroom at a bride. SHE gingerly tests the edge; it is razor sharp. Then she presses the blade into the back of her hand several times, but not so deep as to injure tendons. It doesn't hurt at all. The metal slices her hand like butter. For an instant, a slit gapes in the previously intact tissue; then the arduously tamed blood rushes out from behind the barrier. She makes a total of four cuts. That's enough, otherwise she'll bleed to death" (43–44). The piano teacher feels almost nothing even when she cuts or pricks herself. "She is as unfeeling as a piece of tar paper in the rain" (75). Later she cuts her vagina. "SHE sits down in front of the magnifying side of the shaving mirror; spreading her legs, she makes a cut, magnifying the aperture that is the doorway into her body. She knows from experience that such a razor cut doesn't hurt, for her arms, hands, and legs have often served as guinea pigs. Her hobby is cutting her own body" (86).

Even more disturbing than *The Piano Teacher* is the French film *In My Skin*. Written, directed, and starring Marina de Van, the film is difficult to watch, for it depicts self-mutilation that approaches self-cannibalism. After gashing her leg in a fall, Esther does not realize she is bleeding, but when she does, she begins to pick at the wound and then cuts her arm, leg, and face, smearing blood over her body. We are given no reasons for her compulsive actions; until her accident, she seems to have everything she desires. Nor does the film explain why her savage self-mutilation is more sexually satisfying than making love to her boyfriend. It is hard for viewers not to feel nauseated when she begins to tear greedily at her own flesh, which she devours cannibalistically. Self-cutting is for Esther a deadly pleasure, far more terrifying than Glenn Close's self-injurious behavior in *Fatal Attraction*. Teenage cutters appear in *Thirteen* and *Secretary*. Most cutters in films, as in life, are females, but male cutting may be seen in *Breaking Point,* in which the Viennese Aktion artist Gunther Brus cut his penis with a razor. Several well-known actors and actresses have acknowledged cutting themselves, including Johnny Depp (the eponymous character he plays in *Edward Scissorhands* cuts everything, including his body, albeit unintentionally), Courtney Love, Angelina Jolie, and Fiona Apple. The most famous celebrity-cutter was Princess Diana, who cut herself on the arms and legs with a razor and a lemon slicer. There's even a song called "Bleed Like Me" by the band Garbage that glorifies self-cutting: "Doodle takes dad's scissors to her skin / And when she does relief comes setting in."

The most enigmatic twentieth-century story on cutting is Franz Kafka's "In the Penal Colony." The story opens with the words, "It's a remarkable piece of apparatus" (101), uttered by an officer who waxes poetic over the brutality of the death machine to which he is fatally devoted. The torture machine is used to execute those who are guilty of crimes, however minor, in a penal colony where military discipline is enforced swiftly and ruthlessly. As the condemned prisoner lies on the part of the machine called the bed, a harrow is lowered and inscribes onto his body the commandment he has disobeyed, such as, in the case of a soldier about to be executed at the beginning of the story, "Honor thy superiors!" (197). Only a Kafkaesque imagination could evoke the story's unique blend of realism and surrealism. "The Harrow appears to do its work with uniform regularity," the officer tells a startled explorer who is visiting the penal colony as an observer. "As it quivers," the officer continues, "its points pierce the skin of the body which is itself quivering from the vibration of the Bed. So that the actual progress of the sentence can be watched, the Harrow is made of glass" (200). The harrow is designed to write on the prisoner's body for twelve hours, all the time penetrating deeper and deeper into the flesh. For the first six hours the condemned man remains alive, suffering excruciating pain. "After two hours the felt gauze is taken away, for he has no longer strength to scream" (203). Around the sixth hour, enlightenment comes to the prisoner, a "moment that might tempt one to get under the Harrow oneself," the officer exclaims prophetically.

Throughout the story the officer tries to convince the explorer of the superiority of the regime of the old commandant, who is suggestive of an Old Testament God, to that of the new commandant, associated with laxness and corruption. "How we all absorbed the look of transfiguration on the face of the sufferer, how we bathed our cheeks in the radiance of that justice, achieved at last and fading so quickly!" (209). Realizing that the explorer is horrified by what he sees, the officer frees the condemned prisoner and submits himself to the torture machine, which begins to break down. No sign of promised redemption appears on the officer's face: "What the others had found in the machine the officer had not found; the lips were firmly pressed together, the eyes were open, with the same expression as in life, the look was calm and convinced, through the forehead went the point of the great iron spike" (225).

How does Kafka's ambiguous story relate to cutting? The officer's rhapsodic defense of torture and capital punishment reveals, psychologically, the power of masochistic fantasies that can be gratified only through suffering. So too do many cutters need to experience pain to feel alive. "All self-harm has a strong masochistic element, whether it be a physical masochism, in which pleasure is combined with bodily pain, or moral masochism, in which pleasure is combined with the pain of self-inflicted emotional suffering" (Farber 76). Both the officer and the cutter play the role of victim and self-victimizer, and the conflicts in their lives are literally inscribed on their flesh. The officer's transcendent belief in the old commandant, and the torture machine that he embodies, parallels the cutter's expectation of relief. Both the officer and the cutter are self-sacrificial, wounding themselves in the hope of a desired rebirth. The condemned prisoner cannot defend himself or deny his guilt—the old commandant's guiding principle is that "guilt is never to be doubted" (198). In the same way, many cutters are overwhelmed by guilt, searching for self-atonement through self-punishment. The description of cutting is highly ritualistic, suggestive of a primitive rite of self-sacrifice. As Favazza states, "While some mentally ill self-mutilators consciously believe and publicly declare themselves to be gods or members of the company of saints, others seem to tap unconsciously into such beliefs. In this context acts of self-mutilation and mortification may take on a sacrificial quality" (44). The officer speaks with the same ecstatic vocabulary that cutters often use when describing the act of self-mutilation, which in some cases represents a badge of honor. The officer is both horrified and fascinated by the process, paralleling onlookers' responses in fictional representations of cutting.

There are differences too. Unlike the suicidal officer in Kafka's story, most cutters are not interested in killing themselves: they cut to find relief from inner torture. Their cuts are generally not deep and do not require elaborate machinery. Cutting remains a private act—and art—concealed from the public, though the latter may witness the cutter's scars. Most cutters are adolescent girls, not male officers, and unlike Kafka's character, who shows no signs of what today would be called a mood disorder, they embrace self-mutilation as a remedy for depression. Most cutters experience a shame that is absent in Kafka's officer. Shame is, as Andre Ivanoff and his associates point out, a "critically important emotion in self-mutilation. Clinical observation supports the relationship between self-mutilation and negative attitude toward the self" (153).

"In the Penal Colony" may also be viewed as a metaphor of the creative process—specifically, the art of writing—in which the artist suffers and experiences a loss of life during the act of creation. Writing was for Kafka a form of suffering in which the artist bares himself to an increasingly indifferent audience who, as in his story "A Hunger Artist," grows tired of the performer's renunciation of life. It is not that writing was necessarily hard for Kafka—the hunger artist has no trouble fasting and indeed cannot stop doing so, even if it means death. Rather, the artist needs to fast, to expose himself, in part because he can't find the food or life-affirming sustenance he needs. The artist needs his audience's approval—"I have always wanted you to admire my fasting," he tells an overseer who is in charge of his cage; yet at the same time he says, "But you shouldn't admire it." He fasts, just as Kafka writes, "Because I have to fast, I can't help it" (255). Nor can cutters easily stop cutting. "Chronic self-mutilators are clinically vexing," admits Favazza, "and many treatment modalities have been tried. Occasional successes may occur but no 'magic pill,' behavioral technique, or psychological approach has proven effective, although the habit of self-mutilation may be broken by utilizing a specific inpatient program" (189). One of the many prescient insights of "In the Penal Colony" and "A Hunger Artist" is the close association between cutting and eating disorders. "A most intriguing recent finding is that as many as 50 percent of female chronic self-mutilators have a history of anorexia nervosa or bulimia. In some cases the eating disorder precedes self-mutilation while in others the reverse is true" (Favazza 206).

It is often impossible to disentangle the cultural, historical, and psychological components of cutting. In his book *Vietnamerica*, a study of Amerasian children fathered by American soldiers during the Vietnam War, Thomas Bass comments on the large number of self-inflicted burn marks and scars that are visible on their bodies, symptomatic of poor self-esteem and chronic depression. "They deny problems or avoid them. They are impulsive, needy, clinging. They distrust people, so working with them is difficult. Amerasians act out their psychological hurt with physical wounds. Self-mutilation is the visible sign of their despair" (170).

Cutting has become an inspiration for performance art. An article in the 6 November 2005 "Arts and Leisure" section of the *New York Times* highlights the performance artist Marina Abramovic, who was scheduled to stage a one-woman show at the Guggenheim Museum, where she was expected to carve a star into her stomach with a razor blade, as she had done thirty years earlier. "'In normal life, if I cut myself I cry like a baby because I'm totally emotional and vulnerable, and I don't like pain,' she said. But in a performance, much as in ancient religious endurance rites, 'then the pain is not an issue.'" Staging pain in front of an audience, she told the reporter, helps to get rid of the fear of pain. As if to demonstrate that "art is a matter of life and death," she performed a crucifixion piece in Naples in 1974 that almost resulted in her death. Its premise was terrifyingly simple: "She agreed to stand in a gallery for six hours while anyone who came in could choose any of 72 objects around her—including knives, scissors, a needle, a loaded gun—and do anything they wanted to her with the objects. It was her only work in which she essentially ceded control over her body, and over the pain to be inflicted, to her audience." She was indeed almost martyred by art: the audience burned and cut her body, and a man actually seized the loaded gun and tried to force her to shoot herself in the head.

Writing about one's life as a cutter may not be as dangerous as cutting oneself during performance art, but it poses its own risks. Though Patty hasn't cut herself in years and can hardly remember the troubled teenager who carved her arms and wrists, it is still difficult for her to think about this unhappy period in her life—and even more difficult to share the experience with others. "My own husband does not know I was a cutter." And yet she was willing to make this self-disclosure to a teacher whom she had known for only a few weeks. Moreover, she writes with remarkable clarity and control about one of the most wrenching times in her life.

Cutting, like certain forms of writing, is intended to be a private act, hidden from public view, yet it is almost impossible to prevent scarred arms and wrists from being seen by others. "How this has escaped the notice of people for so long I don't know." Patty's diary entry now draws attention to this aspect of her past, and she seeks greater self-understanding in doing so. Just as reading *Surviving Literary Suicide* has opened her eyes to the seriousness of suicide, her diary opens the reader's eyes to the phenomenon of cutting, a subject that is rarely discussed inside or outside the classroom.

In writing about her experiences as a cutter, Patty discloses violence against the female body, and such writing raises many pedagogical questions that must be explored. Jeff discusses these questions in his section of the book, but for now we may note that only a few college professors encourage this type of writing. Michelle Payne is one of these teachers, and in *Bodily Discourses* she makes an observation about student essays on sexual abuse and eating disorders that also applies to essays on cutting: "Student essays about bodily violence—and our responses to them—are like the proverbial canary in a mine: They hint at the gaps in much of our theoretical work. They challenge the limits of postmodern beliefs that reality is constructed, that selves and the physical body are knowable only through language. Psychologists argue, for example, that someone who has been abused has a fragmented sense of identity—an identity postmodern theory celebrates—yet student essays on abuse have rarely been talked about in postmodern terms. Instead, they are often dismissed as products of an expressivist pedagogy or a cultural focus on individual self-expression and confession" (xix).

The Prevalence of Cutting

The statistics surrounding cutting vary widely. According to Stephen Levenkron, 1 in every 250 people in our society is a cutter (20). Other reports are dramatically higher. The *San Francisco Chronicle* estimates that there are 2 million cutters in the United States, most of whom are women under the age of twenty-five (11 October 1998). A 2003 study by the University of Oxford Centre for Suicide Research reported that more than 1 teenager in 10 in the United Kingdom deliberately harmed themselves, most by cutting (Winkler). The most authoritative study, and one that made national newspaper headlines throughout the country, was conducted by Janis Whitlock, John Eckenrode, and Daniel Silverman.

Appearing in the June 2006 issue of *Pediatrics*, the study, the largest of its kind focusing on the college student population, investigated the prevalence of self-injurious behaviors (SIB), which include not only cutting and carving skin but also scratching, burning, ripping, swallowing toxic substances, and breaking bones. More than 8,000 students from two northeastern universities participated in an Internet-based survey in the spring of 2005. The study does not name the two universities, but newspapers identified them as Cornell and Princeton, where the researchers teach. The findings indicate that 17 percent of the students engaged in self-injurious behavior, three-quarters of whom engaged in these activities more than once.

Whitlock, Eckenrode, and Silverman's study reveals that SIBs are both a symptom of suicidal thinking and, paradoxically, a protection against suicide—the same phenomenon that Patty observes in her diary. By definition, SIBs represent "acts undertaken without suicidal intent" (1940), and for this reason Whitlock and colleagues eliminated from their study those students who stated that they might attempt suicide. Nevertheless, they note that those who injure themselves are at greater risk for suicide than are those who do not injure themselves. "Although most studies suggest that SIB represent a method of temporarily alleviating distress, persons in clinical populations who engage in SIB are more likely also to engage in suicide-related behaviors" (1940). This study found that 34 percent of the Cornell and Princeton students who engaged in self-injurious behaviors indicated they had considered or attempted suicide—far higher than the incidence of suicidal thinking among those students who do not engage in self-injurious behaviors. Yet it is also true that SIBs have an adaptive function, serving as a protection against suicide: "SIB are recognized widely as a method of coping with distress, and some view it as a highly functional alternative to suicide. Our study, like those documenting a relationship between SIB and suicide in clinical settings, showed a definitive link between the 2 behaviors. The findings do not provide evidence that SIB are part of a continuum of suicidal behavior, only that they may signal underlying unresolved distress. Indeed, 66% of all those who had engaged in SIB reported never having considered or attempted suicide" (1945) .

The research by Whitlock and associates yields other important information about cutting. A majority of the Cornell and Princeton students who harmed themselves began when they were fifteen or sixteen years old and ended within five years of starting. Twenty-one percent of all self-injurers reported that they had injured themselves more severely than they had expected; 47 percent of these respondents injured themselves more severely than they expected more than once (1942). Students engaging in SIBs were more likely to have elevated levels of distress than those who did not engage in SIBs, along with a higher incidence of eating disorders. And 53 percent of all self-injurers reported experiencing physical, sexual, or emotional abuse, or a combination of the three (1943).

One of the study's most striking findings is that many students who harm themselves conceal this information from others. "Nearly 40% of all of SIB respondents reported that no one was aware of their SIB"; among repeat SIB respondents, this figure is 31 percent. "Very few self-injurers (3.2%) disclosed SIB to a physician or allied medical health professional, and less than one fourth (21.4%) reported disclosing SIB to or discussing SIB with a mental health professional. Among repeat self-injurers, 5.4 percent disclosed SIB to a physician or allied medical health professional and 25.7 percent reported disclosing or discussing SIB with a mental health professional. Just over half (57.1%) of repeat self-injurers had ever been to therapy for any reason" (1942–43). Whitlock and colleagues conclude from their findings that "SIB generate shame and often are experienced as very isolating" (1945)—a conclusion that Patty also reaches in her diary.

This study raises many questions for future research, such as the relationship between SIBs and psychopathology and whether those who engage in SIBs are likely to have serious problems in the future. The authors end with the observation that it is imperative for physicians and therapists to find strategies for identifying, treating, and preventing SIBs. They are aware of the possibility that information on cutting may contribute to the contagion effect. "SIB communities on Internet message boards are now prevalent and visited frequently, and may provide a means for spreading the practice. The tendency for SIB to follow epidemic-like patterns in institutional settings such as hospitals and detention facilities and to become somewhat addictive may be reflected in nonclinical settings such as high schools and colleges" (1945). Indeed, five articles in their bibliography focus on the contagion effect among those who engage in self-mutilation. The authors are careful to avoid sensationalism in their study, but the nationally syndicated newspaper article announcing the study portrays a smiling coed who acknowledged the pleasure of cutting herself in high school. "It was part of waking up, getting dressed, the last look in the mirror and then the cut on the wrist. It got to be where I couldn't have a perfect day without it" (*Albany Times-Union*, 5 June 2006).

Emotional Contagion

One of the most unsettling observations in Whitlock, Eckenrode, and Silverman's research and in Patty's diary is that reading, talking, or writing about an issue like cutting can be dangerous to others. Patty mentions a student named Mary (a pseudonym, like all the student names in Jeff's books), who found herself becoming at risk as a result of taking a graduate English course in 1994 on literary suicide. The course focused on novels and poems about suicide written by authors who later took their own lives. At the beginning of the semester, Jeff was careful to point out the "Werther effect." In 1774 Johann Wolfgang von Goethe wrote a highly confessional novel called *The Sufferings of Young Werther* in which the autobiographical protagonist kills himself at the end because of unrequited love. The publication of the novel incited many youths to imitate the act: "Sentimental young men sported Werther's costume: blue coat and yellow trousers and vest; some lovelorn creatures followed his example and committed suicide with copies of the novel in their pockets" (Steinhauer 24). Writing the novel proved cathartic to Goethe, but reading the novel proved fatal to many readers, a dramatic example of the danger not only of a reader's overidentification with a fictional character but also of life imitating art. In 1974 the American sociologist David Phillips published a landmark article, "The Influence of Suggestion on Suicide," demonstrating that "celebrity suicides" raise the national suicide rate by an average of 1 percent for about a month. Philips coined the term "Werther effect" to explain how one person's suicide can lead to copycat acts. The longer a story remains on the front pages of a newspaper, the larger the rise in the suicide rate. "In the United States, suicides increased by 12% in the month after Marilyn Monroe's death and by 10% in England and Wales" (306).

The Werther effect is an example of *emotional contagion*, which Elaine Hatfield and her associates define as the "catching" of another person's emotions. The authors emphasize rudimentary or primitive emotional contagion, "that which is relatively automatic, unintentional, uncontrol-

lable, and largely inaccessible to conversant awareness." Implicit is the
tendency automatically to "mimic and synchronize facial expressions, vo-
calizations, postures, and movements with those of another person and,
consequently, to converge emotionally" (5). They quote an apt statement
by the actress Jennifer Jason Leigh: "A character can invade your body
and take over like a virus. When the movie making ends, it's like getting
over a sickness. You slowly but surely get well and come back to yourself"
(76). Though Favazza doesn't refer to the contagion theory, he indicates
how reading the Bible may induce cutting. "A potentially ominous sign
is intensive reading of the Bible by a psychotic person. Time and again
psychotic persons find a final justification for their self-mutilation from
the portentous biblical passage about removing an offensive eye or hand"
(216). Many empirical studies document the existence of emotional contagion. Negative emotions are more "contagious" than positive ones, and
gender is a factor in that women are more susceptible than men to being
"infected" by emotions.

Reading several novels and poems about suicide by writers who later
committed suicide may have contributed to Mary's drug overdose after
the semester ended. Jeff received a letter from her in which she noted
that even as she swallowed a small number of sleeping pills, she recalled
a sentence from Edwin Shneidman's article that was discussed in class:
"*Suicide is characterized by ambivalence.*" As Jeff explains in *Surviving
Literary Suicide*, "Mary knew she was ambivalent about suicide; she did
not wish to die but to find a solution to her pain, guilt, and anxiety. She
phoned her therapist immediately after taking the pills and rushed to an
emergency room where she had her stomach pumped" (260). She subsequently recovered and completed her graduate degree. "Those who argue
that courses like Literary Suicide are inherently dangerous, unleashing
powerful forces that may prove explosive, will find confirmation in Mary's
suicide attempt. Those who counter that these courses are valuable precisely because they allow students to recognize when they are at risk and
take appropriate actions will point out that Mary had the presence of mind
to seek immediate help" (262).

Like suicide, cutting lends itself to copycat behavior. Teachers who
are interested in the pedagogy of self-disclosure need to be aware of the
emotional contagion effect. Students who hear or read an essay about
cutting may find themselves tempted to experiment themselves with self-
mutilation, even if they have never previously thought about it. There

is something in the act of cutting that makes it both fascinating and repulsive, desirable and fearful, self-destructive and self-preservative. As a rule, descriptions of the act of cutting always contain greater aesthetic power than theoretical explanations of why a cutter finally stops cutting. Perhaps this is true of all addictions—beginning is far more exciting and intoxicating than ending. Nor is this true only of addiction: as Jeff notes in *The Talking Cure*, in literature,"evil appears more fascinating than good, sickness more interesting than health" (159). A writer's language becomes emotionally charged when describing cutting: passages contain vivid imagery, incantatory rhythms, metaphorical language, active verbs, brilliant colors. Cutters seem to remember the first but not the last time they cut themselves. Writers use hypnotic and seductive prose as they describe in loving detail their instruments of choice in making themselves bleed. Their razor blades or knives become dependable weapons that can always be counted upon to provide pleasure and relief. Witness Caroline Kettlewell's extended personification, which seems Kafkaesque in its loving attention to detail: "I took my razor blade—my handy razor blade, my dear and trusted and always reliable razor blade—and started at my elbow. An inch, two inches, it didn't seem like enough. Three, four inches, the razor crept down the length of my arm, with the faint *tthick tthick* of its slow passage audible. I got to my wrist, and watched the way the blood faded in, at first so faint that I could wonder if I was really seeing anything at all, then a precise thread of crimson that almost as soon as it appeared began to differentiate into a hundred individual beads" (135).

By contrast, Kettlewell devotes only a few short, unconvincing, and anticlimactic paragraphs to the resolution of her self-mutilating behavior, and she offers no insight as to how, why, and when she was able to stop cutting: "I don't have a tidy narrative conclusion to offer. When I finally stopped cutting, there was no specific day I could mark for this turn, no moment of epiphany when everything became suddenly clear to me and I forsook the razor forever. Instead, the end came as a series of unconnected moments assembling themselves into a whole that is evident only in retrospect" (175).

The contagion effect is not limited to romanticized descriptions of cutting: even an essay that warns against cutting may unintentionally encourage such behavior. One of Jeff's students, Maryann, first learned about cutting when she watched a television program called *7th Heaven*. The program intended to warn viewers about the dangers of cutting, but it had the opposite effect on Maryann, awakening her "love" for an act that she had never known existed. The contagion effect cannot be eliminated, but it can be minimized, especially when teachers and students speak truthfully and openly about dark subjects.

Why read, speak, or write about inherently provocative topics like suicide or cutting, particularly when the risk of "contamination" is ever present? A sentence from Patty's diary suggests an important answer to this question: self-education. "It wasn't until many years afterward, while reading *Reviving Ophelia* and working in a residential school with very troubled kids, and girls who cut themselves, that I began to understand my own self-destructive behaviors." She ends the paragraph by asking the question, "Why would I have ever cut myself? Good question."

It is indeed a good question, one that Patty cannot answer in a brief diary. But the question was important enough for her to ponder. Shortly after completing the Age of Freud, she asked Jeff for his help in selecting a topic for her master's thesis, and he suggested that she explore the theme of cutting in literature, a topic that would at the same time allow her to learn more about her own cutting behavior. She readily agreed. Patty's diary entry on *Surviving Literary Suicide* led first to her 2004 master's thesis at the University at Albany, "Contagion in Cutting," and then to this book.

In part 1 of our book, based largely on Patty's master's thesis, she discusses clinical and theoretical aspects of cutting and then applies these insights to several novels and memoirs, including Susanna Kaysen's *Girl, Interrupted*, Caroline Kettlewell's *Skin Game*, Patricia McCormick's *Cut*, Shelley Stoehr's *Crosses*, and Emma Forrest's *Thin Skin*. Part of the motivation behind Patty's research was the desire to learn more about herself, and she reads these novels through her own experience as a cutter. She thus writes from the point of view of a participant-observer. She also writes from the point of view of a high school English teacher, mindful that a graphic description of cutting in a fictional story may have the unintended effect of encouraging a teenage reader to imitate this behavior.

In part 2, Jeff focuses on the pedagogical dynamics of cutting: how undergraduate students write about cutting, how their writings affect classmates and teacher, and how students who cut themselves can educate everyone in the classroom—including themselves—about a serious problem that has personal, psychological, cultural, and educational significance. Patty's writings are an eloquent example of these benefits. Jeff also discusses the contagion effect in student writings and the protocols he puts in place to minimize the possibility that students who write about traumatic experiences will be retraumatized.

Throughout part 1, Patty emphasizes the risks of reading or teaching stories about cutting; throughout part 2, Jeff demonstrates the educational and psychological benefits of students writing about their own cutting experiences. Educators who encourage students to engage in "risky reading" or "risky writing" are themselves engaged in "risky teaching." They will want to know both the risks and the benefits of this type of teaching. The epilogue contains an essay by Jeff's student Anna, who remarks that she could easily fit the category of being a reader "at risk" for contagion. It is for this reason that her conclusion—the present book did not reawaken the desire to "delve back into the dark world of self-mutilation"—is especially welcome, a conclusion Jeff and Patty hope others reach in their own readings.

Teachers who receive essays on cutting confront many challenges. They must first deal with whatever fear or aversion the subject elicits from them. One of Freud's greatest discoveries was the existence of transference, the patient's projection onto the analyst of feelings and thoughts originating in the patient's relationship to the significant people in his or her life. Countertransference is the analyst's projections onto the patient. An extensive body of psychoanalytic knowledge exists on transference and countertransference, including the recognition that projection exists in all interpersonal relationships, especially unequal ones such as the student-teacher relationship. A paradigm shift has occurred within psychoanalysis in which, as Marvin Krims writes, the "myth of the impartial, authoritative analyst who never projects but only reflects has been replaced by the more realistic notion of collaborative work between analyst and analysand." So too must teachers acknowledge their own projective tendencies—onto both texts and students. Teachers who are horrified by the idea of self-mutilation will have difficulty remaining empathic when reading a diary or essay on cutting. Yet one does not need superhuman empathy to read such an essay and make helpful comments to the author. Like other befriending skills, empathy can be learned, and as Jeff suggests in *Empathic Teaching*, teachers who are interested in learning about the other can do so by trying to suspend disbelief and listening attentively.

Teachers who are aware of transference and countertransference are in a better position to maintain professional boundaries than those who are unaware of these projective tendencies. They will be more aware of their fears and desires, their rescue fantasies, their wish to impose their own social, political, or religious views onto students. Yet teachers need not be trained therapists to respond empathically to a diary entry like Patty's. There is nothing in her entry indicating that she asks Jeff for clinical help: it is clear that she is writing a reader-response diary to her English professor, not seeking therapeutic advice or guidance on "how to live." Nor do teachers need to be therapists to know how to make appropriate referrals to their university counseling service if they believe that a student is at risk. Students appreciate teachers who are concerned about them and who are aware of the campus services that exist to help those who may be in a crisis.

Creative Malady

Patty's master's thesis is an example of literary scholarship that is also deliberate self-analysis. While researching her thesis, she saw a connection between her history as a cutter and other maladaptive behaviors from which she was suffering during her adolescence, including a number of obsessive-compulsive rituals. She discovered for the first time why she had cut herself, and, equally important, she was able to grasp the motivations of teenage girls who cut themselves today. She also learned that she was not alone. Many people cut themselves, which is consoling for those cutters who believe that no one can understand them. Patty's scholarship is an example of what George Pickering calls "creative malady," a term that reveals the relationship between psychological conflict and creativity in such otherwise dissimilar figures as Charles Darwin, Florence Nightingale, Mary Baker Eddy, Marcel Proust, Elizabeth Barrett Browning, and Sigmund Freud: "The illness was an essential part of the act of creation rather than a device to enable that act to take place" (19). Patty knows that her interpretation of cutting-themed literature reflects her own history as a cutter, and she adeptly contrasts her present life as an experienced high school English teacher with her past life as a troubled adolescent. Literary critics who are aware of their own subjectivity and projective patterns are less likely to pretend to an "objectivity" that does not exist. They are also less likely to claim to know the "truth," which is, as Oscar Wilde remarks, "rarely pure and never simple."

Jeff's own scholarship is also an example of creative malady, or what he calls in his book on Joseph Conrad, "writing as rescue." His teaching and writing are efforts to work through the grief arising from a telephone call he received on Labor Day 1968, when his college mentor, Len Port, told him that he had swallowed an overdose of sleeping pills. As Jeff writes in "'The Grief That Does Not Speak': Suicide, Mourning, and Psychoanalytic Teaching," Freud's theory of the "repetition-compulsion principle," the counterphobic effort to master psychological pain, is a striking theme in Jeff's own life and work:

> By converting a passive situation (standing helplessly by as a friend committed suicide) into an active one (becoming a psychoanalytic critic and doing research on self-destructive writers), I have gained a degree of control over a frightening situation. One of the driving forces behind my teaching and scholarship, I now see, is a reparative fantasy in which, by attempting to "rescue" fictional characters, I replay my discussions with Len and strive for a more positive outcome. Although I cannot bring Len back to life nor journey into the heart of darkness, I can play the role of significant other to my students, especially to those whose lives have been touched by suicide or other traumas and who are still burdened by their own private albatross. (43)

Personal criticism may indulge narcissistic inclinations, but these problems can be avoided, as we see in Patty's writings, by an awareness of the distinction between self and other, and by the ability to empathize with others who are not like oneself. As Daniel Rancour-Laferriere observes in the introduction to *Self-Analysis in Literary Study*, "If there is one conclusion that can be drawn from all the essays in this volume, it is this: self-analysis can be a boon to other-analysis, including psychoanalysis of literature. Literary analysis informed by self-analysis is in principle superior to literary analysis not so informed" (29).

The spirit of collaboration has inspired us to work together in writing this book. We hope that it will stimulate teachers and students to learn more about an increasingly widespread act, one that is rarely spoken about inside or outside the classroom. Everything about cutting is risky: performing it, writing about it, and hearing essays about it read aloud in the classroom. Reading a book about cutting is also risky, for it requires the reader to empathize with people who are in great pain and whose actions are not easily understood. More so than nearly any other subject, silence, secrecy, and stigma surround cutting, which is why, paradoxically, it lends itself to pedagogical examination.

We are aware of the ever-present irony that calling attention to a subject like cutting may inadvertently stimulate the curiosity of those potentially at risk readers who find themselves tempted to try it. Jane Wegscheider Hyman's "Warning to Readers" in her book *Women Living with Self-Injury* is apt: "Some of the personal experiences quoted in this book . . . contain graphic descriptions of self-injury that could be upsetting or, perhaps, even trigger self-injury in some self-injuring readers. You may want to pace your reading, skip some passages, and read when you feel protected and can talk about the text with a trusted friend" (23). We confront this problem in different ways. Patty's focus is mainly on the contagious nature of cutting and the ways in which reading literature may render high school students susceptible to infection. Jeff's focus is mainly on the ways in which college students can educate their classmates and teacher about a subject that is unspeakable for most cutters. As Patty illustrates, despite the widely differing theories of cutting, there is widespread agreement that those who cut themselves experience psychological relief. No matter how self-destructive it may be, cutting provides a welcome degree of self-control. So does writing—without the self-destructive implications. We believe that despite the potential for harm, reading and writing about cutting are among the best ways to achieve self-understanding and, in the process, self-recovery.

Cutting and the Pedagogy of Self-Disclosure

Part 1

CUTTING—A Learned Behavior

There has been much research in the past ten years into the self-injurious behavior commonly known as "cutting," which comprises 72 percent of all self-injurious behavior, but many theories continue to attribute cutting and other forms of self-injury to psychological disorders (Engelgau 1). Certainly some who engage in cutting do have diagnosable disorders; nevertheless, I contend that for others cutting is mainly a learned behavior, at times adaptive, at other times maladaptive, and not always triggered by a psychological disorder. Since, overwhelmingly, young women engage in cutting behavior, mutilating their own skin by cutting themselves, it is this population I address.

My main focus and argument are the fact that as so much research, literature, and media attention have been devoted to self-injury in recent years, more and more instances of self-injurious behavior in young women are occurring due to these extrinsic influences. Most cutters are adolescent girls. Considering the cause of their behaviors from a feminist perspective, then, is essential—yet surprisingly, many research psychologists neglect to include feminist viewpoints. Therefore, I provide some insight into a feminist perspective on cutting behavior by taking into account society's harmful impact on female cutters. Health care officials report that self-injury cases doubled between 2000 and 2003 (Engelgau 1). As a former cutter and one who has since worked with a population of students who engage in cutting behaviors, I lend my own experience to my study, too, in order to substantiate what I have discovered in my research.

One belief widely held by scholars from a variety of disciplines is that cutters engage in their behaviors in order to exercise control over themselves and their emotional or psychological problems. However, feminist, behavioral, and other researchers do not generally accept that cutting is always psychopathological in origin. In fact, many researchers believe that cutting is not mainly a symptom of psychological problems. Rather, women engage in the act primarily to stabilize and manage what could otherwise become psychological problems.

Cutting behavior is not a failed suicide attempt and should not be seen as suicidal behavior; however, like suicide, cutting can be seen as a phenomenon spurred by the attention it receives. Therefore, I examine the Werther effect, a term applied to the phenomenon of contagion in suicide that also has relevance to cutting.

While cutting and self-injurious behavior in many females can indicate the presence of psychological illness, the fact that cutting behavior is on the rise among adolescent females in our society compels us to consider other possible causes for the behavior. I began researching this topic to understand my own past cutting behaviors. My reading and experience since have led me to believe that cutting is a behavior that can be learned, influenced, and even initiated because of "learning," "contagion," "peer pressure," "copycatting," "media influence," and "societal influence." I use personal experience to substantiate what I have found in my research, exploring the reasons why girls cut, why the phenomenon is on the increase, and how both these phenomena are represented in current literature. I also examine the pedagogical implications of teaching cutting-themed literature in high school.

CHAPTER 1

Feminist Perspectives
Self-Injurious Behavior among Women

Whitlock and her associates note that although self-injurious behaviors (SIBs) are "popularly assumed to represent a female phenomenon"—some studies suggest that females are up to three times more likely to cut themselves than males—this assumption "is not fully supported by existing literature" (1945). One possible explanation for this assumption, they conjecture, is that most of the research on SIBs has been conducted in clinical settings in which women are overrepresented. Nevertheless, they acknowledge that "compared with those with no SIB incidents, respondents with repeat SIB incidents were significantly more likely to be female than male" (1943). Their research does not seek to investigate the gendered implications of SIBs, but the question cannot be ignored: why do women cut themselves?

"As females grow up in our culture, they are bombarded with intense and conflicting messages about their bodies. Girls and women are the prime marketing targets for the fashion and cosmetics industries, health clubs, diet pill purveyors, and cosmetic surgeons. Even as their bodies are becoming softer and more rounded with sexual maturation, girls are implored by cultural ideals to be 'slim,' 'hard,' and 'in control'" (Conterio and Lader 105). The notion of being "in control" echoes one theory held by the majority of researchers working in the field of self-injury: the cutter uses self-injury as a means of exerting control over her body when her psychological self is in turmoil. This psychological conflict arises, according to feminist scholars, from the impact of social messages claiming that women are inadequate and unable to live up to stereotypical ideals. Despite the gains women have made in a male-dominated culture, they are still objectified, sexualized, and devalued.

"What emerges is a sense of vulnerability that impedes these women from taking a stand, what George Eliot regards as the girl's 'susceptibility' to adverse judgments by others, which stems from her lack of power and consequent inability 'to do something in the world'" (Gilligan 66). When a young woman in our society is made to believe she isn't able to achieve goals, control herself or her life, succeed academically or professionally, flourish personally, meet expectations, or expect affirmation from society, where does she turn? She turns inward. But often lacking the inner strength due to this plague of self-doubt, the cutter seeks to demonstrate her internal pain and turmoil in the form of self-injury, a physical manifestation of what lies within.

Some reports, like *Time* magazine's cover story of June 1998 titled "Is Feminism Dead?" claim that the issue of feminism in our culture is, indeed, dead. After all, women make up almost 50 percent of the workforce, and they constitute the majority of undergraduates in America's colleges and universities. According to the AFL-CIO, median earnings for women ages twenty to twenty-four in 2002 were 93.7 percent of what men in the same age bracket earned—the closest pay scales have reportedly been in the nation's history ("Highlights of Women's Earnings, 2002"). Strict laws and guidelines have been enacted in schools and workplaces prohibiting sexual discrimination and sexual harassment, and the penalties for violating these laws are stiff. Consequently, women have become more confident in their abilities and less concerned with the "old-fashioned" notion that their femininity will prevent them from achieving any real academic or professional success. To some extent, all of this is true. But it is a mistake to believe that feminism is dead and that women are no longer objectified, stereotyped, discriminated against, or oppressed.

Feminists advocate the same rights for women as those granted to men. By definition, then, feminism must be alive and well. However, if we look beyond the laws and overt equality afforded to women of the twenty-first century, we see that women are still regarded as inferior and subjected to oppression in our society. Such attitudes disempower women, creating in them a sense of being out of control, one of the most frequently heralded causes of self-injurious behavior.

Women as Sexual Objects

One example of exploitive objectification is found in the plethora of pornography available and even promoted in our society. There have been exploitive magazines like *Playboy*, *Hustler*, and *Penthouse* for decades, their popularity a testament to the objectification of females. Add to these the accessibility of pornographic material on the Internet, and it is plain that women are still viewed as sexual objects by our society.

Psychological as well as feminist research has been conducted in the area of pornography's perpetuation of female stereotypes and the perception men who regularly view pornography have of women. It concludes that men who frequently engage in the viewing of pornographic images of women can become more prone to viewing women as eroticized objects. According to radical feminist Catharine MacKinnon:

> Pornography, in the feminist view, is a form of forced sex, a practice of sexual politics, an institution of gender inequality. In this perspective, pornography is not harmless fantasy or a corrupt and confused misrepresentation of an otherwise natural and healthy sexuality. Along with the rape and prostitution in which it participates, pornography institutionalizes the sexuality of male supremacy, which fuses the erotization of dominance and submission with the social constructs of male and female. Men treat women as who they see women as being. Pornography constructs who that is. Men's power over women means that the way men see women defines who women can be. Pornography is that way. (148)

Pornography, then, promotes ideas of female objectification and undermines many of the strides we as a society have taken to advance feminism. This objectification is part of the problem some women have in finding a sense of control in themselves. Ironically, one of the goals of the feminist movement in the twentieth century was to give women the right to have control—over themselves and, specifically, over their physical bodies. The movement succeeded in a legal sense. However, some women view having control over one's body to mean they are entitled to exploit themselves in the pornographic industry in the name of freedom and financial gain. They believe they are empowering themselves, taking advantage of a male-dominated culture that rewards them for their pornographic participation. What they fail to realize is that they have simply bought into the reality of male dominance, and the small sense of "power" or control they get from money is minuscule compared to the power and control of men over women, which they have helped to expand.

While pornography is blatantly damaging to a woman's sense of self, more subliminal might be the images in media and advertising presented to us—indeed bombarding us—every day. Mass media advertising promotes antiaging skin products, makeup, and cosmetic surgeries that promise a boost in self-esteem. I suppose that even if a woman's self-esteem were solid before viewing these types of advertisements, it would begin to erode when she realized that she didn't have flawless skin, full lips, or shadowed eyes. She would probably feel inferior to the women with healthier hair, thinner thighs, and bigger breasts because that's exactly what the advertisers want her to feel.

In reality, few women purchase all the products and procedures they are encouraged to, but it is undeniable that we live in a society that constantly reinforces stereotypes of perfection to which women cannot humanly live up. And advertisers now target a younger market. Consumers today are overwhelmingly teenage and female, the very same population that engages in cutting behavior. According to "Understanding the Female Consumer," in the United States alone, "girls aged 8–14 account for $48 billion in annual spending" (186). Moreover, according to a report published in 2002, "The three most important young adult consumer groups for food, drinks and personal care manufacturers to target are teenagers aged between 14 and 17 years old, students aged between 18 and 24 years old and the newly employed aged between 18 and 24 years old in their first year of full time employment"("Young Adults' Consumption Behavior" 1).

While the correlation may not at first be apparent, the pressures young women in our society feel to be perfect in a world that continues to sexualize, stereotype, and objectify them in a host of ways are overwhelming for some. The media impact how women are viewed and treated, and hence how they see and treat themselves. How does a young woman find a sense of herself? How does she assert any power or control over who she is and her life? Perhaps by adopting the feminist philosophy of taking control over her own body. Therefore, a girl's cutting behavior might be one of the only measures of control she feels she has over her body.

Another perspective, adopted by Karen Conterio and Wendy Lader in their book *Bodily Harm*, is that one goal of cutting is to make the girl intentionally ugly. They call this "uglification." They theorize that some young women rebel against the images of unattainable perfection they are surrounded by, choosing deliberately and paradoxically to make themselves as unattractive as they can through cutting and scarification, in order to reject that ideal. This can be viewed as typical teenage rebellion. Or it can be seen as a method of protection. A young girl who rejects our culture's stereotypes and marketing ploys might actually be protecting herself from them by cutting and scarring her skin to the point where she knows no creams or makeup will help. She is protecting herself from the pressure of advertising by distancing herself from its target population (one that will "benefit" from these products), though she is probably not consciously aware that she is doing so.

Similarly, young women who cut might also be protecting themselves from the objectification that comes with being viewed as sexually attractive or the subject of erotic thoughts and images. By scarring their skin, they are attempting to "uglify" themselves to the point of being sexually undesirable. Hence, they might believe they have eliminated the chance of becoming the victims of unwanted sexual advances, harassment, discrimination, or even sexually motivated attack or rape. "One patient of ours told us that she thought all the time about cutting her breasts, because she imagined that would make her safer from sexual predators" (Conterio and Lader 107). Not only, then, does our society sexualize, objectify, and undermine the self-esteem of women through pornography, advertising, the media, and other means, but it also makes some young women believe they are unsafe and must go to extremes like cutting and scarring their flesh in order to feel safer or "in control."

Women and Self-Mutilation

How is female self-cutting different from male self-cutting? Louise Kaplan offers an intriguing theory in her book *Female Perversions*. Like other feminist scholars, she argues that perversions, which she defines as psychological strategies of survival, are "as much pathologies of gender role identity as they are pathologies of sexuality. There is always a subtle collaboration between the individual unconscious with its infantile gender attributions and the structures of the social order with its primitive notions of masculinity and femininity" (14). To study female cutting, she asserts, one must study pathologies of gender role identity. Kaplan then contrasts *delicate self-cutting*, identified with females, with *coarse self-cutting*, identified with males:

> A rare disorder found almost exclusively among females—adolescent girls particularly but also women of all ages—has been given the innocent-sounding diagnostic label *delicate self-cutting*. And since every adolescent girl is struggling with the same emotional dilemmas as the delicate self-cutter, among them separation from her parents, particularly her

mother, trying to come to terms with the uncontrollable physical changes of puberty that are changing her irrevocably into an adult woman with sexual and procreative capacities that frighten her for reasons that elude her, having to suffer the loss of her childhood illusions and with them her dreams of perfection and self-perfectability, she may at times and for a while force these awesome anxieties and mortifications to the background of her mind by tearing at the skin of her cuticles, rubbing the skin off the bottoms of her feet, plucking her eyebrows, splicing the split ends of her hair, pulling out chunks of her hair, even occasionally pricking her skin till it bleeds or making a delicate cut into her wrist. (368)

The difference between the "delicate self-cutter" and the "average" girl, Kaplan argues, is that the latter recovers from the "emotional turmoil of adolescence" while the former does not—largely because the delicate self-cutter has "suffered a childhood where these ordinary troubles of adolescence are experienced as threats to her existence" (369). The male self-mutilator, Kaplan adds, "inflicts his body with more devastating damage," mainly because he "suffers more extensively from the mutilation anxiety and forbidden cross-gender wishes that afflict the female delicate cutter" (369).

Female Perversions was published in 1991, fifteen years before Whitlock, Eckenrode, and Silverman's empirical study of self-injurious behaviors among college students, and we know now that delicate self-cutting is hardly a "rare disorder." Nevertheless, the research by Whitlock and associates confirms several of Kaplan's gender observations: "Female subjects were 2.3 times . . . more likely to scratch or to pinch and 2.4 times . . . more likely to cut. Male subjects were 2.8 times . . . more likely than female subjects to punch an object with the intention of injuring themselves. Male subjects were 1.8 times . . . more likely to injure their hands, whereas female subjects were 2.3 times . . . more likely to injure their wrists and 2.4 times . . . more likely to injure their thighs" (1943).

I was struck by Kaplan's link between female cutting and menstruation, a connection I had not thought about before and one that relates to my own cutting. "Typically, the symptom of delicate self-cutting first appears some months immediately following the first menstruation. Thereafter, the cuttings or burnings or scrapings are a method of relieving the complex assortment of anxieties and tensions aroused premenstrually or during menstruation. Until it is brought to their attention, delicate cutters are unaware of any connection between the mortifications they inflict on their bodies and the mortifications they experience in reaction to their menstrual cycles" (373).

Another explanation for the greater number of female cutters is that women suffer from physical, sexual, and verbal abuse to a far greater extent than do men. "Women are more likely than men to experience sexual abuse, both as children and adults," writes Jane Wegscheider Hyman. "Although boys and girls suffer almost equally from physical abuse, girls are two to three times more likely to be sexually abused, and far more girls than boys are victims of incest. Childhood abuse is also associated with subsequent depression, anxiety, volatile emotions, dissociation, eating problems, and alcohol or other drug abuse, all of which can be familiar experiences for women who self-injure" (14). The study by Whitlock and her colleagues also confirms a link between abuse and self-cutting: "Respondents with repeat SIB incidents were significantly more likely to report a history of emotional, sexual, and physical abuse" (1943).

Sharon Klayman Farber offers still another explanation for the greater number of female cutters: gender differences in brain function. Evidence suggests that men and women differ in their ability to generate and metabolize serotonin, the neurotransmitter linked to depression. Men generate and synthesize 52 percent more serotonin than do women; this may help to explain the fact that women suffer from higher rates of depression than do men, as cross-cultural studies confirm: "It is unclear whether women's lives and experiences cause them to synthesize less [serotonin], whether they are inherently less capable of generating and synthesizing serotonin, or whether some interaction of factors is involved. But if generating and synthesizing serotonin is a crucial issue for more women than men, then perhaps the many women who inflict pain and injury to their bodies have found a short-term 'solution' to the serotonin problem without the help of psychopharmacology. Self-cutting profoundly and immediately is associated with increased levels of serotonin and the resultant experience of well-being" (Farber 292).

Is there also a link between female self-cutting, widely disapproved of culturally, and female cosmetic surgery, generally deemed acceptable by most people? Virginia Blum believes so. In her book *Flesh Wounds*, a cultural study of cosmetic surgery, she asks whether there is a difference between "going under the knife in search of youth and beauty" and covert adolescent cutting. "Just because the culture has normalized our pathology (of course, it's thoroughly normal to want to look rested and vigorous enough to compete in the youth-centered workplace), it doesn't mean that cosmetic surgery isn't like any other practice that has us offering up our bodies to the psychical intensities that angrily grip us" (289). For Blum, there is little difference between those who are "addicted to surgery," and who are often dissatisfied with the results, thus leading to more cosmetic surgeries, and those who cut their bodies as "counterphobic responses to a sense of internal mutilation" (287).

Whatever the precise relationship between nature and nurture, biology and culture, there is consensus among researchers that more females than males engage in self-cutting. So too is there consensus that the number of people engaged in self-mutilation is increasing significantly, especially among high school and college students. And there is also consensus that women cut themselves for many reasons. Hyman lists twenty-five reasons, including obvious ones, such as "to release emotions," "to calm turbulent, racing thoughts," and "to discipline, punish, or show hatred and disdain for oneself, one's body, or a specific body part," to less obvious ones, such as "to stop the internal voices of alter identities," "to prove to oneself that past experiences were true and abusive," and "to communicate a warning from one identity to another in women with multiple identities" (45–46). There is less consensus, however, on how to diagnose and treat cutters, and it is to these questions that I now turn.

CHAPTER 2

Theories and Diagnoses
A Closer Look

Steven Levenkron has written about anorexia, bulimia, and self-mutilation. In his book *Cutting,* he fuses his own theories about the phenomenon with instances of his patients' cutting behaviors. He believes that cutting, like phobias, depression, eating disorders, and obsessive-compulsive behavior, can be traced back to one's inability to form healthy attachments to other people (91–92). Further, forming what he describes as "unhealthy" attachments is the actual problem of which cutting is a primary symptom. He describes cutting and other symptoms of attachment disorder as disorders themselves, ones that "fill the void left by the lack of interpersonal relationships and serve as a replacement for healthy attachments. This is nearly always the case in the personality development of a self-mutilator"(94). He has become a veritable trailblazer among the handful of researchers who work on the mystery of cutting.

Levenkron's theories are heavily Freudian: he blames the parents. He believes that attachment disorders are at the root of the cutter's behavior. He also classifies cutters as pathological, which, by definition, means he has classified those with the behavior as mentally ill. This begs the question, "is it behavioral or psychological?" He seems to think it's both—a behavior caused by a psychological disorder that has resulted mostly from something he calls "love-attachment-abuse," which causes the child (the cutter) to fuse love, attachment, and abuse into a "single complex cluster of feelings" (132). He theorizes that if a parent physically abuses a child while verbally declaring love or care, the child's desire for attachment becomes the "glue that fuses these two contradictory messages. This will result in the self-infliction of pain as a way of dealing with loneliness and the need for parental companionship" (132). He explains that the most common profile of a cutter is an adolescent acting out against herself as a compensatory release against the parent. Since the child knows it's unacceptable to direct anger and aggression at her parent, she turns it instead on herself. Further, he asserts, "it is important to understand that these forms of self-mutilation are not part of group-rituals, [and] are not just an adolescent trend. They [cutters] represent, rather, individual psychopathology: mental illness" (23).

Levenkron distinguishes between adolescent cultural trends like piercing and tattooing, which he deems "goofy," and self-mutilation behaviors, which he deems "sick," in order to establish the significant differences in the psychological motivation behind the respective actions of each group, as well as in the actual experience of individuals who alter their own skin (23). While I agree that it is indeed important to define and identify cutting as something different in intent, motivation, and deed from piercing or tattooing for cultural or social appeal, I believe that, as with tattooing and piercing, some people engage in the behavior because it has become mainstream. "The [self-injury] syndrome has taken the late 1990s by storm: its grip on schools, college campuses, jails, and other sectors of society continues to tighten, and appears to be leaving a lasting impression" (Conterio and Lader 5).

Levenkron does not explicitly mention the possibility of self-injury being a learned behavior or one influenced by contagion. The focus of his research is on the psychological causation of cutting or self-injurious behavior: "The self-mutilator is typically a young woman who has not formed healthy attachments with parental figures. By physically injuring herself, she is making an attempt to redress the pain she was accustomed to as a young child" (58). This passage begins indirectly to describe self-injurious behavior as learned through the pain a child has experienced and subsequently tries to re-create in herself. Levenkron explains his theory of the breakdown in parental attachment in a clear, concise, and understandable manner. However, I cannot help but be taken aback by the terminology, "psychopathology" and "sick," which he applies to the cutter (23, 55). I also cannot help but hypothesize that he holds antiquated notions one can trace to the Freudian theory of hysteria, once commonly applied to women who exhibited any sort of behavior deemed unacceptable or unbefitting a woman of the time. Perhaps Levenkron's labels, like the once common label of hysteria, are loaded with the same antifeminist propaganda that was prevalent in the early 1900s. Such antifeminism can damage rather than heal young women.

In addition to the offensive terminology Levenkron uses in his book to classify the cutter, he includes conversations he has reportedly had with patients who are seeking treatment for cutting. When they ask him if they indeed are "crazy," he invariably answers in the negative. If I were one of his patients and read *Cutting*, I would have to call into question the integrity of my therapist. How can the doctor use the terms "sick" and "pathological" in the opening pages of his book on the subject, while telling his patients they are "not crazy"? The policy he describes in his book of cajoling women in his care with reassurance about their psychological state, then describing these same women as sick or pathological in his writing, patronizes and practically makes a mockery of his female patients. If his objective is indeed to discover the complex causes of self-injurious behavior and treat it successfully, developing sensitivity for his female patients and their mental and emotional frailty should be a goal he works to foster not disregard.

I was reminded too often while reading Levenkron's book of Freud's *Dora*. While the subject matter differs, both psychotherapists are treating young women with disorders they believe stem from faulty parental attachment. Further, both men portray themselves in their work as brilliant, competent, and authoritative, while they portray their patients as silly, overly sexual, and ignorant about the "true" causes of their disorders. I recall Jeff's observation in class that Freud was angry at Dora at the end of his case study *Fragment of an Analysis of a Case of Hysteria* because she had abruptly ended treatment. Freud could not conceal his bitterness when she returned briefly to therapy: "I do not know what kind of help she wanted from me," he writes without irony on the last page, "but I promised to forgive her for having deprived me of the satisfaction of affording her a far more radical cure for her troubles" (122). As neatly as a Hardy Boys mystery, both Freud and Levenkron easily "solve" the cases they profile in their books, while what they tell their patients conflicts with what they tell the reader. Levenkron and Freud may have the best of intentions in treating their female patients, but neither has truly considered the female perspective, one that cannot be overlooked, especially in Levenkron's treatment of cutters.

Self-Mutilation: Maintaining Self-Control

While Levenkron's work has received attention as important research into the "new" phenomenon of self-injury, theorists and psychologists have long held opinions that differ from his. The earliest documentation of self-mutilation in a psychological context appeared in Karl Menninger's landmark 1938 book *Man against Himself.* In Menninger's view, self-mutilation has both erotic and self-punishing motivations. He determined that self-abuse was a result of the conflict between self-destruction and the will to live: cutting gratified the self-injury urges while preventing suicide. Self-injurers, Menninger said, were not ambivalently trying to commit suicide; rather, they were actually trying to heal themselves. "The symptom (even a mutilation) is, therefore, an attempt at self-healing, or at least self-preservation. This gives us a clue to the paradox that local self-destruction is a form of partial suicide to avert total suicide" (237). Like Menninger, most researchers who delve into the study of self-injury have come to understand that the behavior is not an attempt at suicide.

In her book *Secret Scars,* V. J. Turner defines self-injury as "the deliberate mutilation of one's own body, with the intent to cause injury or damage, but without the intent to kill oneself" (15). While it seems universally described as a maladaptive coping mechanism, cutting is not universally agreed upon as "sick" or "pathological." In fact, many researchers assert that people who self-injure are often doing it in an attempt to *maintain* psychological integrity—which can also be seen as an attempt to maintain control. Armando Favazza explains that he had always thought of self-mutilation as pathology, until he began to glimpse other cultures in which people regularly engage in self-mutilation as a means of healing rather than harming themselves. "Here was a situation in which self-mutilation was a positive act performed to promote recovery from illness. Was it possible that young [American] women, like the Moroccans, were trying to heal themselves?" (Favazza 11). Through his study of cutting in other cultures, he found that self-mutilation and the cutting of the flesh were part of the "hadra," or healing ritual, designed to cure the Moroccans he studied and promote health through the "acquisition of a miraculous saintly force called 'baraka'" (67). Favazza explains that the ritual of slashing the skin is done in order to please the saints, who, it is believed, will aid in healing. Having found a new vantage point from which to view cutting, he defines self-mutilation as "deliberate, direct, nonsuicidal destruction or alteration of one's body tissue" (qtd. in Strong x).

New research into cutting is not limited to feminists, psychologists, psychiatrists, and behaviorists. In her book *A Bright Red Scream,* Marilee Strong, a journalist, explores the motivation behind cutting. Her research is balanced, theoretically sophisticated, and experiential. She shares

Levenkron's belief that early problems between parent and child can contribute to adolescent cutting behavior. She explains, "When a child's feelings and perceptions are actively denied or minimized by her parents, the child's ability to develop a language of feelings is stunted, and she is left with a mute hopelessness about the possibility of communicating in a way that will help her to get her critical needs met"(44). She cites Harold Graff and Richard Mallin, psychiatrists who began to study "wrist slash-ers" in the 1960s in a Philadelphia hospital and subsequently published their work in 1967 in the *American Journal of Psychiatry*. They viewed their patients' cutting "as a form of physical communication dating back to the maternal deprivation at the preverbal stage of life." Graff and Mallin state that it is only with great maturity that a child can subsist on the verbal messages of comfort alone. Because a "comforting picture of a mother's nurturing body language does not match the reality" of their patients' childhoods, the researchers believe that cutting is a manifesta-tion of a breakdown in this developmental system (qtd. in Strong 45).

Like these psychiatrists, Strong echoes Freud in recognizing self-mutilation as a concrete expression of unexpressed feelings or body language, rooted in the child's earliest state of psychological awareness, what Freud termed the "body ego" (46). "Comforting and tactile expe-riences help the baby develop a sense of its body as a safe and consis-tent boundary. If the baby is not held and comforted, or is frequently dropped, or handled roughly, or neglected or abused—painful, disruptive experiences British pediatrician and psychoanalyst Donald Winnicott called impingements—the child will not grow to feel like a whole entity, sheltered and contained by her skin" (Strong 46). A child whose body is not treated carefully may grow into a person who equates pain with nurturance. Therefore, it stands to reason such individuals will engage in self-injury when, even as adolescents and young adults, they are craving nurturance and support. Pain, then, becomes comfort. Thus, cutting is, in fact, learned behavior, whether researchers like Levenkron and Strong use the term or not.

Strong avoids classifying cutting as a symptom of psychopathology, saying instead that there is little agreement among psychologists as to how to define cutting. She revisits the work of Graff and Mallin, who were among the first to craft a composite profile of the cutter as a young, highly intelligent woman who is prone to alcohol and drug abuse and who has great difficulty in relationships. They found that most of these women had suffered painful childhoods with cold, rejecting mothers and distant, hypocritical fathers (32). In 1967, Henry Grunebaum and Gerald Klerman, psychiatrists at the Massachusetts Health Center, published similar findings in the *American Journal of Psychiatry*, stating that mothers of cutters "were most often cold, punitive, and judgmental" (qtd. in Strong 33). The majority of the researchers with whom Strong has worked see cutting as a coping mechanism rather than as a form of pathology or psychosis.

Psychoanalyst Maggie Turp also sees cutting as a coping mechanism, and she shares the postmodern assumption that the individual is embedded within the culture. In *Hidden Self-Harm*, she helps her clients construct a healing narrative to understand the sources of their conflicts and possible solutions. "In psychoanalytic psychotherapy with an individual who self-harms, the practitioner's aim is to discover the nature and personal meaning of acts of self-harm through assisting the client in his or her telling and re-telling of a personal story." She takes a more relational approach to psychotherapy than does Levenkron, and she avoids affixing blame. Using the language of Winnicott, she offers herself as a "container" to her clients, providing a "safe environment, where events that are difficult to speak about can begin to be put into words. Gradually, 'showings' of disturbance have been replaced by 'tellings' of a difficult story. Now the experiences in question can be properly thought about and it becomes possible to make sense of physical symptoms, including mysterious actions and eruptions" (165).

While cutting and other forms of self-injurious behavior certainly appear among patients with clinical diagnoses, it hasn't been determined that cutting is linked to psychosis. According to Strong, "it is only in the last sixty years that psychologists and psychiatrists have begun to remove cutting from the realm of possession and masochism and understand it as a complex coping behavior—a measure that, however maladaptive, helps some people manage their emotions and calm the turmoil within" (31). Although much of her book is devoted to exploring and presenting the psychological causations of self-mutilation, Strong acknowledges the opposing views on cutting as well. For example, she includes information about the SAFE program, cofounded by Karen Conterio in 1984 as the first outpatient support group for cutters. "Although Conterio is by training a substance-abuse counselor, she opposes viewing self-injury through a medical or addiction model. She sees cutting not as a disease, but as a behavior, not an addiction one is powerless to control, but a choice.

'They choose to start doing this and they have to choose to stop,' she says flatly"(192–93).

Just as diverse and varied as the reasons people cut are the cutters themselves. Cutters are not necessarily identifiable by their backgrounds, families, or profiles. They come from all walks of life: professional, blue collar, upper class, lower class, educated, ignorant, mentally ill, seemingly normal, physically abused, emotionally abused, or not abused at all. Strong, who profiles primarily women in her book, says that parental abuse lies behind cutting behavior in 50 to 60 percent of the cases. But many cutters were never abused by a parent. Nevertheless, the bulk of research done on the subject of cutting contends that it is often associated in some form with abuse: "Our experience—and the experience of all other researchers in the field—confirms that a large proportion of self-injurers have experienced physical or sexual trauma" (Conterio and Lader 48–49). This is consistent with the finding by Whitlock and colleagues that 53 percent of the self-injurers in their study reported physical, sexual, or emotional abuse, or some combination of these.

Writing about abuse and self-injury, Alice Miller argues in *Prisoners of Childhood* that a child feels emotionally abandoned whether parents are *intentionally* abusive or neglectful or simply inadequate due to their own emotional deficits. The child then has to subvert her own needs to those of her parents. The child locks her true self away in what Miller calls an "inner prison," including all the feelings the child cannot survive without, like nurturance and empathy (53–54). "The sheer intensity of a child's feelings, however, means the feelings cannot be repressed without severe consequences. The thicker the prison walls grow, the more future emotional development is impeded" (12). When the wall becomes impenetrable, and the pain behind it overwhelming, cutting is often used to break through and achieve some sense of control.

Diagnoses

In their 1967 study, Grunebaum and Klerman described how the diagnosis of a cutter often revealed more about the doctors' schools of thought than the patients', "serving as a kind of Rorschach test into which doctors would project their personal feelings and biases" (qtd. in Strong 59). The researchers explain this in terms of the attending physician's school of thought and how it was applied to the cutter being treated. For example, a therapist with experience in treating adolescent "acting out" behavior may be prone to focus on the cutter's own "acting out" behavior. Therapists who favor psychotherapy may be especially aware of their patient's sexual and aggressive fantasies and the use of projection and denial as defenses, making them inclined toward a diagnosis of the cutter as a schizophrenic, while still another therapist, responding to the patient's "theatrical and seductive appeal," might favor the label of hysteria (qtd. in Strong 60). The researchers disagreed with the diagnoses placed on cutters in the late 1960s, citing the fact that cutting patients did not engage in typical kinds of antisocial behavior and did not lack feelings of guilt. Nor, the researchers argued, did cutters manifest a thought disorder or meet the criteria of hysteria.

According to Marilee Strong, there has been a type of labeling going on among those who study and treat cutters—the most frequently given is the diagnosis of borderline personality disorder. *The Diagnostic and Statistical Manual of Mental Disorders IV* (*DSM IV*) lists self-mutilation as one of the eight criteria for the disorder. The trouble with this label, points out Wendy Lader, is that it has become to the psychiatric world what a diagnosis of attention deficit disorder has become to public schools. "Borderline personality disorder," states Lader, "is wildly over diagnosed, applied to anybody who gives you a hard time. And, it is almost exclusively applied to women" (qtd. in Strong 61). David Frankel, psychologist and former program director of the child and adolescent unit at Ross Hospital in Marin County, California, says the problem lies with the way the *DSM IV* focuses on symptoms rather than underlying causes of the disorder:

> The borderline label is so overused they should almost throw out the word. Especially in a hospital setting it has come to mean anyone, particularly female, who is considered real irritating and isn't obviously psychotic. I think it is a useful diagnosis because it implies a certain set of treatment strategies. But it is also pejorative. If someone calls up and says, 'We've got an admission for you: a borderline woman who has cut herself, who is very angry, and this is her fifth hospitalization' a lot of psychologists will say, 'Don't admit her.' They just don't want to deal with borderlines. And insurance companies basically view personality disorders as untreatable. But it's totally untrue. (Qtd. in Strong 61)

The negativity surrounding the label of borderline personality disorder has even reached popular television: on an episode of *ER*, a doctor dismisses the symptoms of a psychiatric patient who complains of numerous ailments as "just the ravings of a borderline."

Thanks in part to those who have recognized the trouble associated with the borderline label, patients who cut themselves are not now automatically diagnosed with a psychological disorder. Many experts believe a more appropriate, compassionate diagnosis for some cutters is PTSD, or post-traumatic stress disorder—once known as shell shock and popularized as a diagnosis given to soldiers returning from the ravages of war. PTSD has become a general diagnosis, applied to those whose experience of trauma in one form or another has rendered them vulnerable to "terror-bound memories that can return or be triggered by other stimuli, but they are never able to effectively process the original emotional memory for reasons that are psychological" (Strong 91). Many people who cut or otherwise self-injure do not fit the criteria for borderline personality disorder—which include anxiety, inappropriate anger, unstable relationships, chronic feelings of emptiness, dissociation, an unstable sense of self, frantic efforts to avoid real or imagined abandonment, recurrent suicidal behavior, and other forms of destructive and impulsive behavior. One can see the trouble with the label. But is there a danger that PTSD will simply replace borderline as an overused, catchall diagnosis? Allan Young, Ruth Leys, and Ian Hacking have all challenged the existence of PTSD as a distinct psychiatric disorder. Psychologists admit there is no one comprehensive psychological theory that explains everything they now understand about cutters. According to Strong, relatively new or changing fields of research are those that are adding the most to what researchers are learning about cutters, fields like developmental psychology, behaviorism, neurochemistry, PTSD, and the psychology of the abused child.

Some psychologists, like V. J. Turner, add addiction to the already confusing world of diagnoses. In her book Secret Scars, Turner identifies herself as a reformed cutter who began scratching herself at the age of six and continued until she was a teenager. Unlike Karen Conterio, she argues that cutting can and should be treated the same way addiction is treated, using a twelve-step program. She claims such a program worked for her, though she admits that traditional therapy was also helpful at times. Turner is among those researchers who find fault with the blanket diagnoses, like PTSD, given to self-injurers. "At present," she states, "there is no diagnostic criteria for self-injury or established guidelines that are used by mental health professionals or medical doctors" (87). She cites the most common clinical diagnoses for self-injurers as PTSD, dissociative disorders, mood disorders, bipolar disorder, anxiety, impulse control disorders and borderline personality disorder (87). She calls self-injury a "syndrome" and asserts that it should be seen as well as treated as an addiction; she even goes so far as to say that "it might be the root to understanding other addictions" (22).

Turner contends that there is a strong correlation between self-injury and other addictive behaviors, pointing out that many who cut themselves also have problems with alcohol, drugs, or food (23). She lists questions in three categories for readers to ask themselves: "Common Childhood History and Background Factors of Those Who Self-Injure," "Common Personality Characteristics Seen in Self-Injurers," and "Self-Injury Checklist." She states, "If you or someone you know can identify with these terms, it is time to seek help" (31).

I wonder if Turner's readers are questioning whether they are indeed self-injurers. Engaging in self-injurious behavior implies, by definition, a self-injurer, just as one who engages in binging and purging has an eating disorder. Those who injure themselves intentionally are self-injurers. The better question to ask is *why* the person engages in the behaviors. The road to recovery, rather than why the behavior exists, is the focus of Turner's book. But Turner does explore some possible causes of cutting. Her theory about cutting as an addiction is a fresh perspective, one that makes a great deal of sense in the manner in which she presents it. She also includes observations surrounding the self-injurer that are consistent with theories of other researchers.

Turner writes, "Deliberate self-injury can be either a method of stimulation to escape depression, numbness, and feeling 'dead inside' or a method to relieve anxiety and agitation" (37). She offers theories from other researchers, like Favazza, Scott Lines, and Alice Miller, all of whom describe the emotional and psychological sides of self-injury. Rather than supporting the traditional belief that cutting is caused by an alteration in brain chemicals, Turner says that self-injury, like other addiction-based behaviors, can be the cause of an alteration in the brain chemicals of the cutter. "Research evidence, most notably the work of Harvard psychiatrist Bessel van der Kolk and his colleagues, suggests that self-injury causes a release of chemicals in the brain that are similar to addictive opiates. Therefore, it may be very difficult for a person who self-injures, once hooked, to stop"(23). Turner further acknowledges the many theories surrounding what actually causes addiction, ranging from abuse to deficits in the self or personality, unresolved childhood issues, spiritual deficits, learned behaviors, peer pressure, genetic predisposition, or the "disease" model (23). She holds that as with addictions to alcohol and drugs, there isn't a single cause of self-injurious behavior; instead, there are many factors involved. But, she adds, "self-injury is initially a learned behavior that may become addictive. Self-injury is usually not learned by direct observation, but rather by picking up on subconscious cues in the environment" (23). Echoing the theories presented by Levenkron and Strong, she is the only one of the three to call cutting "learned behavior." An example of this is a physically abused child who learns to dissociate as a defense during periods of abuse or pain. As the child grows older, she may instinctively long for emotions she cannot produce, due to the defense mechanism she has habitually used. Therefore, self-injury may become a means of stimulating feeling in the form of pain. Paradoxically, the cutter learns to turn to pain whenever she wants to get away from pain.

CHAPTER 3

My History as a Cutter
Losing Self-Esteem

I first cut myself when I was twelve. I did it because someone told me to. That sounds typically adolescent, I know. I used an old, dull jackknife and carved a cross into the side of my right shin. It was summertime, and I wore shorts almost every day, so I knew people would notice it—but that's what it was about at the time—people noticing.

I didn't cut myself due to physical abuse by my parents, intense self-loathing, or suicidal ideations—I cut myself because a teenage boy who lived in the neighborhood told me to. Looking back with the hindsight of a thirty-three-year-old woman, I now realize this boy was a sadist. More about him will come. For now, let me try to take myself back to that twelve-year-old girl I have trouble believing now I ever was.

"The Time I Lost Myself"

I was like the nearly 40 percent of those in Whitlock, Eckenrode, and Silverman's study who never told anyone about their self-injurious behavior. Nevertheless, I wanted my parents to notice the cuts. Maybe not right away, but I know I wanted them to notice. This was the beginning of my "phase," a strange and difficult part of my life that began slowly and peaked when I was about fifteen. It was over by the time I was a senior in high school. I call it my "phase" because that's what my parents called it. A more apt and accurate name for it might be "the time I lost myself" because that's what happened.

At twelve, I struggled to fit in. It was the summer between sixth and seventh grade, and I was preoccupied with my appearance, my friendships, and my incompetence. I was thin, probably about eighty-five pounds and about four feet ten inches tall. I was prone to exaggeration, and I was so sensitive to others' criticism that I was a slab of marble to these would-be sculptors, becoming the shape they wanted me to become. My best friend's brother once told me my thighs were fat. This one comment reshaped my body image irreparably. I had stringy brown hair that wouldn't do a thing, and I had no athletic ability, nor did I particularly care to develop any. I was supposed to wear glasses, but I refused to do so in the name of vanity. I had begun to menstruate, and I believed the old wives' tales about one's body having grown to its adult size once a girl began her period, so I was mortified to think I would be short with fat thighs and a flat chest forever. I became obsessed about my body and compared myself to the images of perfect girls I saw in magazines such as *Teen*. I couldn't live up to these models, and I failed to realize that few girls could. Being bombarded with societal messages that I was inadequate produced my inner turmoil. I felt I had little control over myself because I lacked the power society equated with beauty and perfection. As Gilligan suggests, my sense of vulnerability, preventing me from doing "something in the world," had begun to paralyze me. I was convinced that those who complimented me were lying or were just trying to be nice for whatever reason. My self-confidence had always been shaky. By twelve, it was gone.

According to Mary Pipher, "America today is a girl-destroying place. Everywhere girls are encouraged to sacrifice their true selves. Many girls lose contact with their true selves and once they do, they become extraordinarily vulnerable to a culture that is all too happy to use them for its purposes" (44). I agree with this assertion, but I wonder whether each of us has a "true self" rather than a self that is constantly influenced by a variety of cultural and genetic forces.

I was adopted when I was three months old and grew up in a family of four, consisting of me, my parents, and an older brother, who was also adopted. All I was told about my birth family was that I was Catholic and my birth mother had allergies. Adoptions were closed when I was born in 1970, meaning no information that could identify birth parents was given to adoptive families. I grew up imagining many details about who my "real" mother was. As a small child, I pictured her as a princess. My image of her grew as I did, and its incarnations included a movie star and an author. Until I met the boy, the sadist, I had never entertained negative images about my birth mother. The boy told me she was probably a whore.

My adoptive parents were educated people, both teachers, who were much older than the parents of my peers. In fact, they were closer in age to my friends' grandparents. This always bothered me. When I was a small child, I had fears of my parents dying. I was paralyzed with thoughts of their dying, and spent much of my mother-imposed, before-bed prayer time begging God to let them live. I am not sure where this fear came from other than my parents' age. They were both almost thirty-nine when I was adopted. Today, this isn't as unusual as it was then.

The relationship at home between my brother and me was always strained. We were like peanut butter and mustard, and we fought so much that my parents would not allow us to sit next to each other in the car or at the dinner table. I think I resented him for being so "weird." I think he resented me for simply being. He once told me he that liked his life much better before my parents adopted me (he was two and a half when they brought me home) and that he wished I were dead. He once threatened to chop me up and bury me in my mother's vegetable garden. I was hysterical and ran screaming and crying into the house. My parents were both at work, so I called my mother. When I told her I had locked Bill out of the house because of the threat he made, which I believed at the time he was completely capable of carrying out, my mother grew angry with me, telling me I was lying and that it was a "sin" to lie about my brother like that. She told me for what must have been the thousandth time in my life, "There is something wrong with you, Patricia" and hung up on me. Not only did my own brother verbally threaten me, but my cries for protection were unheard. I felt powerless to ensure my own safety, and ignored by a mother whose job it was to make me safe.

My parents believed that an adopted child was born tabula rasa. This was a popular theory in the 1950s and one my parents did not abandon until they tried raising strangers as if we were family. My father was smart, athletic, and what he called "a self-made man." He came from humble beginnings, and he put himself through college after serving in the navy during the Korean War. He was a successful educator in our city and well liked. He taught English with passion and fervor, but often lost patience with my brother and me. My mother had grown up in a small family. Her father was a pioneer in the invention of plastic (I grew up in Pittsfield, Massachusetts, once the plastics capital of the world), and he made a comfortable living. My mother was used to obeying her parents, the nuns at her school, and just about anyone else who told her what to do. Unfortunately, I was nothing like my mother.

I was an insecure child, the kind who clings to her parents and fears everything unfamiliar. This didn't bode well for me when I started school, particularly because my mother had been in the hospital battling breast cancer the previous summer, and my aunt had to bring me to my first day of kindergarten. I was instructed to wait for my brother to meet me after school and walk me home. My teacher, Ms. Rosenbaum, would not allow me to leave that first afternoon with my brother. Instead, she insisted I take the kindergarten bus with my classmates, a bus that was supposed to carry me home. I bit her hand, and she finally released me from her grip. I remember escaping out the school door, running and crying. The turmoil of having my mother ill and my father at wit's end most of the time was apparently enough to rattle my sense of security and rendered me highly anxious. I was also given to rocking back and forth, which I did often at home and in school. My mother thought I was disturbed, and she tried to get me to stop this behavior, somehow believing that would stop the disturbance. I also began stealing once I entered school. I stole little items from the classroom, like plastic teddy bears used to help kids count. I guess I was suffering from the change in structure at home, and the fear of my mother dying and leaving me with a brother who was mean to me and a father who couldn't begin to fathom raising two children alone. This stress was manifesting itself in behaviors we now term "acting out," since I had no sophisticated coping skills, or indeed any coping skills at all at the tender age of five and a half. As my fears and behavior grew more unreasonable, my self-image deteriorated. I became a creature of habit, and any deviation from my regular routine troubled me. Add to this the fact that older girls in the neighborhood began hazing me, bullying me, and making fun of my clothing, and I was already well on my way to losing my self-esteem.

Cutting Myself

By the time I was twelve I had begun cutting myself. I was trying to fit in. I was hanging around with a crowd of kids who did not have the best reputation. They smoked cigarettes and pot, and carried on in a fashion my parents disapproved of: staying out late, committing petty crimes like bicycle theft, and playing loud music past nine o'clock. They were also older than I was, in some cases by as much as six years. But these kids seemed to accept me.

It began with that first cut, the cross in my leg. Soon there were more cuts and crosses. This was approximately the same time that I had told my mother I was no longer interested in attending catechism and that Sunday mass bored me. Perhaps there was rebellious symbolism in the crosses. To early Christians, the cross was a symbol of salvation and victory. Later Christians viewed the cross as a symbol of shame and torture, reflected in the phrase "a cross to bear," which comes from the story of Jesus Christ carrying his own cross to his crucifixion ("Colum Cille Cross Symbolism"). For me, the cuttings symbolized both: my cutting was a victory over the lack of control I felt, as the crosses I carved appeared to empower me and give me control over what I felt was unacceptable in myself, particularly my changing, awkward body. However, I was indeed torturing myself by inflicting pain, albeit temporary. The shame didn't come right away but gradually emerged as I began hiding and covering my scars. I was afraid of being different, of not attaining the physical beauty society demanded. My crosses made me different from others around me who didn't cut themselves, and my scars were like graffiti on a building's facade, making the structure appear repulsive.

My parents did not seem to notice the cuts, so I made more. These, too, went unnoticed, or at least unaddressed. I was yearning to be what society and my parents wanted me to be: pretty, well behaved, attractively shaped, smart, well mannered, athletic, and most importantly, accepted. I was having little success. I was smart, but I had begun doubting this in the third grade, because I could never keep up with my classmates in math drills. I could read and write well, but that didn't seem to be enough. I struggled with math and science, and I also had a history of strep throat, which resulted in frequent school absences. I wanted so much to be liked by my peers that I would do almost anything to fit in. I took violin lessons because my friends did. I took up the flute when my best friend took up the clarinet so we could go to lessons together. Alas, we had drifted apart by the time I was twelve. I grew distant from most of my friends. I was changing, becoming different from most people. I was afraid of being rejected by my peers and by my parents, whose approval I so desperately wanted. My behavior assured that I would be rejected by almost everyone.

The sadistic boy was one of those older kids with whom I had started spending time. He was tall and blond and loud and controlling. He seemed to like me and persuaded the other kids to allow me to spend time with them. For this I was immensely grateful, and I became whatever I thought I needed to be in order to remain in his good graces. When he told me to cut myself, I did. I am not sure why he told me to do this—it was long ago and much of it seems to have been mercifully blotted out by my memory. The cutting wasn't all of it, either. I began drinking alcohol and dressing like those older kids did, fitting the profile of a cutter created by Graff and Mallin. My parents tolerated my new companions for the summer, confident I would return to middle school and my peers in the fall, and, they hoped, normalcy. But I wasn't normal, and I wouldn't be again for several years to come.

I became a cutter to please someone else but remained a cutter to please myself. I was suffering in so many ways. I was afraid of failing, so I failed. I was afraid of displeasing my parents, so I displeased them. I was afraid of not fitting in, so I turned to a group who didn't fit in. I was afraid I would never be smart enough in school, so I stopped trying. I was fearful of being too fat, too short, not pretty enough, and I succumbed to all these societal pressures by scarring my own skin. I did it in an attempt to manifest what I felt on the inside at a place on the outside where people would see it—and help me. Or in Hyman's words, I was cutting myself "to make the outside look the way the inside feels" (46). But the right people didn't see it. As I began cutting myself more, on my legs and forearms, I began hiding the cuts and the scars. I guess my desire for a response from my parents was short-lived. I realized they were not going to intervene; they were not going to help me, and so I began to see cutting as a way of helping myself. To the noncutter, this must sound strange. How did slicing up my arms and legs help anything? Oh, but it did.

According to the psychologist Scott Lines, "The skin becomes a battlefield as a demonstration of internal chaos. The place where the self meets the world is a canvas or *tabula rasa* on which is displayed exactly how bad one feels inside" (qtd. in Strong 29). I was in control of my cutting as I was in control of nothing else in my life. I could shape the cuts into whatever form I chose. I could bleed, then clean the wounds, and then bandage them until they became the scars I so desired. Like Jesus Christ, I had my own crosses to bear, but for me, it was all about the scars. I could hurt myself and heal myself, as Favazza observed in the Moroccan women, but nothing could take away the scars. They were medals of honor, of courage, of control and facility that I could achieve nowhere else in my life. The Sufi Indians regarded cutting and scarification in much the same way: as initiation rites, tests of strength, courage, and endurance that help make the transition to adulthood. Scars, like blood, are richly symbolic. They provide a permanent, physical record not only of pain and injury but also of healing (Strong 34). They were beautiful to me, perhaps replacing the other parts of me I felt weren't. I was creating something beautiful: scar tissue.

CHAPTER 4

Kettlewell, OCD, and Me
Keeping One's Beasts at Bay

In her memoir *The Skin Game*, Caroline Kettlewell beautifully narrates her own adolescent and young adult struggles with a razor blade. For Kettlewell, cutting was about the blood, yes, but like me, she also wanted the scars that came with the damage. "I cut to lay down a line between before and after, between self and other, chaos and clarity. I cut as an affirmation of hope, saying 'I have drawn the line and I am still on this side of it'"(176). This passage, which is as eloquent as the rest of her book, uses the metaphor of a line or border to symbolize her inner feelings about her outer scars.

Cutting is about more than bloodshed, more than scar tissue; cutting is a way to keep one's beasts at bay. It makes the invisible struggles inside the cutter visible to him or her, and that visibility alone seems to make the problem real enough, legitimate enough, and physical enough to mean something as significant as it *feels* like it means. "Cutting was my defense against an internal chaos, against a sense of the world gone out of control," writes Kettlewell (176). Her memoir traces her development as a young woman. She writes of her overwhelming childhood fears, like being afraid of the dark, afraid of not fitting in, afraid of her own lack of self-confidence. However, nowhere in her book does Kettlewell describe problems with attachment, nor does she write of having any other symptoms Levenkron and others describe. In fact, she does not mention abuse, childhood trauma, or psychological dysfunction anywhere in her memoir. She does, however, write about seeing the evidence of cutting on the arm of a teenage boy on whom she had a crush:

> One afternoon he slouched against a wall, arms folded, to engage me in the usual dialogue of innuendo. He shifted position, absentmindedly shoving up the frayed sleeve of his yellow button-down shirt, revealing on his forearm a series of ugly gashes, dried and crusted. He wanted me to ask.

"What'd you do?" I gasped, riveted by the raw slashes, the blood-rusty stains on his shirt.

"Razor blade." He laughed, dismissive. It was lurid, livid—beneath his notice. Who knew what games he and his friends had been up to, who were always double-daring each other with buck knives and bravado?

I couldn't stop staring. I knew how the skin would feel with the feverish burn of those wounds. Of course, razor blades—why had this never occurred to me before? (26)

Kettlewell admits in this passage that she had never considered cutting herself until she saw the results from the actions of a cutter. In her case, cutting was clearly a learned behavior and probably involved copycatting as well. The boy she mentions does not resurface in her book—instead, he moves away. But she continues the behaviors in his absence, having found what she felt was the perfect outlet for her inner turmoil and disordered world. She had made the connection. She engaged in cutting to heal herself. Her failure to include in her memoir accounts of physical, sexual, or verbal abuse or even neglect is important because it is the only story I have read that fails to do so. Her memoir presents only the influence of a peer to which her cutting behavior can be attributed. She does not present herself as mentally ill, either, and although she mentions seeing several therapists, she never went with the intention to address the cutting. Instead, her book is an account of an adolescent searching for a means of control, finding it in cutting only after being introduced to this coping mechanism by someone who had already engaged in it. Of course, one person's experience cannot dispel the many theories of researchers who link self-injury with abuse and mental illness, but it can encourage consideration of the power of peer pressure and contagion; they may be as influential in initiating a person's cutting behavior as the more universally recognized causes.

When I began my own research, I focused on what I was reading more than on what I was thinking; I wasn't examining my own cutting behavior and its causes. Then one day it hit me that there had to be a connection between my own history as a cutter and other maladaptive behaviors in which I had engaged. I was given to rocking back and forth, a behavior I continued until I was in my midtwenties, though I did it only in private. Like Kettlewell, I was afraid of the dark and often slept with a light on. And I was an obsessive-compulsive child. Levenkron mentions that obsessive-compulsive behavior is akin to cutting. He believes that cutting, like OCD, is a maladaptive behavior a person engages in to "pro-tect" herself (85). He also believes that "the length of time the patients used their maladaptive defenses for relief from psychological confusion, insecurity, or pain increased their dependence on their psychological behaviors" (87). According to Scott Turner of Brown University, "some OCD disorders may be triggered by infectious bacteria that cause strep throats" (1). I believe my obsessive-compulsive behavior was a result of strep infections.

Obsessive-Compulsive Behavior

I had strep throat four times during first grade. Like many young chil-dren, I could not swallow pills, so I was written a prescription on every occasion for liquid penicillin. Liquid penicillin tastes like vomit. I had a great deal of trouble taking the antibiotic because of its taste, and I often swallowed far less than I was supposed to. My strep throat would continue to plague me longer than it should have. As a result, I believe I developed obvious and common signs of obsessive compulsion. I washed my hands constantly, and I had to dry them in a particular fashion or chance having to rewash. My hands became flaky and scaly. My mother tried to make me sleep with Vaseline and gloves, but I couldn't stand the feeling of the petroleum-based product on my hands and under my fingernails, so I washed it off. I also began rituals involving counting and the wearing of particular clothing. For example, I had to count the rotations of my bicycle pedals, and I had to wear a shirt with clowns on it every Monday and Wednesday. I also had to walk home the same way every day, eat the same snack every day, and go to bed at the same time each night. Devia-tion from any of these rituals made me extremely anxious and irritable.

My strep infections became frequent the year following my mother's cancer, and I think the two factors—emotional anxiety that arose from my mother's condition, coupled with the physiological changes we now know strep infections can have on their hosts—led to my obsessive-compulsive behaviors. As I grew older, the hand-washing lessened, as did the intensity of my other rituals, and I eventually outgrew my clown shirt. However, I began to brush my teeth so frequently I eventually wore the enamel from them. (I had veneers attached to my eight front teeth when I was thirty.) When I was under extreme stress or fatigue, the rituals and the physi-cal rocking intensified, though I realized once I left kindergarten that

I should not rock in public. Had I been capable of obtaining an object with which to cut myself before my twelfth summer, I might have done that, too.

Like Kettlewell, I was introduced to cutting by a teenage boy—and I had never thought about cutting myself before that incident occurred. My obsessive-compulsive behaviors were a way for me to corral my wild thoughts and put order and sense into a young girl's world that seemed to have none. The behaviors were not conscious choices but unconscious necessities. At the time, I could not stop the behaviors on my own, though I could decide where and when to engage in them. I was always good at keeping up appearances, and I made sure that I never let even my best friends know about my behaviors. I knew my rituals were odd enough to make me different, and I certainly didn't want to be any more different than I had to be. So, with some control over my cutting behaviors when I felt I could control little else, I guess I was doing what I could. Curiously, the cutting replaced some of my obsessive behaviors. While I do not believe OCD behaviors are learned as much as they are a result of organic factors, I am sure that once I adopted the learned behavior of cutting myself, I used that, rather than my other rituals, to protect myself and manage my internal chaos.

Although I engaged in self-abusive behavior, I was never physically abused by either parent. In fact, my parents did not employ corporal punishment in any form. My mother was the primary disciplinarian in our household. I suspect this was because my father became too emotional when he tried to discipline either my brother or me. I remember once when my brother refused to go to school. He locked himself in his room and would not come out or even speak to my father through the door. My father, who didn't use profanity, began to swear and pound on my brother's door. Eventually, he tried to break the door down by repeatedly throwing himself at it. He was purple in the face, and I thought he would have a heart attack and drop dead then and there. I vaguely remember another incident for which I was punished. I was very small, and I have no idea what I did, but I remember my father attempting to take me over his knee and spank me. When I began to scream, cry, and wail, my father, with tears in his eyes, gave up his halfhearted attempt to spank me. I was never physically struck by either parent, nor did I witness my father lose control again to the extent he did while attempting to get my brother out of the bedroom.

Alarmed by the emotional toll that punishing his children took on my father, my mother decided she was better equipped to handle such parental obligations. She prided herself on her strength, resolve, and composure. She was not an emotional woman, and she discouraged displays of emotion in all of us. Because I was an emotional child, I often became the object of her scorn and ridicule as I cried and carried on over issues that bothered or hurt me. True, I was overly sensitive, the type of child who cried because she felt her stuffed tiger was actually in pain while being pulverized by her brother's fist, or because the mother on the Hallmark commercial received the kind of card from her son that made her hug and kiss him. My mother's reaction to my tears was typically sarcasm. Children can feel emotionally abandoned even when parents are not intentionally abusive or neglectful.

Psychiatrist Frank Putnam, a leading researcher at the National Institute of Mental Health, believes the ability to regulate our emotions and behave appropriately gives us a sense of self-control. People who have difficulty regulating their emotions develop problems controlling their behavior. A chronic feeling of being "out of control" is, for researchers like Putnam, a signal that something may have happened in childhood that disrupted the ability to care for oneself in an appropriate way (qtd. in Strong 41). His theories, like Levenkron's, claim that a secure attachment bond is one of the most important elements of protection against traumatization. Emotional attachment helps a child feel connected and supported rather than alone and helpless. Abused and neglected children don't learn from their parents how to soothe themselves, and they cannot trust anyone else to help them do this. They may turn to cutting or other forms of self-injury as a means of soothing themselves and reestablishing a temporary psychological equilibrium. When this happens, cutting can be seen as a learned albeit unconscious behavior.

For the first three months of my life I was cared for by strangers—who and how many I don't know. Because there were several infants at the adoption facility, time spent being held, fed, and nurtured by staff members must have been limited. Subsequently, I was adopted by parents who were never particularly affectionate, and while they were indulgent in terms of material things, that indulgence didn't extend to rich physical or emotional nurturance. As an adopted child, I may have had trouble with bonding, but I have been unable to find any connection between adoptees and self-injury in my research.

I was a sensitive, emotional child being raised by a mother who had a great deal of difficulty understanding or accepting this, and she tended to reject me when I was emotional. Perhaps the emotional attachment I lacked contributed to my eventual, maybe inevitable, cutting behavior. I personified Grunebaum and Klerman's theory that cutters often have cold, punitive, judgmental mothers. I have learned that abuse doesn't have to include breaking bones, slapping cheeks, or sexually molesting children in order for it to damage and define their psychological state. Children subjected to emotional abuse are often damaged in deeper ways, and sometimes they grow to wish, as I guess I have, that it was only a slap in the face or a fractured arm. Once I "learned" about cutting, I initially engaged in the behavior to get the attention and sympathy I so craved at home. It was a deliberate, learned behavior in which I chose to engage, unlike the OCD behaviors of my childhood. Ronni S. Stefl, a psychologist working with SIB patients, describes a behavioral model of self-injury: "Behavioral models provide convincing evidence for the motivation of SIB indicating that the behavior may be reinforced by extrinsic sources of positive reinforcement such as attention, negative reinforcement, escape from demands, or that the behavior may produce intrinsic reinforcement such as sensory stimulation or pain reduction." I was searching for those extrinsic positive reinforcements, but I didn't receive them from my parents. Instead, I acquired them from the boy who introduced me to cutting—the only person in whom I confided my cutting secrets. Perhaps my upbringing and the emotional problems I had at home caused me to seek approval from external sources, like a peer group. Once I began to derive that sort of approval, I engaged in self-injurious behaviors, like drinking and cutting, that allowed me to continue receiving that approval.

Like the overwhelming majority of the students in Whitlock's study, I never disclosed my cutting to a physician or therapist. Indeed, I never disclosed my cutting to anyone except that one boy—until I wrote my reader-response diary in Jeff's course. No one discovered my cutting, and those who may have noticed turned the other way. Despite this, somehow I developed more appropriate coping mechanisms and abandoned cutting. I think much of it had to do with breaking the hold that boy had on me and developing healthier friendships. That took me several years, but I eventually realized he was a destructive influence on my life. It wasn't just the cutting, either. He did not want me to engage in school-related activities once I entered high school. He tried to alienate me from my other friends. He monopolized my time, and when I had to do homework or attend algebra tutoring, he coaxed me into neglecting my schoolwork. As I deteriorated, he grew more pleased with his influence on me, reminiscent of the antifeminist influence male-dominated society can have on young women. In all the research I've read linking cutting and abuse, parents or guardians are the identified abusers. In my own case, I theorize that if I was indeed a victim of deliberate abuse, I suffered at the hands of an older male cohort rather than my parents.

Girls Who Cut

Many years after abandoning most of my OCD behaviors and all of my cutting, I graduated from college and began searching for a teaching job. Like so many English teachers, I was unsuccessful in my quest for a position in a public school in the early 1990s, and so I took a job in a residential treatment facility in Lenox, Massachusetts. Initially, I worked as a residential counselor. My duties included waking the facility's young population, making sure they completed their morning showers and dressed themselves appropriately, and escorting them to breakfast. After breakfast, we attended a site-based school, then went back to the dorms at the end of the school day to engage in scheduled activities, work on students' issues, and learn about appropriate ways of living and interacting with others. The ratio of students to counselors was 4:1. These students had been placed at the facility either by court order or by their local school systems due to "out of control" behaviors. Many of the students, in particular the adolescent girls, cut themselves.

While students were never to be left alone or "out of eyesight," they had privacy in bathrooms. This is where most of the cutting occurred. When I was employed there, the facility had just begun treating adolescent girls, and most employees and even administrators were naive about cutting. Having been a cutter myself, and having read Mary Pipher's *Reviving Ophelia*, I was not surprised when students began to self-injure. One student, Molly, had been at the facility for several years. She displayed classic symptoms of OCD, including rituals before and after meals of sitting on her bed, and frequently going through a complicated series of slaps and touches of her head, her arm, and her shoes, which always reminded me of a baseball coach's signals. As Molly entered adolescence, she would previously have been "transitioned" to another type of facility; the one I worked for had never kept adolescent girls. But an influx of referrals for adolescent female students from Chicago, New York, Connecticut, Maine, and Vermont prompted the school to change its policy.

The girls were divided into three "teams" of between seven and nine students each. Molly was in a team of girls who functioned at a lower academic level and had what we referred to as "issues," like sexual abuse trauma, bed-wetting, OCD, and the like. But they were not considered dangerous to themselves or others. One evening while she was alone in the bathroom, Molly cut her forearm. From that point on, she cut herself in the same spot whenever she had an opportunity to do so, with pens, combs, any object that would reopen her wound. She was to be watched constantly, even while in the bathroom. One morning as I sat in the bathroom doorway while she readied herself for a shower, another student came down the hall toward me. I turned my head to acknowledge the girl and explain that I would have to talk to her later, because I had to watch Molly. In the seconds it took me to do this, Molly retrieved a comb with broken teeth that she had stashed under the trash basket earlier. She concealed it under her arm when she entered the shower, where she proceeded to cut herself again. I felt horribly guilty when it was discovered that afternoon that she had reinjured herself. She confessed where and how she had done it. Thinking I would lose my job, and overwrought with guilt, I cried as I drove home after work. That evening, she did it again. A supervisor who was with her turned away to answer the telephone. Molly was determined to cut herself and took every opportunity to do so. I had not been at fault nor had the supervisor. Molly wanted to cut herself—perhaps she *had* to cut herself. Interestingly, once she began cutting herself, she abandoned her OCD rituals, something none of us recognized until her clinician pointed it out to the staff.

Molly was sent to the facility's intensive treatment unit (ITU) for stabilization. In traditional copycat fashion, other girls on Molly's team began scratching and trying to cut themselves. Girls who had never before demonstrated any type of SIBs were now collecting and hiding sharp rocks from the ball field, taking the hinges off the doors in the dorms to get the screws, and even biting themselves on the arms and legs. After several minor incidents, the SIBs faded in most of the girls, maybe because Molly was sent from the ITU to a psychiatric hospital and they didn't want to follow suit. Perhaps she was indeed in need of treatment for psychological concerns. However, what of the other cutters? Girls in the team and even others at the facility stopped cutting and scratching when it was no longer "the thing to do." I completed my master's degree in education and left the facility three years later. I never learned what became of Molly or what kind of treatment she received for her cutting behaviors in the hospital.

Like me, Molly suffered from OCD behaviors that were eventually replaced by cutting behaviors. I have been unable to find research that specifically links OCD and cutting, if indeed a link exists. But I believe I engaged in OCD behaviors in order to control myself and the world around me—as did Molly. Once we began to engage in cutting, it brought a degree of self-control and we could both, therefore, abandon our OCD behaviors. Molly's case also illustrates how contagious cutting can be.

CHAPTER 5

Cutting Influences
Peer Pressure and Out-of-Control Lives

"The phenomenon known as 'contagion' is growing. Teens are learning about the behavior from one another, from the press, and from popular culture, and it is giving them ideas. Several popular singers and rock groups portray self-injury in their lyrics and album art" (Conterio and Lader 23). The researchers add that many children and teenagers may begin self-injury by accident—literally. Following an accidental cut, however, these adolescents "were surprised when they were flooded by feelings of relief" (22). Cutting then becomes a deliberate pattern of behavior. One survey of 245 college students found that 12 percent admitted to having harmed themselves deliberately (qtd. in Conterio and Lader 21). And Whitlock, Eckenrode, and Silverman's study of 8,300 hundred Cornell and Princeton students found that 17 percent engaged in self-injurious behaviors (1945).

With the emerging work of researchers like Conterio and Lader and the memoir written by Carolyn Kettlewell comes the theory that the increase in SIBs in our culture can be attributed, at least in some women, to conscious, learned, or deliberately imitated behavior. And what of the media's contributions to cutting behavior? "Music groups are now expressing themes of self-injury, and even popular television shows like *Beverly Hills 90210* and *7th Heaven* are giving exposure to the problem" (Conterio and Lader 6). Celebrities including Johnny Depp, Roseanne Barr, and Princess Diana all admitted publicly to cutting behavior. Particularly during the 1990s, the decade to which most researchers attribute this veritable wave of self-injury's emergence, those celebrities were quite popular, particularly among adolescents.

"I think there is a great deal of copycatting in the rise we see in cutting," says Katherine Jensen (personal communication). A psychologist who practices in Pittsfield, Massachusetts, she has treated several clients, especially in the past ten years, who engage in cutting behaviors. The typical cutter, says Jensen, is a young adolescent female being raised by only one parent. While abuse, particularly sexual abuse, is certainly a factor in the majority of cases of self-injury, Jensen believes that cutting has become as popular a method of "fitting in" and being accepted by peer groups as wearing the right clothing. "The emulation of the behavior, whether it is emulation of someone who actually has these behaviors caused by some psychopathology or the emulation of behaviors in others who are doing it to seek status among their peers, is a factor in the counterculture of certain adolescents." She agrees that media influence probably has an effect, but she was not aware of young-adult literature with cutting as the theme.

"I Needed Relief Fast"

Several books have been written on the theme of cutting, most notably two works of fiction geared toward the female, young-adult audience: *Cut* by Patricia McCormick and *Crosses* by Shelley Stoehr. Both books are written in the first person, narrated by female adolescent cutters who chronicle their out-of-control lifestyles. *Crosses* includes accolades on the front cover from the *School Library Journal*, "Reminiscent of *Go Ask Alice*, the powerful portrayal of Nancy and Katie will be read again and again," and citations from the American Library Association for "Best Book for Young Adults," and "Recommended for Reluctant Readers." Knowing that the theme is self-injury, I recall thinking quizzically about these citations even before I read the book. While *Crosses* doesn't tout cutting's virtues, it certainly does, in my opinion, feature an unhealthy main character who not only cuts herself but also engages in sex, consumes alcohol and drugs, lies to her parents, and witnesses the overdose and subsequent death of her best friend and cocutter. I don't recall books as racy as this one being recommended by librarians when I was a teenage reader. In fact, as I recall, *Go Ask Alice* was an underground book—the kind my high school and local libraries considered contraband. I heard about the book for years before finally getting my hands on a copy.

The narrator of *Crosses*, Nancy, is fifteen. The book, set in the mid-1980s, was published in 1991. It belongs to a subgenre known as the "problem novel," popular with young adults. I was intrigued by the title because I recalled my own experiences with cutting. Aside from two brief descriptions of Nancy cutting crosses into her skin and one mention of

Katie having a similar scar, the title has little to do with actual crosses, unless one thinks in symbolic terms of Nancy having "crosses" to bear. Otherwise, there is no Christ-like symbolism or religious reference. I wondered about this the same way I have wondered about my own choice to begin cutting by making a cross. The two main characters attend a public rather than parochial school, and neither character has a devout family. Much of the character development in the novel, however, supports theorists' profiles of the stereotypical cutter.

A single mother is raising Katie, Nancy's best friend. Nancy, on the other hand, has two parents, both of whom are alcoholics. They are so consumed by their own behaviors that they fail to notice their daughter's deviant behavior, unless it has to do with her clothing. Nancy, then, is a child of distant, practically negligent parents. The two main characters' behaviors have been learned through interactions with their parents and the influence the characters now have on each other. Nancy narrates, "I always kept sharp things in my bag for emergencies. Sometimes I carved designs—mostly crosses—but the way the day was going, I really felt like I might cry. I needed relief fast and this was how I was brought up. When I was little, my mother used to slap me across the face when I cried, 'to give me a good reason,' but once I got older, I found that wasn't enough. I began to use glass when I needed a reason to break down" (6). The girls meet at school, and their friendship forms quickly when Katie asks Nancy for a cigarette. Nancy is slightly nervous about the new cuts on her arms, fearing Katie will notice. "I think she read my mind because she smiled and showed me her shoulder, which had a scabby cross about an inch long carved into it" (7). Perhaps one aspect of the "crosses" in the title has to do with the characters "crossing" paths. The reader later learns that Katie has other scars, particularly one in the shape of a K on her abdomen, and Nancy describes her own arms as being "covered with many different shapes and designs" (10).

Katie states that the K scratched on her stomach is "so my boyfriend, when I get one, always knows who it is he's sleeping with" (10). This is the first reference in the book to either of the characters being or planning to become sexually active, and it is an indiction that the girls view sex casually. Later in the book, the reader learns that Nancy is sexually active and does whatever her boyfriend wants her to do. This is further evidence of the extent to which her self-esteem has been compromised. Levenkron observes, "The person who chooses this action [attacking one's own skin] is someone who experiences herself as powerless. . . . The self-mutilator has very little physical and emotional security about herself" (46). Clearly, both main characters feel insecure and lack power over their lives. Katie's willingness to have sex with someone who might forget who she is demonstrates a severe lack of self-esteem, as does Nancy's desire to keep a boyfriend even if it means compromising herself sexually. Nancy is also influenced by others in her life: by her parents when she chooses to abuse substances and by Katie when she chooses to cut herself.

Other characters in the novel are also susceptible to cutting because of peer pressure. "Since Tom was even geekier than I was," Nancy says in an early scene, "and I knew he had a crush on me, it was easy to convince him to play the game," the "game" being scratching their arms in science class to see who could make the most cuts and, hence, draw the most blood (11). This episode demonstrates the contagion in adolescent cutting and how easily teens can be manipulated by their peers. Nancy uses acceptance to manipulate Tom into cutting. The book does not state clearly why Nancy began cutting, but her cutting behavior is certainly reinforced by Katie's. Katie's nonchalant attitude toward cutting—and her message that it is not only acceptable to cut but also something the girls need to do as a means of bonding—reinforces Nancy's behavior. In turn, Nancy promotes cutting as a game, and she uses peer pressure to influence Tom to cut himself. Cutting, then, becomes a way of identifying friends and making new ones.

The book demonstrates camaraderie among cutters. Nancy expresses an immediate liking for Katie upon seeing that she, too, has scars. The boy who likes Nancy gives in easily to her game of scratching as he succumbs to the desire to be liked and accepted by her. Young readers of this book might well succumb to the act as well, even if it is only out of curiosity. The book presents cutting as a method of fitting in with peers: "Media exposure of the problem [cutting]—while fantastically helpful in getting self-injurers the care they need—may also inadvertently give people ideas they may not have had before . . . more significantly, people who tend to take their cues from one another—particularly teens—who are desperate to fit in with their contemporaries—and we hear more and more reports from self-injurers who picked up the behavior from a classmate, a sibling, or someone else they know" (Conterio and Lader 6).

Peer influence in cutting is also expressed in the following scene: "Back in the world of ninth grade and Katie, I wasn't laughing anymore.

I was almost crying, remembering two years ago when cutting was only for fun. I didn't seem to need it then, but all of a sudden I thought, I can't stop! Then I thought, I don't even want to. 'What are you so worried about?' Katie said, 'You can stop cutting whenever you want, just like me. It's just that you don't want to, because it's good for you. It keeps you from being overwhelmed by all the shit around you'" (12–13).

The common cutting philosophy is also evidenced here, as Katie expresses what researchers have theorized is at the root of cutting—control. Control can be a powerful allure to adolescents, many of whom feel their young lives are out of their control. Kids from dysfunctional homes, who have trouble making friends, fitting in, and are no longer able to tolerate rules imposed on them at home or at school, often turn to other means of control in an attempt to regain a hold of themselves. However dysfunctional cutting may seem, and despite the differences in theories behind cutting, one link common in most research done on the subject is that it does, indeed, facilitate a sense of control.

"The adolescent who self-injures confronts these issues of separation [from parents] and identity formation with great alarm," write Conterio and Lader. In their discussion of what they term the "underparented child," the authors describe an adolescent who has established autonomy in some senses, like holding down a job, cooking, and cleaning for herself, and who takes responsibility for what the authors think in many cases are "inappropriate duties." This adolescent secretly resents having to take on the responsibilities she feels her parents should be shouldering for her, and she turns to self-injury as a means of coping, by "forcing others into caretaking roles and impeding independence. The underparented adolescent has already experienced, in the emotional or physical absence of care, too much separation and autonomy. This occurs before she is mature enough to assimilate it as a natural part of her growing personality" (99).

Nancy, in reaction to her parents' drunken fight one evening, reaches out in a dysfunctional attempt to regain parenting. "I'll show her [Nancy's mother] slashed wrists, I thought, reaching into my night table drawer and taking out a big piece of broken glass left from when she broke a vase of flowers over my head a few months before. Flipping off the light, I bit my lip and pressed the glass hard into my wrist. I kept saying to myself as I dragged it up and down, fuck you, fuck you, fuck you. Eventually I started to cry, dropped the glass on the floor and fell asleep" (33).

Nancy's mother does not minister to her, and the daughter's reaction in the morning is simply to clean up the blood and make up an excuse should her parents notice the soiled sheets. Because Nancy's parents are alcoholics, they cannot adequately manage adult responsibilities, like caring for themselves or their daughter. Nancy witnesses her parents' physical conflicts time and again, and she even sees her mother resort to threats of suicide. Nancy cannot ensure her own safety, as we see in her spiral down a path littered with self-destructive behaviors, so she certainly cannot shoulder the burden of her parents' behaviors. Likewise, they are setting for Nancy an example she seems destined to follow, one of substance abuse and instability. This out-of-control home life is reflected in Nancy's behaviors, which seem to symbolize not only a cry for help from her parents but also a genuine need for control amid the chaos.

Nancy cannot communicate her pain to her parents. So she turns to cutting as a means of gaining control by physically manifesting her internal pain. The behavior is an extension of what she fails to express in other ways. Cutting is only one way in which troubled adolescents use their bodies as vehicles for expression when inner turmoil is too much to bear. By presenting the idea of cutting as a coping mechanism, the novel creates a dilemma for readers. On one hand, it suggests that cutting is a behavior that requires both understanding and intervention; on the other hand, it presents cutting as a coping mechanism, one for which some readers might opt.

The idea of gaining self-control through cutting may not be enough to make an adolescent reader contemplate the idea, but most adolescents have an intense need for acceptance. Nancy isn't accepted at home, and her parents are guilty of what Conterio and Lader would surely deem "underparenting." Nor is she accepted by her boyfriend, who she theorizes is with her only because she is "good in bed." Other girls at school call her a druggie and think she is a "sicko" for cutting herself. But Katie accepts Nancy. "In only a month, Katie had completely accepted me for what I was, which was amazing to me. In fifteen years, my parents had yet to accept anything about me" (16). The narrator's statement sends a powerful message to readers: finding someone who cuts, and continuing to cut yourself, is one way to gain friends and acceptance. Nancy has found a way to "fit in."

The pressure to fit in is strong. Young women, and increasingly young girls, are bombarded with the message that they need to change their appearance to fit society's expectations. Pressure from advertisers, along with images of young women in music, television, and movies, sends the message to adolescents and preadolescents that they must look a certain way in order to gain popularity and power. Entertainers such as the Olson twins, Britney Spears, Shania Twain, and Beyoncé have found popularity, fame, wealth, and power by promoting an idealized sexual image that panders to the male notion of what is sexy in a woman. In *Crosses* Nancy has sex with a boyfriend who is with her only for that purpose. Nancy's character is being demoralized, objectified, and sexualized, and she is compromising herself in order to be accepted by a male. To land the coveted popular, good-looking boyfriend, she is willing to objectify herself to please him sexually. She has given up power and self-control, and she struggles to regain it through cutting and self-destructive behaviors.

Another detail the main character includes about herself is the fact that she likes to read—perhaps the novel's readers can relate to this as well. "That was my hobby, reading books about teens in trouble. . . . I filled in the extra hours before bed with stories about drug addicts, anorexics and alcoholics" (17). She tells us in the same passage that she has learned to replace the alcohol that she secretly drinks in her parents' home with water. "I didn't think of the replacing booze with water trick on my own. I read it in a book about a teenage alcoholic." The ability to identify with a character, especially the first-person narrator in a novel or book, makes the literature more appealing to young readers, particularly what the American Library Association considers "reluctant readers," or those who do not see reading as an activity they can successfully engage in and enjoy. While the book almost certainly wasn't written to promote self-injury as a means of coping or gaining acceptance by one's peers, it may do just that. Nancy and Katie are portrayed as teenage girls using drugs, alcohol, sex and cutting as recreation. They quickly become solid friends, finding solace in each other's company. Nancy and Katie are painted as bold characters who succeed academically despite being intoxicated in school. Even when a teacher notices they are under the influence of alcohol, they manage to keep him from reporting them by using their stellar academic records as proof that they "don't have a problem." The message that girls who take drugs, drink alcohol, and cut themselves are still capable of achieving excellent grades in subjects like English and science is dangerously misleading to readers. And considering that so-called reluctant readers are not typically students who excel academically, is it too much of a stretch to think they might try to emulate Nancy and Katie's unrealistic approach to scholastic success?

It would be overstating the case to say the book glamorizes self-injury, but it does present Nancy and Katie as girls who are likable and who are coping with life's problems through self-injury. When Nancy's boyfriend breaks up with her, Katie is there with hallucinogenic mushrooms and cheese-doodles to make things better. "I wanted to be with Katie, because she did more good for me than any idiot shrink. . . . I just needed to lie there on the floor with my best friend until I died, and that'd be good, and that's all I needed. I was sick of people calling us crazy when it was they who were fucked up" (138). The passage foreshadows Katie's death by overdose, not Nancy's. And despite the fact that Katie's death pulls Nancy out of her self-injurious behavior, the bond that was created between the book's main characters could be seen by readers as something to envy.

Nancy and Katie's friendship was based on the discovery that both characters cut themselves. The book continues to develop the friendship based on the characters' shared mutual experiences, but these mutual experiences are detrimental. As the girls cut themselves more, drink more, and take more drugs, they become closer and begin to see themselves as two young women against the world. What high school student doesn't desire a best friend like that? The danger in this novel is not just in its themes but in their delivery. A contagious theme should be used carefully, so as to avoid making the behaviors it presents seem appealing to readers.

"It is a psychologically vulnerable person who may seize on something she views as a fad, and fashion it into a strategy to deal with preexisting agonies" (Conterio and Lader 6). It seems that cutting has, indeed, become something of a fad. Celebrities have admitted to engaging in the behavior; cutting has emerged as a theme in literature; and 1 March is now recognized as "Self-Injury Awareness Day" in the United States.

As a high school teacher, I see ninth graders who identify with Elie Wiesel as a fifteen-year-old narrator in the autobiographical *Night* develop such an interest in the book they routinely tell me they couldn't put it down. Thrilling as this may be to an English teacher hoping to present the Holocaust through literature in a way my students can grasp, that kind of identification with a character is alarming considering the themes in *Crosses*.

"Low Self-Esteem. Poor Impulse Control. Repressed Hostility"

Patricia McCormick's novel *Cut* features another adolescent first-person narrator. Her name is Callie, and like Nancy and Katie, she is a cutter. Scholastic, a company renowned for its young-adult literature, published this novel in 2000. It too contains praise from highly regarded publications and organizations like the *New York Times Book Review* and the New York Public Library. The novel has also received a citation from the American Library Association as a "Quick Pick for Young Adult Readers," as well as a recommendation from Robert Cormier of *I Am the Cheese* fame. Credibility, quality, and heightening reader interest seem to be the focus of the back and inside covers. The front cover is eye-catching, too, with gray script lines from the book on a black background: "Then I placed the blade next to the skin on my palm. A tingle raced across my scalp. The blood tipped up at me and my body spiraled away. Then I was on the ceiling looking down, waiting to see what would happen next." In the center of the cover, the title is printed in large white letters with three red lines drawn through it. This book was mentioned again and again in various sources when I began researching the topic of cutting. The aesthetics of the cover were intriguing, and I couldn't wait to read the book. I read the 151-page novel in one evening, and I kept hoping that I would like the content as much as the cover. But the novel was disappointing; it reminded me of *Girl, Interrupted* for the younger reader.

Cut, like *Crosses*, features informal first-person narration by an adolescent female. The narration is primarily an inner monologue, as the narrator, Callie, suffers from elective muteness. She is an athlete, a runner to be precise, who cuts herself on page 3, apparently in reaction to an empty house, after no one showed up to watch her compete in the high school cross country meet. The author has established Callie as an "underparented" adolescent from the beginning, but in a much more subtle fashion than Shelly Stoehr did with Nancy in *Crosses*. Callie's parents aren't screaming, negligent alcoholics. Instead, they have immersed themselves in work and other people, especially Callie's brother, Sam, who has chronic health problems. Because her mother has to work outside the home, as does her father, Callie is often left in charge of her severely asthmatic and allergic brother. She is expected, at the age of fifteen, to care for him properly by making sure his environment is free of allergens and to monitor him constantly for exhaustion. Her mother, seemingly as a result of her son's frail health, is afraid to drive long distances and is overly protective of him. She is home more than Callie's father, and when she is, her son is her primary focus. Callie is thus thrust into what Conterio and Lader termed "inappropriate duties," or responsibilities too demanding for an adolescent who still requires parenting. She cannot express her frustration or need for attention to her parents, and, like Nancy, turns to cutting as a coping mechanism. The narrator feels she cannot talk with other characters in the book about her behavior or the incidents that led up to her self-injury and she refuses to speak—to anyone, about anything.

Callie is put into a facility for adolescent girls with problems, Sea Pines, which she always refers to as "Sick Minds." No other cutters are initially present—instead, the "group" features anorexics, substance abusers, and an overweight girl who presumably uses food for comfort. Callie doesn't speak in group, nor does she speak to anyone out of group. She won't even speak to her therapist for three-quarters of the novel. When her mother (who made the sacrifice and drove to the facility) and her brother visit, Callie doesn't speak to them. The suspense builds slightly for the reader; we don't know why she won't speak, nor whether she will attempt to cut herself again. She wrestles with cutting throughout the book, as when she contemplates taking a piece of a foil dish from the hospital's kitchen.

Rather than being the center of attention from the start, as many first-person narrators are, Callie acts as the eyes and ears of her group in a fly-on-the-wall fashion. She focuses her narration on the other girls' problems, dialogue, and actions, but rarely on her own. She includes glimpses into her own past experiences, but cutting isn't featured frequently. Instead, we are supposed to wonder what has really put Callie there, and why she is cutting herself in the first place.

It isn't until another cutter arrives at the facility that Callie begins to emerge as a whole character. She begins to tell her therapist, albeit cryptically, about her brother's health and a time when he was hospitalized. Therapy triggers memory and insight for Callie, and finally the reader can begin to sense that Sam's hospitalization is an important piece of the puzzle.

Amanda, the newly arrived cutter, seems to be the antithesis of Callie. While both girls are cutters, they share none of the symbiosis that Nancy and Katie did in *Crosses*. Amanda is talkative and unabashed about her cutting behavior, proudly showing her scars to others in group. Callie reports to her therapist (to whom she has begun speaking), "They're gross," and adds that "it's not fair" to show others your scars, for fear of upsetting them. Amanda sees Callie as a "friend," or at least a comrade in self-injury, but Callie is put off by Amanda's brash behavior and her attempts to cut herself at Sea Pines (83).

In one scene, Callie and Amanda are left alone in a locker room. Callie had previously broken a metal strip from the trim of the dining table and had put it in her pocket, "just in case" (106). Amanda retrieves the metal strip when it falls from Callie's pocket and hands it back to her without a word. I am not sure this can be construed as peer pressure or as an example of one cutter's influencing another, but it certainly indicates to the book's protagonist that a fellow cutter isn't going to stop her. Callie knows that Amanda will break the rules and keep a secret even if it means a fellow patient might injure herself again.

Perhaps the appearance of another cutter, one whom Callie does not admire, was just what Callie needed to help her overcome her cutting. Until Amanda's arrival, Callie had been surrounded by staff members, other patients, and a psychiatrist who were supportive and proactive in trying to help her with her treatment. Sensing that the new patient is willing to allow Callie to harm herself is enough to awaken in her a desire to change. Even though she does manage to cut herself once during her hospitalization, she eventually tells her therapist about Sam's trip to the hospital and that she felt overwhelmed by the responsibility of caring for her brother and responsible for Sam's illness. One evening, when her mother was visiting Callie's grandmother in a nursing home and her father was at a bar, Sam had a severe asthma attack, and Callie couldn't help. Being a runner, she sprinted from the house, leaving Sam alone, and tried desperately to find her father. She located him at the bar, and he managed to drive them both home in time to call an ambulance. Callie, who had been thrust into the role of parent by the underparenting adults in her family, was ill equipped to handle a difficult situation, proving she needed more guardianship than she was getting. She felt unable to express her feelings and turned to cutting to manage them. It isn't clear whether Callie had cut herself prior to this event or if she began afterward, but McCormick seems to be stressing primary motivators for her protagonist's behaviors, such as the inability to control a situation, insufficient parenting, too much responsibility, and guilt. This book also includes an important element missing from *Crosses*; her therapists are presented as helpful without the criticism of therapy that readers often see in similarly themed books such as *Girl, Interrupted*.

Through therapy, Callie gains insight into her behavior, and she discovers a means to recovery when she finally begins to talk to her therapist. This is a positive aspect of the book. The number of reported cases of young women who injure themselves comes primarily from those who have sought treatment for their behavior. However, we have to wonder how many more cases, like Kettlewell's and my own, go unreported. If young women who injure themselves feel comfortable seeking help for their problem, perhaps the number of cases will start going down rather than up. And books like *Cut* that demonstrate therapy as a nonthreatening, nonjudgmental, and truly therapeutic aid might make cutters more willing to turn to it when they are searching for ways to cope with their problems. Even V. J. Turner, the psychologist who believes cutting is an addiction and should be treated as such, admits that traditional therapy helped her overcome her cutting behavior.

Therapy is no guarantee of recovery, however, as Amanda shows. She speaks the language of psychobabble, demonstrating familiarity with the vocabulary of psychotherapy. When asked why she cuts herself, she replies, "Beats me. . . . Low self-esteem. Poor impulse control. Repressed hostility" (37). Embodying intellectual but not emotional intelligence, she lacks the ability to empathize with others, and she cynically interprets a fellow patient's compassion for others as "being co-dependent again" (115).

While *Cut* doesn't feature overt peer pressure on the characters the way *Crosses* does, the novel does seem to tout cutting as a coping mechanism to young readers. The book's physical appearance is appealing, and commendations from reputable sources like the *New York Times* and *Publishers Weekly* imply that the content is suitable for young readers. Like *Crosses*, it is written specifically for the young adult audience. Since it features a fifteen-year-old female narrator, it is likely to draw more adolescent female than male readers. As Patricia McCormick explained, "When I read stories, I see, or hope to see, aspects of my life reflected in them" ("Interview with Pat McCormick"). Given that the cutting population is overwhelmingly female and that most cutters begin the behavior during adolescence, I believe the book's theme of cutting may be seductive to its target audience.

Fortunately, *Cut* refrains from incorporating other types of self-injurious behavior, like substance abuse and promiscuous sex. However, the novel provides a highly superficial treatment of a deep subject. Callie, the cutter in the story, could easily be replaced with an anorexic or bulimic narrator, and the story wouldn't change much. The book fails to probe deeply into the psychology behind Callie's cutting behavior and treats her problem as something that will miraculously go away thanks to her eventual willingness to speak with a therapist. The simplicity with which the novel treats cutting is misleading and could even prove dangerous for readers who cut themselves. The book not only exposes the reader to a maladaptive coping mechanism but also suggests that such behavior can be overcome without tremendous effort.

Aside from treating the subject matter with simplicity, *Cut* also takes a stock approach to solving Callie's problems. She is hospitalized, develops friendships with others who care about her, encounters a complication when she cuts herself, confronts a foil in the shape of Amanda, and starts talking, which leads to her cure. The book doesn't glamorize cutting, but it does not try to demonstrate the dangers of cutting in a realistic fashion. Instead, it presents a difficult theme flatly in a book that reads like a formula. That may be stylistically acceptable for the young adult audience, but it fails to handle the theme of cutting with substance. Cutting has become increasingly common in young women. Perhaps treating the subject lightly is one reason it has grown in popularity. Once, anorexia and bulimia were seen as self-destructive and appalling behaviors in which young women didn't wish to engage. Now, some girls in the public high school where I teach throw up their lunches in the bathroom daily. I had a student in a creative writing class who included her eating disorder in two of last semester's poetry compositions, but she did so in a nonchalant way, using "bulimic" as a descriptor like blond, or tall, or thin. Bulimia, it seems, has become an accepted weight-control activity.

It is possible that raising public awareness about behaviors like bulimia or cutting also raises the curiosity of those willing to try it. Certainly not all young women who are exposed to behaviors like these will adopt them, but those who are vulnerable for whatever reason are prone to imitate them. If researchers like V. J. Turner are right in suggesting that cutting is an addiction, it stands to reason that cutting could become the next cigarette, the next bottle of alcohol, or the next harmful vice that young women are unable to break. And, like smoking and drinking, there is peer pressure surrounding cutting. Apparently, there is contagion in eating disorders, whether it is due to overt peer pressure or not. I contend that the same is true of cutting; literature that is going to use it as a theme must confront the gravity of this behavior. Authors must recognize the potential problems of treating the subject lightly; otherwise, readers who are introduced to cutting will receive the impression that the behavior is not problematic.

In my community, there is a popular program presented in elementary and middle schools by the police department. It's called DARE, or Drug Abuse Resistance Education. It has been around for about fifteen years, and it continues to present drug abuse education to young people through films, live demonstrations that show common street drugs and how they are bought, sold, and used, and methods for saying "no" to drugs. I have had older students in my high school classes who have been through the DARE program. One told me point-blank that the program didn't achieve its goal; instead, it taught him how to locate and use illegal drugs. By the time this student was a freshman in high school, he had spent time twice in a detoxification center. I suggest that presenting cutting-themed literature to susceptible young adults could have the same effect on potential cutters that DARE had on this student, and perhaps many others.

There is power in suggestion. Once the mind becomes aware of a concept, it can then think in terms of that concept in a way it could not do before. Consider the Dodge Viper. In 1996, I taught summer school. During a class discussion, a girl explained that her favorite car was a Dodge Viper. Having never seen a Dodge Viper, I couldn't conjure its image, nor could I conceptualize the car, even after a fairly good description from the student. However, that very afternoon while driving home, I saw a Dodge Viper! Within the next week or so, I saw at least three more Dodge Vipers. I had probably seen a Dodge Viper before the student in my class mentioned the car, but because I didn't know anything about it, the car didn't receive recognition from my brain. The same thing happens with students and new vocabulary words. Once we study a new word, they come to class days, even weeks later, telling me the word was used in their history textbook or on *The Simpsons*. The newly acquired information or concept, be it a Dodge Viper, a vocabulary word, or the idea of cutting one's skin, has now been recognized by the brain, and it can be incorporated into conscious thought from that point on.

Jeffrey Berman observes in *Surviving Literary Suicide*, "Curiously, although students do not generally romanticize suicide in life, they often do so in literature" (15–16). Jeff, who has taught a course called Literary Suicide at the University at Albany, finds the Werther effect common in response to literary works members of the course read, including those by Ernest Hemingway, Sylvia Plath, and Kate Chopin. Named for a Goethe character who commits suicide due to unrequited love, the effect refers to imitation of suicides that receive a great deal of publicity. The term was coined by David Phillips who, in 1974, wrote an essay entitled "The Influence of Suggestion on Suicide." Though Phillips's research was devoted mainly to Hollywood celebrities who had committed suicide, Jeff points out the copycat suicide committed following the death of poet Sylvia Plath, notably by Assia Wevill, the woman for whom Plath's husband, Ted Hughes, left her. "In 1969 she gassed herself and her two-year-old child, Shura, who was fathered by Hughes, in the kitchen of her flat. She was severely depressed about her relationship with Hughes, whom she feared would soon leave her, as he had left Plath. There is little doubt among biographers that the suicide imitated Plath's" (170). Jeff also cites the incidence of copycat suicides following the death of Ernest Hemingway. Given this impact on readers, it seems that a variation on the Werther effect could be responsible for the rise in cutting behavior among adolescent girls who may read books like *Cut*, *Crosses*, or Susanna Kaysen's *Girl, Interrupted*.

"We Have Something to Hide"

Kaysen's popular memoir is peppered with self-injury references. In the beginning of the story Susanna describes picking her pimples in a psychiatrist's office. "'You have a pimple' said the doctor. 'You've been picking it,' he went on. 'You've been picking yourself,' the doctor said. 'Trouble with a boyfriend?' It wasn't a question, actually; he was already nodding for me. 'Picking at yourself,' he repeated" (7). Of course, picking one's pimples seems minor compared with cutting one's flesh intention-ally, but picking, biting, and other SIBs that result in scarring are closely akin to cutting. "Scar tissue has no character. It's not like skin. It doesn't show age or illness or pallor or tan. It has no pores, no hair, no wrinkles. It's like a slipcover. It shields and disguises what's beneath. That's why we grow it; we have something to hide"(16). This comment can also be interpreted as a reflection on the pressures on women in our society to be stereotypically beautiful, meaning they have no unsightly blemishes on their skin, no unwanted hair, no visible pores, and certainly no wrinkles. This reinforces Conterio and Lader's theory of "uglification," or perhaps cutting is an unconsciously self-abusive attempt to attain the skin we are all supposed to covet. After all, women have surgical procedures to burn hair from their bodies, laser away wrinkles, age spots, and blemishes, and abrade the surface of their skin in an attempt to achieve flawlessness. Is intentional cutting really much different?

In other references to self-injury, Kaysen reveals behaviors characteristic of a cutter. "I began scratching at the back of my hand. My plan was to get a hold of a flap of skin and peel it away, just to have a look. I wanted to see that my hand was a normal human hand . . . but I couldn't get my skin to open up and let me in. I put my hand in my mouth and chomped. Success! A bubble of blood came out near my last knuckle, where my incisor had pierced the skin" (102). She is relentless in her quest to break the skin, and she seems pleased in this passage with the results of her scratching and biting. Given that she was hospitalized and denied access to sharp objects, her method of self-injury was probably the closest she could come to cutting at the time.

Going to a bookstore on an outing from the hospital, Kaysen discovers a "diagnosis *Manual*" (she gives no complete title) and locates the definition for borderline personality disorder; a psychiatrist with whom she had met for only fifteen minutes made this snap diagnosis that changed her life forever. "Wrist scratching! I thought I'd invented it. This is the sort of stuff you get locked up for. Nobody knew I was doing it, though. I never told anyone, until now" (152). During this portion of the book, Kaysen begins to disclose some of her self-injurious behavior in an attempt to understand her diagnosis and decide whether she concurs. "I'd had an earlier period of face-scratching. If my fingernails hadn't been quite short, I couldn't have gotten away with it" (153). She adds that she was in pain and that nobody knew it; in fact, she says, even she had trouble knowing it. "So I told myself, over and over, you are in pain. It was the only way I could get through to myself ('counteract feelings of numbness'). I was demonstrating, externally and irrefutably, an inward condition" (153).

While Kaysen's book is autobiography rather than fiction, not written specifically for a young adult audience as *Crosses* and *Cut* were, the narrator is young and writing in the first person. She is female, intelligent, sexually active, and self-injuring. The risk of identifying with the narrator, in this case Kaysen, is present for young female readers. Perhaps the book would not have become as widely read had a movie not been made based on it in 1999, at the height of the cutting "epidemic." Kaysen was a young woman who had difficulty in school, difficulty with her parents, and difficulty in her romantic relationships. She had become outwardly lethargic, and her parents became alarmed. She was placed in a psychiatric hospital in Massachusetts and given the borderline diagnosis. Yet Kaysen never felt there was anything "wrong" with her. She learned to cooperate with therapists and her parents, realizing that this would lead to freedom. However, in her book she presents herself as almost a norm against which the other patients can be measured, and all seem to have more severe conditions and behaviors than Kaysen's. The author is also skeptical about the type of therapy she receives, portraying psychiatrists as curt, cold, unresponsive, and prone to making snap judgments about patients.

When I read the book, long after I had ceased cutting myself, I felt I could relate on many levels to her, though, thank goodness, I had not been hospitalized. I was in my twenties at the time and, like Kaysen, I didn't see too much wrong with her. I am sure that other readers have reached for the book because they can relate to the story. But, given a reader who is impressionable, looking for a way to manage her pain, searching for an outlet for her emotion, and wanting a means of feeling "in control" of herself, the idea of self-injury might seem appealing, perhaps inducing the contagion effect. Kaysen has written two novels as well as this memoir. She must make a comfortable living, and she has received media exposure and acclaim for writing her life story. The celebrity involved seems alluring, as does the reassuring thought that she turned out seemingly "normal." To those who read *Girl, Interrupted* and share the author's penchant for self-injury, Kaysen's position in life might lull them into a false belief that they, too, could have success because they cut themselves. Having success and money can create a sense of control, much like cutting can.

Sylvia Plath wrote a poem titled "Cut" in which the narrator accidentally cuts her thumb instead of an onion and experiences a "thrill" to see the top "quite gone": the cutting is a cause for "celebration" (235). "Thrill" and "celebration" are odd choices to describe an injury. But keep in mind Conterio and Lader's theory that accidents can trigger self-injury in people. Plath, like Kaysen, was pleased with the results of her cut, be it intentional or otherwise. Given her history of suicide attempts, Plath clearly had a death wish, and she might see any type of physical harm as a "celebration." But self-injury and suicide are not the same in their intent, so Plath may have seen the cut on her thumb as a release. Or perhaps Plath, like Kaysen, saw it as a means of "counteracting feelings of numbness." People cut to manage feelings and to control their psychological states. That type of control might extend to the control of one's feelings of numbness, as described by V. J. Turner and others, just as easily as it might be used to control one's feelings of pain.

"I Like the Cuts—They Comfort Me"

I had not heard of Emma Forrest before discovering *Thin Skin*, but I had heard of the publisher, MTV Books, owned by the music channel that remains a favorite among teens. *Thin Skin* is an interesting, well-written book by a British author who penned her first novel at twenty-one. The book's heroine is a New York model named Ruby who lacks self-esteem. Once again, we have a first-person narrator who is young and female. Her problems began with her parents. Ruby grew up with an overly emotional mother and a distant, judgmental father. Her parents, like Nancy's in *Crosses*, were so wrapped up in their own melodrama that they scarcely acknowledged what was happening to their daughter, even when she was engaging in sexual relations with their twenty-three-year-old house guest while she was only twelve.

This sexual relationship sets the stage for the remainder of the book. Ruby is beautiful but seems the last one to notice—or care. She narrates a story filled with self-destructive behaviors including the use of drugs and alcohol, overeating, and cutting her skin. The most notable difference between this book and others I have discussed is that Forrest's cutter is a model. Ruby embodies, then, society's ideal. She is not just beautiful but ravishingly beautiful—so attractive that she finds work even while strung out on drugs, bloated and acne-ridden from bingeing, and sporting visible cuts and scars. No one seems more surprised by this fact than Ruby herself, whose self-effacing qualities make it easy for the reader to both identify and sympathize with her character. Ruby is, in fact, a mess. She is on the brink of breakdown throughout the book, and she is persistently drawn to the wrong lovers. While most men she comes in contact with admonish her for her scars and cutting behavior, only one actually leaves her because he can no longer emotionally stomach behaviors he deems self-destructive.

At one point in the story after a photographer notices her scars, Ruby cryptically explains to him why she cuts herself. "'And I know you've been cutting yourself,' he added, gathering courage. 'That too,' I agreed, smoothing out my skirt. 'Well, if you know what you're doing, well, then why?' I didn't move my hands as I answered his question: 'I've started so I'll finish'" (33). Later in the novel, Ruby provides a more in-depth explanation for her cutting behavior: "I like the cuts—they comfort me—I can't lie. My thoughts are messy, my emotions are messy, my body goes in and out at will. The raised white scars on my arms and legs are the only aspects of my being that come close to minimalism. They come from chaos, but it is hard to carve frustration and unease into flesh. Only straight lines. Every fear, every night terror, every hour I cried, every fight with Sebastian is registered as a neat white scar" (52). Ruby has the chance to live the American dream—as America tells us it should be lived. She is a model, highly paid, in demand, who struggles, not with the pressures from society about idealized beauty to which she cannot live up, but with the pressures that come with being beautiful.

At an early age, Ruby was too beautiful for her first lover to resist. He felt guilty about having a relationship with a twelve-year-old, and he eventually left. Ruby grows to resent her beauty, because it drove away the first man she ever loved. In fact, she not only seems to resent her beauty but also tries to undermine it any way she can, such as overeating and getting tattoos, while frequently turning back to it in order to make a living. This suggests that beauty does not equal happiness, but it is so contrary to the messages most often sent to young women—to be beautiful is to be happy—that it produces for the impressionable reader a catch-22 situation.

Paradoxically, Ruby is damned for her beauty, the only attribute for which she has ever received any recognition, attention, or success. It made her a victim of statutory rape, and because of her feelings about her first lover she is unable to find love and happiness in a relationship. She does not go to college or consider any career besides modeling, buying into the notion that her beauty is all she has. Rather than empowering her as a woman, this disables her and empowers the male-dominated culture that objectifies her. She is so miserable that she turns to drugs, food, and cutting as means of coping. When she finally meets Sebastian, the one man who treats her well and who appears to love her for who she is, she cannot give up her cutting behaviors, which drive him away. Her character embodies Conterio and Lader's theory of "uglification," in which a cutter rejects the ideals of beauty and protects herself from objectification through scarring. As she admits, "Everyone asks how I'll feel about the tattoos and scars in thirty years. I'll always say: 'I'll like them.' I've always loved damaged monuments, in architecture and in humans. . . . I was trying to be a ruined beauty then, at twenty. I wanted to know how ugly I could get, how ruined and ugly and spoiled, before they stopped trying to fuck me" (52).

Ruby is the modern novel's equivalent of the tragic beauty, but one to whom readers can relate. She never presents her life as glamorous, exciting, or enviable. Instead, she comes across as a troubled girl who struggles with demons no one sees, and who turns to cutting as a release and as a defense mechanism. Unlike most other cutters I have read about, either real or fictional, Ruby doesn't try to hide her self-mutilation.

More skillfully narrated than *Crosses, Cut,* or *Girl, Interrupted, Thin Skin* doesn't seem to be written specifically for the young adult audience. Nevertheless, I am troubled that the novel is published by MTV Books. This shouts, "teenager, read me." The book features a bright pink cover with a drawing of shoes, legs, and a cloud shrouding the body to which they belong. Pink suggests that it is intended for the female audience, as does the picture of women's shoes. The narrator is a young woman who begins her story by recalling her childhood. She tells most of the story in the past tense, but she is in her early twenties when the novel ends. These factors add up to a book that is intended for a young female reader, perhaps in late adolescence. Like the others, it is likely to draw readers who can relate to the topic or the narrator, probably women who have once engaged in or are in the process of engaging in cutting behavior. The book, though darkly comedic, is depressing, and there were points in it when I felt so close to the narrator that I could have spoken the very words Forrest wrote. I did not have this strong a reaction to the other books I read, perhaps because they did not present a character as realistic, fully formed, honest, and human as Ruby. Or perhaps I also identified with Ruby, like the teens who will identify with characters such as Nancy and Katie. This was both an enthralling and frightening experience for me, someone who is sixteen years removed from her own cutting, because I felt dangerously close to the character. If I am typical of other cutters who might read the book, I suspect it will evoke in readers memories of a difficult time in their history, if not reinforce behaviors in which they still engage. Either way, the novel's influence is palpable. Forrest writes Ruby's story in direct, matter-of-fact prose that speaks directly to the reader, thereby engaging her to the point that she cannot put the book down, for fear of abandoning a character in need of help.

CHAPTER 6

Cutting Literature
"High School May Not Be the Place for Books Like These"

I once used cutting as a coping mechanism. I know firsthand how powerful a device it can be, whatever the reason someone turns to it. As a teacher and as a member of our society, I have a responsibility to recognize the epidemic of cutting among teens. I want to do what I can to help decrease cutting—now and in the future.

Nevertheless, as a high school English teacher, I would hesitate to teach works featuring cutting behavior. I teach primarily ninth grade, and I believe that my students might have a great deal of difficulty resisting the appeal of copycat cutting. Students readily identify with characters who share their sex, approximate age, habits, likes, and dislikes. While I haven't noticed any scarred ninth graders in my classes, any one of them could be cutting or at least contemplating it. I worry that exposure to cutting-themed literature might produce something akin to the Werther effect. I routinely see literature's influence on my students' behavior. When I teach *West Side Story*, for example, I have students shooting each other with their fingers, exclaiming, "pow pow" and "wacko jacko" for several weeks.

Parents are another part of the equation. Undoubtedly, some would object not only to the cutting chronicled in the books but also to the other types of self-destructive behaviors, such as drug use and promiscuous sex. High school may not be the best place for books like these. If I were to teach books about cutting, I would be certain to present the types of information I have presented in this book. To avoid creating a "how-to" effect similar to that of the DARE program, I would stress the theories behind cutting by various researchers and have students select one they felt offered the most compelling argument. Then I would have them research the theory further and present the dangers involved in self-injury and cutting to the class from their own perspectives. This would force students to think about cutting in a clinical and objective sense, while raising their awareness about the phenomenon. Teaching others about a subject is often the best way to learn about it. Perhaps deeper examination of the subject would dispel the myths and allure some students might associate with cutting. It is better to allow students to learn the truth about cutting in an academic environment rather than have them exposed to a romanticized version of cutting from peers or the media.

However, I would not be inclined to divulge my own history to a high school class. While we are, of course, human, it is important for teachers to maintain themselves as positive role models for their students and not to acknowledge anything that causes students to lose respect for them, question their stability, or cross personal boundary lines. Just as I don't believe teachers should confess past drug usage to students, I do not think past cutting behavior should be revealed in the classroom.

If I chose to teach books like *Cut, Crosses, Girl, Interrupted,* and *Thin Skin,* it might be in a college course. While I have no teaching experience at the college level, I imagine the maturity of the students reading these books, coupled with the freedom from parental and administrative censorship, would make it a more suitable environment for examining cutting-themed literature. An interesting topic might be comparing the Werther effect as it pertains to literature or literary figures and similar effects stemming from cutting-themed literature. I would expect students enrolled in the class to have at least one prerequisite psychology course as well as other upper-level English courses.

Under ideal circumstances, teaching similar themes could prove enlightening for students and interesting for me, and if I taught them properly and attempted to stress the dangers of copycatting or the Werther effect, I might be able to prevent students from being influenced to the point that they themselves attempted cutting. I would have to consider the possibility that a course of this nature could draw students who were cutters or had been at one time. I suspect that the complications that could arise for those who confront this theme, such as dredging up powerful emotions in them or me, might be difficult to manage. I am not a trained psychologist, and my minimal experience with counseling students was in a controlled environment.

Perhaps books like these would serve best in a psychology course that dealt with self-injurious behavior, taught by someone with a more suitable background than mine in presenting and dealing with this issue. In any case, I question whether cutting-themed literature, classified as young adult or not, is appropriate for the young adult. If high school teachers who felt equipped and ready to present such literature did so using approaches that lessened the danger involved in the subject matter, and if they employed techniques that served to counteract any contagion of cutting, perhaps the books could be used as positive teaching tools. Ideally, parents of high school level students would need to be involved, offering their children support and insights when they are reading at home. Perhaps having a psychologist or at least a school counselor speak to the class would help in the teaching process. Because the topic is both publicized and controversial, I am fairly certain a public school teacher would have to receive administrative approval to teach cutting-themed literature. The teacher must also be prepared for difficult discussions and questions that could arise in the classroom. Students who might begin entertaining the idea of cutting themselves, or students who had already engaged in self-injury and were feeling uncomfortable with the emotions the theme brought up for them, would definitely need appropriate channels, supports, and outlets for their feelings.

Adolescents in our culture have become fascinated with cutting behavior. According to the latest statistics, these behaviors have grown to alarming proportions, and those statistics deal only with discovered and reported cases. I wonder how many more cutters, like me, have silently dealt with their own problems, never reaching out for help or intervention that resulted in treatment. Had I not taken a course in the summer of 2003, fifteen years after creating my final scar, and then studied the issue of cutting as it pertained to a study of literature, I am fairly certain I would not have made my cutting known to anyone. Through that course, I discovered that others around me had cut themselves too. What were the chances of that, I wondered. In a response diary students kept during the course, I wrote of my reaction to others' cutting behaviors, and disclosed my own, something I had not done before. Prior to composing this diary entry, I had all but forgotten that I once cut myself. The person who did that seemed like a friend I had lost touch with, or a character who once portrayed me in a strange play that was just a small, forgotten segment of my life. Even my scars, long faded and barely noticeable, had become such a part of my skin, like the freckle on my index finger, that I no longer paid attention to them. Once I stopped cutting, I saw it as a part of my past, something that had no bearing on the person I later became. But that part of my past reemerged in my diary, and again when I met with

Jeff to ask that he work with me on my master's thesis. It was he who suggested I probe into the phenomenon of cutting, and so I have. Through the research I've conducted and the books I've read, I have learned that I was never alone in my cutting. I now realize that I have the power not only to revisit and understand my own motivations for cutting but also to grasp the motivations of the twelve-year-old girls who are living with their own cuts and scars today.

Jeff had created in that course a safe method for disclosure by assigning those diaries. Rather than feeling overwhelmed, scared, confused, or haunted by issues I had to confront, I felt fully capable, for the first time, of writing about my cutting behavior. I never felt influenced by the literature we studied or the writing of classmates to revisit cutting as a behavior, nor did I feel uncomfortable about sharing my own experiences in my diary. Perhaps I was far enough removed from cutting and the shame I once struggled with finally to admit my behavior. Perhaps I was intrigued at the kinship I felt after learning that others in that class had cut themselves, too. And, perhaps Jeff has discovered a way of making the theme of cutting safe for his students to think about, write about, and disclose without fear of the Werther effect. Because the class was examining literature from a psychological perspective, I think it was easier for students to distance themselves from the themes in the literature and focus on both the authors' methods and the characters' psychology. Our diaries were used for personal thoughts and reflections, but they remained separate from the analysis of the literature we conducted in class and in our formal writing. This separation helped me to focus on the literature and interpret it, applying Freudian or other psychological theories, while at the same time having an outlet for my emotional reactions.

Writing my thesis was both a trying and a cathartic process. When I was writing a first-person narrative, I found it surprisingly simple to compose my ideas and words. I wrote quickly and rarely edited the work. My writing seemed to flow as if I were writing one of the diary entries for Jeff's course. I didn't worry much about others reading my work. My husband had no interest in what I was writing, and aside from Jeff and the other professor on my master's thesis committee, I doubted anyone would read my thesis. I had no intention of showing it to anyone else, so I had no problem being candid and honest.

I am reminded of one of my favorite stories, Charlotte Perkins Gilman's "Yellow Wallpaper" and the reaction my junior honors students have to it when I pose the question: "Is the narrator reliable?" This is a great question to spur discussion and debate. Students often come up with many reasons we might not be able to trust the narrator entirely: perhaps she has bought into her husband John's ideas about her, or maybe she is indeed crazy or suffering from sleep deprivation or postpartum depression. Nevertheless, students never suspect the narrator is trying intentionally to misguide or deceive the reader. When I ask students why they don't think she is simply lying, I always get the same answer—people don't lie in their diaries. Isn't that so true? I've heard it said that we are most truly ourselves when no one is looking at us. That's what diary writing does for us—it makes us honest, and it gives us the opportunity to be our true selves. The narrative portion of my thesis became a diary for me, and I still have some reservations about letting everyone see who I truly am, since I wrote it, like Gilman's fictional protagonist, thinking no one was looking.

The cathartic parts occurred as I wrote. I was able to let so much of myself out, parts of myself I didn't realize were there anymore. I remember crying a little during portions of my composition, as well as feeling ashamed, hurt, and victimized.

"Cutters Are Everywhere"

Doing the actual research, reading many scholarly and clinical books, and formulating my preliminary plan weren't difficult. In fact, the reading was interesting and enlightening. I had no idea cutting was epidemic. I felt some comfort in the fact that others shared my deviant behavior. Misery loves company. I discovered why I had cut myself a long time ago, and I found the research empowering. I became concerned for others who cut, especially when I learned that many cutters engage in behavior far more damaging than my own. My cuts were never terribly deep and weren't disfiguring. Others I read about cut far deeper and risked more than I did.

I was struck when reading Jeff's section of the manuscript by the idea of six degrees of separation—like the old email that everyone is separated from Kevin Bacon by a maximum of six degrees. I thought about how each of the writers Jeff featured, including myself, is only one degree away from each other. We have all intersected in his classroom, and, with his guidance and understanding, we all managed to find a way to disclose our cutting. It proves what I have suspected since I began writing my thesis—cutters are everywhere. We could be almost anyone: student, teacher, daughter, son, wife, husband, former classmate, or bank teller. How would people know?

Cutting now seems almost as common as eating disorders—and indeed, many cutters have eating disorders too. I wonder whether more people cut themselves as a form of self-healing than actually enter therapy. Cutting certainly isn't a new practice; it has been around since humans have had skin to cut. But in our culture, cutting was taboo—it still is. And like other taboo practices, it cannot be understood, much less cured, if it cannot be openly discussed. Perhaps increased exposure and a new understanding of cutting and other SIBs will allow people who practice them to seek help, to discuss what has been unspeakable. What will happen then? I don't know. I hope that increased understanding will result in fewer cutters. But that may be wishful thinking.

I hope the other cutters in Jeff's class, whose stories seemed strangely familiar to me, have the transformation I had many years ago, the one that lets us abandon our self-destructive ways. I still feel so far from my own cutting that I don't think I could describe the practice in depth and in vivid detail, as some of the other writers did. I suspect my mind is protecting my body: I don't want to remember the pain. I have done the best I can to portray my own cutting self, and I hope my narrative helps those who read our book to know that they are not alone, not freaks of nature or psychos. I hope that Jeff's discussion of the Werther effect will allow people to read our book without becoming "infected" by it. I also hope that our book opens the eyes of those who romanticize or sensationalize the behavior to the dangers that are just a novel, film, or TV show away. Writing is an outlet, like cutting, and perhaps even scarier to those who, like me, have chosen to reveal the truth. I don't know whether to hug Jeff or hit him for suggesting I write about my cutting experiences, but I believe that all things are meant to serve a purpose. It may be years before I can see this project clearly, but I believe that some good must come from so much suffering. I hope that those who think they haven't been touched by cutting will take a look around—so that they can see the six degrees of separation from a cutter.

I found much evidence, both from my research and from Jeff's students, to substantiate what I already knew—cutting isn't attempted suicide. I was glad to find so much research in this area; I know most laypeople don't know the difference between cutting behavior and suicide attempts. I remember in high school being very conscious of this fact, and doing my best to camouflage my cuts so people wouldn't think I was trying to kill myself. Having them think that of me would have been far worse than having them know I cut myself, but even then I understood what they would not: the difference.

I learned from my research that I was still a teenager inside a thirty-something woman. I learned that I still carry scars no one can see. I learned that my past is integral to the person I have become: trying to deny, hide, or forget that is easier said than done. I learned that understanding one's past, however difficult that might be, is the key to feeling confident enough to say, "OK, I did it, and it didn't kill me. So what has it done for me?" It has made me aware of the fact that cutting behavior can be overcome with personal strength. It has also made me aware of the self-respect component. When I had no self-respect, no self-esteem, I was willing to damage myself in ways I couldn't dream of now. As I grew, learned, and accepted myself, not the labels others put on me, I gained self-esteem, and thereby became a person who helps herself, and strives to help others, rather than someone who wallows in pain.

I was apprehensive when Jeff suggested I write my thesis on cutting, specifically my own cutting. Did I want to put myself into the equation? It seemed easier to focus on others, which I had originally thought of doing. I was fascinated by the idea of damage done to women and how that is portrayed in literature, so that was what I wanted to focus on in my writing. But myself? Could I do that? And where would I even start? I was scared, but knowing that I felt comfortable with Jeff as my adviser, and felt safe presenting my ideas and history to him, I agreed that it would be an interesting angle to take. The diary entry I wrote for Jeff's class, the one that started all this, was so offhand. I simply wrote what I was thinking, and I was thinking how interesting it was that I had all but forgotten about my own cutting. It didn't matter anymore, and I had grown so far from it that I was surprised when it came back to me during his reading of another student's diary entry about cutting. This, coupled with Jeff's book about literary suicide, brought back my own behavior and feelings about it. But then, I had no idea anyone else would ever read about it. I think anonymity, or at least partial anonymity, gives some people the strength to disclose things about themselves they never would otherwise. It reminds me of Paul Lawrence Dunbar's "We Wear the Mask."

I wore the mask until recently. I think it's because I fear being misunderstood, just as I did during my days as a cutter. It is so difficult to explain the behavior to others that it becomes easier to remain silent.

There is a stigma attached to cutting that I don't want. I don't want to be called crazy, suicidal, or unstable. I do not want to be labeled a borderline personality, even though I am almost twenty years removed from cutting behavior. I don't think I ever had a death wish, nor do I believe I was disturbed or even unstable in the clinical sense of the word. I believe I cut for the same reason others take drugs, have breakdowns, engage in risk-taking behavior, become self-deprecating, fail in school or on the job, become alcoholics, or abuse others. It is escapism, but rather than engage in any of the more prevalent behaviors I just described, I chose to cut myself. At the root of the behavior was the same feeling of worthlessness and lack of self-respect druggies and alcoholics feel and seek to numb. And I don't think others in my life are capable of understanding that without judging me negatively. I am not now nor have I ever been crazy—just misunderstood, primarily by myself. While we were dating, my husband once asked me what my biggest fear was. "Being misunderstood," I answered.

Until Jeff proposed turning my work into a book, I hadn't felt the need to tell my husband about my cutting history. He hadn't asked many questions about my thesis, nor had he asked to read it. But once Jeff and I began mailing additions, deletions, and revisions back and forth, my husband grew curious, and he must have read at least a portion of an early version of the manuscript. He told me one evening he couldn't believe I had ever cut myself. I told him I couldn't believe it, either. He then asked why I wrote about myself in my thesis, and I explained Jeff's faith in the value of self-disclosure, about which I was understandably skeptical. You see, my husband doesn't handle weakness in others very well, especially when I am that other person. He tends to hold a person's weakness against her, and I knew I had not heard the end of the cutting from him. But I also knew I could no longer keep my cutting a secret from him when I was contemplating going public with the information. In a way, I felt better than I thought I would after he found out because I had passed the first test (second, really, if I count Jeff's approval, which I do). Another person who knows me now can forgive me for the adolescent I was then. He can more than forgive: he can now accept.

My reluctance to tell my husband about my past is similar to my birth mother's reluctance to tell her husband about me. During the time I was working on my master's thesis, I was also working on locating my birth mother. It was a slow process, or at least it seemed slow to me. I had waited for thirty-three years to find the woman responsible for my being. Once I found her and we began writing to each other, she told me she was afraid to tell her family about me for fear of what they would think of her. She did not know how they would react to such a deeply buried secret. Other people I confided in thought it odd that my birth mother would have such a hard time revealing her past and, in the process, revealing my existence. But I understood. It meant going back to a place she had tried to forget—a place that was painful and that she did not want to acknowledge in the present. It also meant reconnecting with the person she was thirty-three years earlier. The truth is frightening for those who spend their lives trying to conceal mistakes and decisions that have had such a huge impact on their inner lives. Eventually, she gained the courage to tell her husband, who was supportive of her and accepting of the news, though she has not yet told her other children. I have to respect the decisions she makes for herself, because I know what it means to keep a secret from those closest to you. I know how the imagined impact of divulging that secret can be enough to render it ironclad.

Writing my thesis helped me to understand myself and others who cut, but I don't think people removed from cutting are capable of fully understanding, like a nondrinker doesn't get alcoholism, and a nonaddictive person believes a junkie has a choice. While professional intervention can certainly help some people in need—fragile people, those who injure themselves—the only help that truly works is the help people have the power to give themselves, through whatever avenue they find it. So, self-disclosure of this magnitude is scary, but if it does anything for others, I hope it gives them the message that the solution isn't a pin, a knife, a piece of glass, a cut, or a gouge. It lies within, and understanding that is the only way out.

Part 2
STUDENT-CENTERED TEACHING

If, as Patty suggests, cutting is highly contagious and likely to "infect" others who come into contact with it, how can teachers prevent students from becoming at risk when they *read* essays and stories about self-mutilation? And how can teachers prevent students from becoming at risk when they *write* about cutting? *Should* they be permitted to write about it? What are the educational and psychological benefits of allowing—or encouraging—college students to read stories about cutting and to write about their own experiences? Are college students susceptible to the same contagion that threatens high school students, and, if so, how should teachers address this problem? These are some of the questions I explore in the next chapters.

Before doing so, I should describe my experience with the "pedagogy of self-disclosure." As Patty states, the reader-response diaries gave her and her classmates a "safe haven" so that they could write about experiences they could "never say aloud—to anyone." To understand how she and her classmates could write safely about cutting and related topics, I need to summarize briefly how I became interested in "risky writing," "risky reading," and, by implication, "risky teaching."

I have been using reader-response diaries in my literature-and-psychoanalysis courses since the middle 1970s. *Diaries to an English Professor*, published in 1994, is based on the diary entries that students wrote over a period of several years. The diaries are both private and public: private in that I am the only person who reads and comments on them, public in that I read aloud three or four entries each week before returning them to the diarists. I always read the diaries anonymously, and there is no discussion of them. Students draw their own conclusions about the entries they hear me read. In effect, the students speak through me in their diary entries. Students who do not want me to read aloud their diaries write the word "no" at the top of their entry. Each semester, several students do not want their diaries read aloud during the beginning of the term, but only one or two deny me permission by the end of the semester, when trust has been established.

Over the years, thousands of my literature students have written tens of thousands of reader-response diaries. Students tell me, in both signed and unsigned evaluations written at the end of the course, that they enjoyed this aspect of the course more than any other. Since they write on topics of great personal importance to them, the diaries are often better written than their formal, graded essays. I am careful not to "psychoanalyze" my students when reading their diaries. I limit my comments to supportive remarks, suggestions for further readings, and grammatical and stylistic suggestions.

For example, I wrote on Patty's diary that I was not familiar with the Web site Half.com on which she had bought her copy of *Surviving Literary Suicide*. To her statement that she found it helpful to learn the statistics of suicidal thinking, I wrote, "Yes, this is important for a high school teacher to know." Her wry comment that she often contemplated suicide in her youth but decided to "wait and see if things get better. If not, I can always kill myself later!" prompted my response, "good decision!" Struck by her admission that her husband did not know about her history as a cutter, I wrote, "Then you'll need to be careful about this diary." And when she thanked me for the course at the end of the diary, I wrote, "Thank you, Patty, for your *excellent* contribution to the course. Your diaries, especially this one, have been outstanding."

Since the publication of *Diaries to an English Professor*, my writing and research have focused largely on pedagogy. Students in my graduate and undergraduate literature courses write weekly reader-response diaries in which they discuss their feelings and thoughts about the texts on the reading list. The diaries help students make connections between their own lives and those of the imaginary characters we discuss in class. Most of my scholarship in the past fifteen years has been collaborative: reading and commenting on student writings, interviewing students during and after the semester, coauthoring scholarly articles with them, and exploring how reading and writing have affected their lives. For the past forty years I have been a student of psychoanalytic theory, and I find myself most drawn to attachment theory, which helps to explain the great importance of the student-teacher relationship.

Many of my writing assignments are student-centered (as opposed to subject-centered or teacher-centered). Patty's reader-response diary on *Surviving Literary Suicide* demonstrates students' freedom to comment on the relationship between literature and life. They are able to write on any topic that they wish, and equally important, they can avoid writing on any topic they deem too personal or threatening. Student-centered theories of learning imply, as Elaine Showalter suggests, collaborative learning in which the teacher is more of a facilitator than the center of attention. "The teacher still performs, but the class is not primarily about the teacher's brilliance, omniscience, personality or originality on the podium" (36).

In the mid 1990s, I began to teach personal writing courses in which students signed their names to essays that were then read by their classmates. Students write on a wide variety of topics considered too controversial for the classroom, including family problems arising from divorce, drug and alcohol addiction, sexual abuse, eating disorders, depression, and suicide. My students have educated me about the reality of growing up in contemporary America, and they have given me permission to use their writings in my articles and books. These signed essays expose the writers to greater risk than do anonymous reader-response diaries. As I observe in *Risky Writing*:

> What are the risks of personal writing? There are dangers for the students, classmates, teachers, and even college administrators. Students may feel pressured to disclose personal experiences; even if they are willing to disclose an experience, such as drug or alcohol addiction, they may later regret the disclosure because of a teacher's or classmates's criticism.

Students may fear that a self-disclosure will later come back to haunt them. In addition, students who write about traumatic experiences may find themselves retraumatized by the process of writing. There are risks for classmates too. Risky self-disclosures may produce anxiety or depression in the reader who witnesses suffering. The fear or anger in an essay may be contagious, infecting susceptible readers. Teachers who encourage personal writing may find themselves emotionally or legally unprepared for their students' self-disclosures, fearful that controversial pedagogical assignments or methods will render them vulnerable to criticism from their departmental chairpersons, who themselves may fear phone calls from irate parents complaining about their children's inappropriate self-disclosures. All these risks are real and should never be underestimated or ignored. (10)

I did not know when I wrote *Diaries to an English Professor* that it would be the first of several books on the pedagogy of self-disclosure. Nor did I know how controversial such an approach is, eliciting not only healthy skepticism from educators but also open hostility. Before we appreciate the benefits of this approach to teaching, we must acknowledge the risks, beginning with the contagion effect, to which we now turn.

CHAPTER 7

The Contagion Effect
"Teachers Ought to Be Careful in What They Assign"

I first encountered the contagion effect when I was teaching a graduate course called Literary Suicide in 1994, from which arose *Surviving Literary Suicide* in 1999. The more I learned about the suicides of Virginia Woolf, Ernest Hemingway, Sylvia Plath, and Anne Sexton, the more examples I discovered of copycat deaths. Hemingway, for example, never forgave his father for committing suicide. The act haunted him his entire life and compelled him to write stories in which he attempted to exorcise his own obsession with suicide. Carlos Baker quotes in his biography a revealing canceled passage of *The Green Hills of Africa*. "My father was a coward. He shot himself without necessity. At least I thought so. I had gone through it myself until I figured it in my head. I knew what it was to be a coward and what it was to cease being a coward. Now, truly, in actual danger I felt a clean feeling as in a shower" (809). Hemingway regarded this suicide as a moral failure, and despite statements to the contrary, he felt little empathy for his father and none for his mother, whom he held responsible for his father's death.

Copycat Suicide

Though he often wrote about suicide, sometimes autobiographically—Robert Jordan's fear of committing suicide, as his father had done, is the underlying motivation behind his "heroic" death in *For Whom the Bell Tolls*—Hemingway did not want biographers to intrude on his privacy. "The suicide of my father," he states sardonically, "is the best story I never wrote" (Mellow 570). It is no exaggeration to state that Clarence Hemingway's suicide was a major factor in the formation of his son's hypermasculinity and in his repeated defiance of death, whether it was on the battlefield, in the bullring, or on the plains of Africa. His disdain for those who killed themselves concealed the fear that he would share his father's fate. One senses that his father's suicide was a lifelong contagion from which the novelist never could escape. After Ernest Hemingway's suicide, his son John recalled a promise that the novelist obliged him to make several years earlier when John was confronting a personal crisis. "After I left the army and was married, I was very depressed about what I was going to do, very gloomy. And Papa said, 'You must promise me never, never . . . we'll both promise each other never to shoot ourselves.' He said, 'Don't do it. It's stupid.' This was after quite a few martinis. I hadn't said anything about shooting myself, but I was obviously very depressed. He said, 'it's one thing you must promise me never to do, and I'll promise the same to you'" (Brian 262).

The antisuicide pact did not prevent a severely depressed Hemingway from shooting himself in 1961. Within a few years his brother Leicester and sister Ursula also died by their own hand, as did his granddaughter Margaux Hemingway in 1996 of a drug overdose. Copycat suicides followed the novelist's death. Upon being told of Hemingway's suicide, the Spanish bullfighter Juan Belmonte responded succinctly, "Well done," and not long afterward he shot himself in the same way (Meyers 564). In one of the most haunting stanzas in his poem *The Dream Songs*, John Berryman, who committed suicide, as did his father, believed that fathers who kill themselves condemn their sons to the same fate:

> Save us from shotguns & fathers' suicides.
> It all depends on who you're the father *of*
> if you want to kill yourself—
> a bad example, murder of oneself
> the final death, in a paroxysm, of love
> for which good mercy hides?
>
> .   .   .   .
>
> But to return, to return to Hemingway
> that cruel & gifted man.
> Mercy! My father; do not pull the trigger
> or all my life I'll suffer from your anger
> killing what you began. (254)

Like Ernest and John Hemingway, Sylvia Plath and Anne Sexton also had an antisuicide pact. The two young poets met in Robert Lowell's

1958 graduate seminar at Boston University and soon disclosed to each other the details of their suicide attempts. Plath's self-asphyxiation in 1963 was devastating to Sexton, who felt that her rival had done something magical and forbidden that she too had long desired. Acknowledging that Plath's suicide deepened her own longing for self-extinction, Sexton romanticizes the act in "Sylvia's Death." News of the death has created a "terrible taste for it, like salt" (*Complete Poems* 127): "Plath's suicide had a permanent influence on Sexton, planting a seed, or at least fertilizing one that had already been planted, and that would bear terrible fruit a decade later. [Biographer Diane] Middlebrook quotes a statement Sexton made to [her psychiatrist] Dr. Orne confirming her fascination with Plath's suicide. 'Sylvia Plath's death disturbs me. . . . Makes me want it too. She took something that was mine, *that* death was mine! Of course it was hers too. But we both swore off it, the way you swear off smoking'" (*Surviving Literary Suicide* 192).

Assia Gutmann Wevill, too, understood Sexton's competition with Plath. Plath's life and death were so intimidating to Wevill, who felt inferior to her famous rival both as a poet and a woman, that she regretted her six-year relationship with Hughes, whom she feared would abandon her, as he had abandoned Plath. "I should never have looked into Pandora's box," Wevill confided in her diary, "and now that I have I am forced to wear her love-widow's sacking, without any of her compensations. What, in five years' time, will he reproach me for? What sort of woman am I? How much time have I been given? How much time has run out?" (qtd. in Koren and Negev 126). A. Alvarez theorizes that Wevill's "only way of outdoing her dead rival was in the manner of her death" (qtd. in Koren and Negev 214): that is, whereas Plath killed herself but not her two children—though she dramatizes her own death and those of the two children in her last poem, "Edge"—Wevill killed herself and her daughter, Shura, thus creating a double tragedy. Wevill's biographers, Yehuda Koren and Eilat Negev, report that news of the two deaths gave the "final blow" to Wevill's father and his own mother, both of whom died shortly afterward. Plath's and Wevill's deaths also had a devastating effect on Hughes. "With two suicides on his back, Hughes felt as though he was cursed. There was something in him that was fatal for every woman who got involved with him. He infected them with his black moods, but they did not have the immunity that he had, and could not cope" (215).

Just as Wevill and Sexton viewed Plath's suicide as an outcome to which they were drawn inevitably, like a moth to a fire, so did Elizabeth Wurtzel see Sexton's suicide as having a formative influence on her. She describes in her 1994 autobiography *Prozac Nation* an elaborate suicidal fantasy to her psychiatrist. Horrified, the psychiatrist insists that she be hospitalized immediately, upon which Wurtzel panics, thinks of the lines from Sexton's poem "Wanting to Die"—"But suicides have a special language. / Like carpenters they want to know *which tools.* / They never ask *why build"*—and then rushes to a bathroom, where she locks the door and swallows a full bottle of powerful antipsychotic medication.

Sexton was not a household name when she committed suicide, and so there was little national attention to her death by carbon monoxide poisoning in 1974, an outcome long anticipated by her poetry. But Kurt Cobain's death on 5 April 1994, three weeks before the end of my Literary Suicide course, made newspaper headlines across the country, and there was a sharp spike in suicide crisis calls in the Seattle area, where he lived. The *New York Times* reported the suicides of two French teenagers who shot themselves a month later. Near their bodies were several Cobain lyrics; the police would not say which songs for fear of their impact on other vulnerable youths.

Because suicide rates increase after self-inflicted death, newspaper editors have learned to be cautious when covering these events. Those who work with children also need to be cautious. "Suggestible young-sters," Sharon Klayman Farber writes, "are all too prone to idealize and romanticize the successful suicide," especially around the anniversary of a suicide. "There are suicide watches in some local schools in my area in March, as suicides and suicide attempts have occurred around this time for a number of years. They increase as spring arrives, the time of Christ's crucifixion and resurrection, when desperate people believe that they will be reborn after they have died" (61).

Students Becoming at Risk

The first two students whom I noticed becoming at risk were members of the Literary Suicide course. One was Mary, about whom Patty wrote in her reader-response diary. The other was Ultra, who found himself becoming at risk while reading *Darkness Visible*, William Styron's account of his suicidal depression and recovery.

Sadly, I fear the one thing you'd taken precautions against all semester which I'd dismissed as a possibility has happened. Shortly after reading Darkness Visible I found myself slipping into a depression the likes of which I have not experienced in years. Styron's descriptions of what his depression felt like disturbingly matched my own experiences with depression. In fact, his accuracy was uncanny.

Oddly, and for reasons I can't determine or explain, reading his work proved not purgative but pernicious. It seemed to literally "stir up" feelings that hadn't plagued me in at least two years. The effects were swift and encompassing, and while there are other factors that could have served as proximate causes (a deteriorating relationship), there's something so familiar to this depression that I know it's not just due to outside influences.

To allay your concerns, the intensity of these feelings has decreased over the past few days and will hopefully subside. I'm hoping that the letter Julie [a classmate] will read in class will help us as well.

So, no, I'm not in danger of suicide or anything, but Darkness Visible *had a pronounced and immediate effect upon me, one I had no way of foreseeing, and it's something you may want to consider in future classes. I really hate ending on a note like this, because I felt the diary writing was an incredibly beneficial experience for me, and truly appreciated your consistently insightful and empathic comments. Thanks and take care.* (Berman, *Surviving Literary Suicide* 258)

Ultra's response to *Darkness Visible* mystified me, for the memoir was the only story we read with an affirmative ending. Instead of committing suicide, as Woolf, Hemingway, Plath, and Sexton did, Styron institutionalized himself and recovered thanks to the enforced safety of the hospital and the passing of time. Ultra sent me a letter a month after the course ended, and while it still remains unclear why he found a recovery narrative so threatening, he told me he was feeling better:

Dear Jeff,

Having put aside my final diary for a few weeks following our discussion, I've just finished rereading it and have some comments to offer.

In the weeks that have passed, the depression I had feared approaching has faded away. My last diary now strikes me as hyperbolic, if not hysterical. I can, however, remember how I felt at the time clearly enough to know these emotions were genuine when written.

When we met, we discussed other possible causes for my reaction to Darkness Visible; *the end of the semester, for example. I'm still certain that what I felt was distinct from the stress brought on by papers coming due or something similar, but again, it's gone. Hearing Julie read her letter to Styron helped a great deal, as did speaking with you about what I had experienced.*

In a sense I now consider reading Darkness Visible *as a kind of inoculation against depression. You know the way inoculations work: you get infected with a little bit of a virus and your body develops a resistance to it that protects you from it in the future. (Right?) In doing so, however, you may come down with some symptoms of the disease you're being immunized against. So I suppose in this analogy, my evanescent depression was simply a side effect of the inoculation. (Or something like that.)*

That's about all I have to say on the subject for now. Thanks for this chance to elaborate on my last diary. Moreover, thank you for the concern you showed. It was very much appreciated.

Other students have also become at risk in my writing and literature courses. In *Risky Writing* I discuss in detail three female students who found themselves becoming depressed while reading novels on the syllabus. Chrissy told me that she experienced nightmares and insomnia while reading D. M. Thomas's *White Hotel*, which describes in graphic detail the protagonist's rape and murder during World War II at Babi Yar, the infamous ravine located near Kiev, the capital of Ukraine. After the course ended, she wrote a letter revealing that *The Diary of Anne Frank*, which she read when she was ten, was the first story that terrified her. "As I read the book I noticed that I was more afraid of the dark than normal. I had trouble sleeping, and often had nightmares about being hunted and captured by the Nazis. I would hear sirens in my sleep, and at night, once it was dark outside I would sometimes have the sensation of being stalked like some kind of prey" (*Risky Writing* 239). She never finished the book.

The White Hotel evoked similar nightmares in Chrissy. "As Lisa tried desperately to save herself and her son, I was reminded of my nightmares where I was being hunted and I had to try to outwit and escape those who would capture and kill me. Every part of that section from the rape to the description of the layers and layers of murdered corpses in that ravine sickened and frightened me." She finished the novel but was angered that she was forced to read it. She ended her letter by stating that she did not believe her responses to literature are unusual. "Anyone who can read a book as though they are seeing a movie in their mind could be similarly affected, and I think for this reason teachers ought to be careful in what they assign. Professors ought not to take it for granted that because students are past a certain age that they can handle anything. Why should anyone assume that at a certain age you become jaded enough that you are unaffected by death?" (*Risky Writing* 239).

Not long after speaking with Chrissy, I began to ask my students on the first day of the semester to visit me during my office hours if they found themselves becoming anxious or depressed over a reading or writing assignment. Two students told me the next semester that this was precisely what was happening when they read Plath's *The Bell Jar* and Kate Chopin's *The Awakening*, both of which describe female protagonists who attempt or commit suicide. The novels reminded Justine of the suicidal depression she experienced the summer before, when she placed an iron in the bath tub in an effort to electrocute herself. With her mother's help, she recovered, but she became depressed again when identifying with Esther Greenwood in *The Bell Jar*. She was alarmed by the many similarities between herself and Plath's autobiographical heroine, and she was distressed further when she learned that Plath committed suicide shortly after completing the novel. Viewing these similarities as portentous, Justine noted in her essay on *The Bell Jar* that teachers should take precautions with certain novels. "He or she should be prepared if a student is feeling depressed or suicidal during and after reading these novels. Talking to their students before and after is therapeutic and essential in assuring that students do not get the wrong message. If a student is showing signs of serious illness they should be directed to the appropriate practitioners" (*Risky Writing* 241).

Reading *The Bell Jar* and *The Awakening* had a similar effect on Olivia, reminding her of the depression she experienced five years earlier, when she was sixteen. She found that the novels were altering her sleep patterns and darkening her moods. Like Chopin's heroine, she began to lose herself in "mazes of inward contemplation." Like Plath's heroine, she began to feel an indescribable oppression. "I could sense the boundaries of the transparent bell-shaped glass; within it, I was trapped in this feeling, this mood of unsettlement and extreme anxiety. This was the way I felt in high school, not even comfortable in my own skin." The mood lasted for two weeks and then began to lift. She thanked me at the end of the semester for alerting her in advance to the possibility that the novels might put her at risk. "He left the door wide open and gave a fair warning of what may happen. His availability comforted me while I was trapped in this spell. Though I experienced such haunting things, I am glad to have read the material. I know that I am not alone. Nor does this hinder me from putting *The Awakening* on my shelf as one of my favorite novels" (*Risky Writing* 243).

As I report in *Empathic Teaching*, two students found themselves becoming ill while reading Primo Levi's *Survival in Auschwitz*. (A third student, Christine, I discuss in a later chapter.) "Talk about literature having the power to traumatize," Patrice states at the beginning of her reader-response diary:

> *Now, books have made me laugh aloud as well as cry, but I cannot remember ever reading a book that gave me a nightmare. Last Wednesday I finished the final chapter, "The Story of Ten Days," and went to bed. That night I was haunted by those very same images I have seen at least a couple of dozen times in documentaries. However, not one of those documentaries ever gave me a nightmare; Primo Levi's book did. Human figures so emaciated I could see their bones through their gray skin. I felt scared, as if these lifeless bodies were ghosts, although none seemed to be aware of my existence. They all bore heavy loads of various types (one was pushing a huge boulder, another was carrying an old car on his back), and their heads were listlessly pointed towards the ground. It seemed like a sort of purgatory, with the putrid smell of human suffering that no stomach can handle. I honestly woke up scared! I think the last time I had a bona fide nightmare before this was about 14 years ago, when Freddy Kruger intruded into my unconscious.* (334–35)

Mac was the other student who found himself haunted by dreams as a result of reading *Survival in Auschwitz*. The Holocaust memoir evoked memories of the time when he was incarcerated wrongly for a drug charge:

> *Reading all about Primo Levi's experience serves as a reminder to me as to why I get so scared when I see a police officer. Being held captive against my will was definitely the most traumatic thing to happen to me. I never looked*

*at things the same way; not my friends who would put me in such a situation,
my relatives and other friends who felt I was every bit as guilty as the law
believed me to be, nor myself who has never been so scared before and will
never let myself forget. To hear Primo Levi's accounts made me sit and think
about those dreams I always have; the one's when I wake up in that cell,
wearing the bright orange of County, in a pool of my own sweat, trying to
keep myself awake, and most of all afraid of every single shadow that passed.
I never want to be just a number again. One loses all sense of self-respect
and one loses his identity. Primo Levi was one among the masses persecuted
against by the German's. No one believed he would survive the experiences
at Auschwitz but he somehow gathered the strength to pull through. I have
so much respect for this man. He has endured more than I can ever imagine
and when I try to imagine it, I get sick, I get nervous, I start to sweat and I
just can't talk about it anymore.* (336–37)

Emotional Contagion

Most of my students who have reported becoming at risk during a reading
or writing assignment are women, which is consistent with their greater
susceptibility to the contagion effect. Elaine Hatfield, John Cacioppo,
and Richard Rapson argue that although men and women may *feel* the
same way, there are significant gender differences in how they *express*
these feelings: "Women are generally more open and expressive than are
men. They are better encoders of friendly, unfriendly, and unpleasant
affect, of happiness, love, fear, anger, surprise, and dominance. They
spontaneously smile and laugh more, engage in more eye contact, touch
more, and show more body movement, and are freer about expressing
negative emotions as well. Even when men and women are both *trying*
to communicate nonverbally, women are the far more expressive send-
ers" (143).

Significantly, those who are able to read others' emotions are especially vulnerable to contagion. "Awareness of others' feelings," Hatfield
and her associates theorize, "is a predictor of sharing those feelings even
if it is not a necessary condition for contagion" (154). Females are more
sensitive than males to emotional expressions, and they are also better at
interpreting nonverbal clues of emotion. "Women were simply better at
reading what is meant by the awkward glance, superior smile, or hesitant
speech. Their advantage was most pronounced for facial cues, less pronounced for bodily cues, and least pronounced for vocal cues" (162).

The authors describe many studies that confirm the contagion effect. One experiment demonstrated the effect of an interviewer's warmth on the interviewee's reactions. "Interviewers who were to behave warmly were instructed to lean forward as they talked, smile, and nod; the others, who were to be reserved, were told not to do so. Interviewer warmth was reciprocated in kind: Warm interviewers' subjects smiled, nodded, and leaned forward more than their peers did. Warm interviewers also elicited more intimate self-disclosures and less hesitant conversations" (37). Infants are remarkably attuned to other infants and seem to catch their pain. "From a few months after birth through the first year of life, studies have shown, infants react to the pain of others as though it were happening to themselves. Seeing another child hurt and start to cry, they themselves begin to cry, especially if the other child cries for more than a minute or two. But around one year of age, infants begin to realize that the distress is being felt by someone else. 'They recognize it's the other kid's problem, but they're often confused over what to do about it'" (82). Parents catch their children's emotions. One study found that "parents who were asked to observe a sad or angry newborn reported feeling more 'annoyed, irritated, distressed, disturbed, indifferent, and less attentive and less happy' than those who viewed a smiling infant. When parents viewed a sad or angry child, their diastolic blood pressure rose and their skin conductance increased" (86). Depressed mothers tend to convey their sadness to their children, who themselves become depressed.

Adults can also catch the depression of others: "Students entering Florida State University for the first time were assigned a roommate. Before they entered college, the students took the Beck Depression Inventory; they took it again periodically over the three months they lived together. Those who had been assigned to live with a mildly depressed roommate themselves became more and more depressed over time." The researchers found these results unsettling because "depressed physicians, nurses, and teachers, for example, might have a depressing effect on their charges, at a time when they are especially vulnerable" (Hatfield, Cacioppo, and Rapson 102). The authors quote a statement by Carl Jung indicating that emotions are contagious to the therapist. "In psychotherapy, even if the doctor is entirely detached from the emotional contents of the patient, the very fact that the patient has emotions has an effect upon him. And it is a great mistake if the doctor thinks he can lift himself out of it. He cannot do more than become conscious of the fact that he is affected. If he does not see that, he is too aloof and then he talks beside the point. It is even his duty to accept the emotions of the patient and to mirror them" (89). My doctoral student Matthew Pangborn reminds me that Freud also knew about the contagion phenomenon. In *The Psychopathology of Everyday Life,* he remarks that the "forgetting of names is highly contagious. In a conversation between two people it is often sufficient for one of them merely to mention that he has forgotten such and such a name, and the result will be that it slips the other's mind as well" (40). Slips of the tongue, Freud adds, are also highly contagious (62).

There are many examples of the contagion effect, beginning with the Werther effect, which Hatfield and associates curiously omit. But they document cross-cultural research describing "hysterical contagion," including the "madness" of crowds, hysterical laughter, and hysterical illnesses mysteriously sweeping over communities. Emile Durkheim observes that the "idea of suicide may undoubtedly be communicated by contagion" and documents many examples (131). Perhaps the most famous example of hysterical contagion is Orson Welles's infamous radio broadcast of H. G. Wells's *War of the Worlds.* Tens of millions of Americans panicked on 30 October 1938 when they heard Welles and his actors read the science fiction novel as if it were a live news story. "Thousands telephoned family and friends to warn them of the attack from Mars, fell to their knees in prayer, or packed up their families and drove aimlessly for miles, not knowing where they were headed" (Hatfield, Cacioppo, and Rapson 108). Stanley Kubrick's 1971 A *Clockwork Orange,* judged by *Entertainment Weekly* to be the second most controversial film of all time, contains a violent rape scene during which "Singing in the Rain" is played; the film resulted in copycat crimes that led to its withdrawal from distribution in Britain (*Albany Times-Union,* 10 June 2006).

There are many documented cases of mass hysteria affecting schools and entire communities. "Between 1973 and 1993," writes Margaret Talbot in the 2 June 2002 issue of the *New York Times,* "there were 70 reports of mass hysteria in medical journals; most took place in self-contained communities, like schools, barracks and factories. Sixty percent of the incidents of epidemic hysteria written up in the English-language journals this century occurred in schools." Talbot concludes her article with a paradox: "Suggesting that symptoms might be psychogenic can help stop them, but it often does so at the risk of alienating, even embittering people." Entrainment, or sympathetic vibration, is another example of emotional contagion, as Mitchell Gaynor describes in his book *Sounds of Healing*:

> The seventeenth-century Dutch scientist Christian Huygens noticed that the pendulums of two clocks, hung side by side, would begin of their own accord to swing to the same identical rhythm. The reason that entrainment occurs is that the more powerful rhythmic vibrations of one object, when projected upon a second object with a similar frequency, will cause that object to begin to vibrate in *resonance* with the first object. We human beings also react in resonance with the vibrations and fluctuations in our surroundings, so it follows that our physiological functioning may be altered by the impact of sound waves, whether produced by our own voices or by objects or instruments in our environment. (49)

One of the most curious examples of the contagion effect occurs when the husband of a pregnant woman develops symptoms of morning sickness. According to Armin Brott, "somewhere between 25 percent and 90 percent of dads-to-be in this country experience couvade syndrome (from the French, 'to hatch'), or 'sympathetic pregnancy'" (*Albany Times-Union*, 29 September 2005). These expectant fathers apparently experience the same symptoms as their wives, including mood swings, food cravings, and weight gain. The symptoms nearly always end with the child's birth. Among the many theories of couvade syndrome is the belief that the husband tries to ease his wife's pain by sharing it. David Morris notes in *The Culture of Pain* that the couvade phenomenon may be seen in societies throughout the world and that its influence can be traced on literature from the *Argonautica*, written in the first century, to James Joyce's 1922 novel *Ulysses* (278).

Who are the people most susceptible to emotional contagion? Hatfield, Cacioppo, and Rapson offer several insights here. People are more likely to catch others' emotions "if their attention is riveted on the others than if they are oblivious to others' emotions"; "if they construe themselves in terms of their interrelatedness to the others rather than in terms of their independence and uniqueness"; "if they are able to read others' emotional expressions, voices, gestures, and postures"; if they tend to "mimic facial, vocal, and postural expressions"; if they are "aware of their own emotional responses"; and if they are "emotionally reactive people" (148). One of the "dismal" conclusions of contagion research is that "it is happy people who are most receptive to others and most likely to catch their moods; the unhappy seem relatively oblivious to others' feelings and to contagion. Thus, when Good Samaritans venture out to cheer up the sad, anxious, and lonely, there looms the horrible possibility that they will make themselves miserable while accomplishing little for the suffering recipients of their good works" (152). Close relationships lend themselves to emotional contagion: couples passionately in love; mothers of infants ("the mother-infant relationship may be a prototype of the kind of relationship in which people 'lose their boundaries'"); people "who have a psychological investment in others' welfare," such as psychotherapists, teachers, and caregivers; and children of alcoholics, who are "especially sensitive to the changing moods of their troubled parents" (166).

There are advantages to being able to infect others with one's emotions, according to Hatfield and associates. "When we try to distract an irritable child, when we go to the hospital to 'cheer up' a friend, when we try to liven up a dull party, we are trying to dominate an interpersonal encounter." So too are there advantages and disadvantages to catching other's emotions. "Sometimes people benefit from being able to read and share others' feelings. At other times, however, contagion is too much of a good thing. People may wish to build a glass wall around their feelings when they must act coolly in a 'hot' situation or respond with verve and energy in a cool, dead environment. They may not wish to share others' feelings when their interests are opposed. In such situations, it may be a good thing to be able to resist" (202–3).

Contagious Texts

Like people, texts can be contagious or noncontagious. Contagious texts are more likely to infect readers than noncontagious texts. Contagious texts communicate emotions more intensely than do noncontagious ones, eliciting in particular negative emotions, such as anger, sadness, or fear. Contagious texts provoke stronger reader identification than noncontagious texts. They romanticize acts that have disastrous personal and interpersonal consequences, such as suicide, homicide, rape, or war, all the time failing to describe the destructive aftermath of these events. Contagious texts evoke reader responses that are either similar ("as when smiles elicit smiles") or complementary ("as when a fist raised in anger causes a timid person to shrink back in fear, a process sometimes called *countercontagion*") (Hatfield, Cacioppo, and Rapson

5). Contagious texts are more likely to be mimetic than noncontagious texts, perhaps because it is easier for readers to identify with realistic characters. Insofar as women are more susceptible to contagion than men, contagious texts are more likely than noncontagious texts to contain female characters who suffer from anxiety, depression, suicidal ideation, or sexual abuse. They are more likely to show than to tell, to dramatize rather than merely to summarize human conflicts or illnesses. They may dramatize traumatic events so powerfully that they actually reawaken similar traumas in readers.

Because of their graphic and often hyperrealistic nature, films are more likely than literature to be contagious. As I point out in *Surviving Literary Suicide*, "Many films and television shows have provoked acts of copycat violence, including *The Deer Hunter, Taxi Driver, The Burning Bed, Boulevard Nights, Colors, New Jack City, The Program, Natural Born Killers,* and *Beavis and Butt-Head*" (202). The suicide rate rises following television broadcasts of fictional stories portraying suicide (Gould, Shaffer, and Kleinman), and suicide stories "trigger deaths that would not have occurred otherwise" (Phillips and Carstensen 101). War films can prove traumatic to soldiers who have been in battle. Stephen Spielberg's 1998 film *Saving Private Ryan* traumatized not only soldiers of World War II but also of Korea, Vietnam, and the Persian Gulf. "Across the country, veterans' hospitals have been inundated with calls from men seeking help coping with disturbing memories uncovered by the movie's realism. In some cases, the film's stark portrayal of torn flesh and frightened soldiers watching their friends die triggered post-traumatic stress disorder in veterans who had never experienced such difficulties before, counselors said" (*Albany Times-Union*, 31 July 1998).

Based on the reader-response diaries I have received over a period of many years, I have learned that Freud's case study *Fragment of an Analysis of a Case of Hysteria*—the story of Dora—may disturb, anger, or infuriate readers with its antifeminist bias, but rarely does it depress them. Readers may feel more sympathy for Dora than Freud intends, but they do not identify with her to the degree that they begin to experience her "hysterical" symptoms. Nor have my students reported becoming at risk while reading novels by Virginia Woolf or James Joyce, perhaps because their stories are so linguistically challenging. Readers may find Kafka's stories grim and nightmarish, but they rarely find themselves at risk while reading them, perhaps because of the allegorical and fablelike quality of his writing. I regularly teach a course on F. Scott Fitzgerald and Ernest Hemingway, and I cannot recall students telling me that they have become at risk while reading novels such as *The Great Gatsby* or *The Sun Also Rises*.

Some students in my course on Thomas Hardy and D. H. Lawrence find themselves feeling depressed while reading Hardy's late novels, especially *Jude the Obscure*, which is the most despairing story I have read. Female students who identify with Hardy's entrapped female characters— the eponymous heroine of *Tess of the d'Urbervilles*, Eustacia Vye in *The Return of the Native*, and Sue Bridehead in *Jude the Obscure*—sometimes feel as if they too are trapped in a patriarchal society. Female students also reported that while reading Hardy novels they suddenly recalled old memories they thought they had long forgotten. "Each novel related in a way or another to my life. I remembered scenes from my childhood which I thought [were] forever forgotten—and some characters brought back to life people I loved. I do not think that I am a depressed person but reading Hardy I became one (just for a while)." Students report feeling infected by the gloom and doom of these novels, though not to the extent that they do while reading *The Bell Jar* or *The Awakening*, both of which produce intense feelings of anxiety or depression in certain readers.

Reading-Induced Post-Traumatic Stress Disorder: Deana

Some female students who have been sexually abused find themselves experiencing symptoms of post-traumatic stress disorder when reading *Lolita*. One graduate student, Deanna, found herself identifying so strongly with Dolores Haze, Humbert's "nymphet," that she began having flashbacks and nightmares. She gave her oral presentation on the ways in which the novel reawakened so many of the traumatic memories she was trying to forget, and she later wrote an essay on *Lolita* in the form of a letter to the author:

Nabokov,

Such is my anger that I cannot finish a letter to you. Several times I have begun to write and each time my pencil and my courage fail me in my desire to rant and rage at you. I am held back by my feelings of inadequacy in the face of an author considered by many to be one of the greats. After all, who am I, a mere graduate student, to criticize you? What right do I have to question your authority and skill as an author? My right lies in the fact that I was once a Lolita with a Humbert in my own life. My right lies in my experience and in my role as a reader. This is the first time that I have read your novel. Originally my interest was piqued by the incredibly positive reviews from various critics, including some who I greatly respect. Needless to say, this text has affected me like no other; it is, however, not in the manner which I expected. I thought I would be awed by what many have called your magnificent prose, introduced to a novel that I could read time and again and treat as an old friend. Instead, I have found the first novel that I have ever despised. As for you, I have very little respect for you and cannot bring myself to call you either "Sir" or "Mister."

What disturbs me most is your treatment of Dolores (I refuse to call her by the other name which you and Humbert gave her), and the other girls that you have deemed nymphets. You would have one believe that there is an essence or aura lurking around these girls that entreats a man to rape or molest them; something in the way they walk; the shape of their limbs, and so on. You write as if these girls are "asking for it." I assure you that there is nothing in them that secretly asks for the perverted attention of any man. The fact that you treat Humbert as a sympathetic character and Dolores as a seductress is impossible for me to accept. The lightness with which you treat abuse, mental, physical, and sexual, and the suffusion of your sick humor throughout this novel make me physically ill. A crime committed against a child is the most abhorrent crime that can be committed in any society. You, in your desire to push the boundaries and taboos of society, have belittled the pain that abuse victims suffer from by making Dolores appear to be partially responsible for the torment inflicted upon her.

It took two days a week, every week for a year, for my therapist to help me realize that the abuse I had been suffering under was not my fault; the problem did not lie with me, but with my abuser instead. Your novel, Nabokov, seemed to push me to question the potentially life-saving realization that it took me so long to come to. It is obvious to me that you are lacking both understanding and sensitivity regarding your subject matter. Perhaps my letter can bring you some knowledge of the terrible pain that your novel has caused me and, doubtless, many other men and women.

From the time I was fourteen until I was nearly eighteen years old, I was sexually abused by an older man. The age difference was not as great as that between Dolores and Humbert, but it was enough. In the beginning it was treated as a boyfriend-girlfriend relationship. I do not know how my family was so completely sucked in by this man, but it didn't take long for him to sever me emotionally from them and insert himself between us. While I was still physically near my family, in all actuality I could not have been more alone. Like Humbert, he made me believe that he was the only one person in the world that I could turn to. When you believe that there is only one person in the world who "cares for you," you cling to that person because without them there is no one.

You have no idea what it is to be touched by hands that drive shame into you like a spear that then spreads throughout your entire being with a deadening chill. If you knew what it is to lie crushed beneath a man as he steals away every last vestige of innocence that you had left, then you would not have written this novel in that manner that you did. I know what it is to dry heave after that man leaves the room, to have to burn incense because any trace of his smell brings your stomach to your throat and causes the shrinking of your very essence until you know that you are a black hole. But you can't escape because NO ONE ELSE WILL EVER LOVE YOU. That person is the only one who will have you now that you are tainted. I know what it is to scour my body so hard that I left raw patches of skin all over. I know these things and you do not so you have no right,

NO RIGHT, I scream at you, to write of such things. Until you have been forced to do things that no girl, woman, boy, or man should ever be forced to do, you have overstepped your bounds.

Because I know. I KNOW. I know what it is to die inside. To numb myself so thoroughly that I could turn my smile on and off like a light switch, that I forced myself to make others laugh because if they were laughing they couldn't see the deadness in my eyes, the same disgust that I knew surrounded me like an impenetrable, black cloud.

I never would have known that reading *Lolita* was such a torture for Deanna had she not trusted her teacher and classmates enough to give her oral presentation on the novel. She later described the presentation as a "purely emotional response to a disturbing novel." She felt that during her presentation it was "nearly impossible" for her to "step back from the text and view it from a distance." Her fifteen-page essay written a week later was more analytical, though she still could not appreciate the novel's "aesthetic bliss," which so many critics have experienced, including myself. She discussed persuasively in her essay many important issues in the novel, including Humbert's relationship to his dark double, Claire Quilty, and the last encounter between Humbert and Dolores, in which the reader's sympathy appears to shift toward the broken-hearted lover, who gives her all his worldly possessions, without preconditions. "Her behavior in his presence and the manner in which she speaks to him," Deanna concedes, "does not coincide with her status as a victim of his lust." She agreed reluctantly with my observation that one of the most disturbing aspects of the novel is that it is hard for the reader to find textual evidence indicating Humbert has traumatized Dolores. One crucial issue that Deanna does not explore in her paper is Nabokov's relationship to Humbert: the question of narrative distance has bedeviled literary critics since the novel's publication in 1955.

Deanna told me in an email six weeks after the course ended that she intended to write in more detail about her experience of sexual abuse. The *Lolita* paper was excruciating, she added, but in retrospect she believed that the writing was helpful for her ongoing recovery. I told her that I would be happy to read whatever she wrote and suggested that she might consider the topic for her doctoral dissertation. I then asked her if she could elaborate on what it felt like to read and give her class presentation on *Lolita*:

The best teachers of literature are those who can create a bridge, a connection, between the student and the text. It is true that some of this may be a painful connection, but it is always enlightening. Literature is not written for the purpose of being analyzed, deconstructed, and placed within scholarly categories. It is written to make the reader feel. Whether the author writes from "sheer egoism," "aesthetic enthusiasm," "historical impulse," or for a "political purpose," the desired effect is achieved only if the reader connects with the text, if the distance barrier erected by previous styles of pedagogy can be broken down or circumvented. The atmosphere that permeates your classroom allows students to recognize or cultivate emotional attachments with texts. These ties are by no means less scholarly than a purely analytic criticism. They allow for a greater, broader understanding of the words on the pages.

Having said this, I do recognize that addressing the literature you teach in the personalized, self-disclosing manner in which you do is certainly risky. I did not realize just how risky until I took your course on the Age of Freud this past summer. It was during this course that I read Vladimir Nabokov's Lolita for the first time. As someone who has been a victim of sexual abuse, [I found] the experience petrifying, horrifying, and shame-filled. Every word of that novel dredged up from my deepest vaults the memories and accompanying emotions that I believed I had successfully locked away years ago. Humbert Humbert's descriptions of his relationship with Dolores Haze caused me to feel nauseous, alone, vulnerable, naked, shamed, disgusted, and scared. I was scared because something as commonplace as a novel was able to break through every safeguard that I had erected. Even now, the calm I felt only moments ago has dissipated and been replaced by the once again familiar, frantic squeezing in my chest. I dreaded every page of that novel. I was sickened by it and yet I read on. Why? Why am I doing this? Why keep reading? I repeatedly asked myself these questions. The answer is this. I continued reading out of the hope for an ending that would redeem the novel for me and that would redeem you as a teacher in my eyes.

I had previously taken a course from you and respected you a great deal as both a teacher and a person. Your approach to litera-ture and your students has always been empathic, nonjudgmental, and sensitive. Yet you kept repeating that Lolita was one of your favorite novels: a masterpiece. With those words I felt utterly be-trayed. There were moments when you spoke in praise of the novel in which I hated you. I actually felt a surge of pure anger and hate flow through me. I wanted to scream at you and demand an answer for your foolishness. How could anyone, especially a teacher as em-pathic as yourself, not recognize the anguish that Nabokov's words caused me? I had struggled for years to combat the fierce bouts of anxiety, the nightmares, the crawling sensation when touched, and there you were presenting Lolita, a novel that buried my hard-won freedom from torment, as one of your all-time favorites. Such a sense of betrayal I had not felt in years.

While feeling these emotions, I knew in my head that there was no way you could have known about the abuse I had suffered. You were entitled to your opinion about the text, although it was not an opinion that I could fathom having. At first I believed I wanted to present my experience to the class so that they would not be seduced into viewing Lolita as you had. I wanted them to recognize how great the agony was that the novel caused me. There was a feeling of desiring revenge on anyone who could possibly view the novel in a positive light, as if a positive reading of it were somehow a personal betrayal. Somewhere inside me, from a dark place came the wish to wound others with my tale so that they could never read it the same way again. I guess it was more a desire to lash out at the author for writing such a thing. No. That is not it either. So much of the anger that I had condensed and compressed, anger at my abuser and the fact that I had been abused surged swiftly to the surface and I wanted to hurt anything that was around me to rid myself of it. More than anything, I felt the need to have my reading of the text validated. This is why I feel the way I do. These are my reasons. Please understand me. I had brought something to the text that was essential to my reading of it, and your permission to present that to the class helped me to achieve the validation that I needed to continue onward with the class. The presentation also helped me to release pain and anger in a manner that was not harmful to myself, nor do I believe to anyone else. I do not remember exactly the comments that were made directly following my presentation; I do recall a sense of sympathy and understanding rising from my fellow students. Shame warred with an awkward sense of peace. My silence had finally been broken and I have both you and Vladimir Nabokov to thank for that.

In the "Risky Teaching" chapter of your book Empathic Teaching, you write of your students, "I do not rescue them; they rescue themselves." This is true. It has been over a month since that course ended. I am not who I was before the first day of class, nor am I the same person who walked out of class because I was either going to vomit or faint during the discussion of Lolita. Dark shadows have fallen over my soul for days at a time. I have had bad dreams. Lately a certain familiarity in a man's shape is enough to reduce me to fever-pitch anxiety that I can only control by counting to five on my fingers and taking the same number of steps in each square around campus until I feel better. Reading Lolita was extremely risky for me. It was like a whirling vortex that sapped me of good feelings and plummeted me into blackness. I feel now that it was worth it. The class response to my risky writing gave me a platform from which I could begin a crawl towards healing. The support that I had from you in allowing me to present my experience and in providing a setting in which I could explain and validate my emotional response to the novel is something that I am abundantly thankful for.

To anyone who would jump to criticize your teaching methods

I would say this. Come and sit through a class. Experience the freedom of being encouraged to personally connect with a text and being allowed to share those connections with others. You will learn that literature is more than groups of paragraphs to be analyzed for plot, diction, and structure. It is life in words, both affecting the way we read and live and affected by our lives and pasts. You will learn to read all over again.

Deanna's class presentation and writing are not only confessional but, more importantly, transformational, helping her to release much of the pain, anger, and shame that had burdened her for many years. Postmodern scholars are suspicious of confession, agreeing with Michel Foucault that it has long been associated with coercion, accusation, and torture. "One confesses—or is forced to confess. When it is not spontaneous or dictated by some internal imperative, the confession is wrung from a person by violence or threat; it is driven from its hiding place in the soul, or extracted from the body. . . . Confession frees, but power reduces one to silence; truth does not belong to the order of power, but shares an original affinity with freedom" (59–60). Talk shows have also sensationalized and trivialized confessional discourse. But voluntary self-disclosures like Deanna's can be a crucial step toward self-awareness and self-mastery, affirming the power to understand and control one's life.

I agree with Deanna that one of the purposes of reading is to make us *feel*—and, I would add, as she would, to make us *think*. I also agree that we can experience the power of literature only if we connect, emotionally and intellectually, with our reading. I try to "cultivate emotional attachments with texts" by speaking personally about literature and by encouraging students to express their feelings and thoughts in reader-response diaries, class presentations, and formal essays. These ties, as Deanna reports, "allow for a greater, broader understanding of the words on the pages."

Such teaching is risky, however. Until she wrote to me, I did not know how furious Deanna was at me when I expressed my admiration for *Lolita*. I believe that all people are entitled to their feelings: this is one of the cornerstones of the empathic classroom. I would never presume to tell students how and what they should feel. Teaching is an intersubjective experience in which teacher and students share interpretations that inevitably reveal aspects of themselves. Every interpretation reveals something about the interpreter: there are no objective readings of literature. Reader-response critics have been proclaiming this for years, but a theoretical understanding of subjectivity does not adequately prepare one for the actual demonstration of what readers bring to a text, as we can see in Deanna's writings. Nor does a theoretical understanding of subjectivity necessarily make it easier for teachers to accept the intense emotions, both positive and negative, that students project upon them.

Stunned by her presentation, I did not want to invalidate Deanna's point of view. Yet at the same time, I felt compelled to point out that *Lolita* is not only considered one of the greatest novels of the twentieth century but has also been embraced by some (though certainly not all) feminists. During the next class, I read aloud passages from Azar Nafisi's best-selling memoir, *Reading Lolita in Tehran,* a moving account of a teacher and her seven Iranian female students who met in secret to read and discuss forbidden Western fiction. Nafisi, who is now a literature professor at Johns Hopkins University, reads *Lolita* not as a glorification of pedophilia, as Deanna does, but as a story in which the novelist takes revenge on solipsizers. "The desperate truth of Lolita's story is *not* the rape of a twelve-year-old by a dirty old man but *the confiscation of one individual's life by another.* We don't know what Lolita would have become if Humbert had not engulfed her. Yet the novel, the finished work, is hopeful, beautiful even, a defense not just of beauty but of life, ordinary everyday life, all the normal pleasures that Lolita, like Yassi [an Iranian woman] was deprived of" (33; emphasis in original).

Reading Lolita in Tehran is a stimulating book, but I don't agree with Nafisi that the separation between Nabokov and Humbert is always clear. Novelist and narrator are alike in many ways, including their fiercely held antipsychiatric belief that the difference between "therapist" and "the rapist" is a matter of spacing. (Anyone who finds psychotherapy helpful, not to mention life-saving, such as Deanna, would object sharply to Nabokov's detestation of mental health professionals, which he expresses, often gratuitously, in the preface to every novel.) This problematic narrative distance makes it impossible to tell at times when Nabokov is implicated in our hatred of Humbert. But I do agree with Nafisi that literature is always disturbing. "Most great works of the imagination were meant to make you feel like a stranger in your own home. The best fiction always forced us to question what we took for granted. It questioned traditions and expectations when they seemed too immutable. I told my students I wanted them in their readings to consider in what ways these works unsettled them, made them a little uneasy, made them look around and consider the world, like Alice in Wonderland, through different eyes" (94).

I suspect that not even Nafisi would have predicted how unsettling *Lolita* was to Deanna. I learned of the intensity of her anger toward Nabokov only from her class presentation. I learned of the intensity of her anger toward *me* only from the paper she wrote six weeks after the end of the course. I did not want Deanna to hate me, but I was grateful that she expressed her feelings so that I could understand her reaction both to the novel and her teacher. She did precisely what I ask all my students to do: engage with literature. Part of this engagement involved her displacement onto both the novel and me of her pent-up rage toward her abuser. The intensity of her feelings frightened and almost overwhelmed her, but she experienced relief through speaking and writing—the talking cure and the writing cure. Nor was it only relief that she experienced. She felt validated by expressing her point of view, one that was moving to everyone in the classroom.

Reading, writing, and speaking proved transformative for Deanna, and I do not believe she exaggerates when she says that she is now a different person. Her risky self-disclosure before a class of strangers was a turning point in allowing her for the first time to speak publicly about a previously unspeakable subject. Reading the novel felt like reliving a terrible nightmare, or, to change the metaphor, like battling a virulent contagion that has never left her body, but she felt strengthened by the experience. In Ultra's words, she was inoculated against disease. In Michelle Payne's words, her anger was resistance to pain:

> Women's anger at being sexually assaulted has been dismissed, seen as a symptom of hysteria, and ridiculed as evidence women can't control their emotions; yet, in therapy and feminist theory it is often seen as the source of resistance to the pain inflicted by such violence—an emotion that, combined with a historical, psychological, and sometimes feminist perspective, can help a victim (a subject) become a survivor (a Subject). This process of healing and resistance occurs when the outlaw emotion is placed into a different context, offering an alternative interpretation of its meaning, reeducating the emotion and the sense of self and world that has been constructed by or around it. (29)

One doesn't ordinarily think of literature as analogous to a flu shot, an antibiotic, or an antidepressant, but under the right classroom conditions, both reading and writing can lead to what Richard Tedeschi and his associates have called "posttraumatic growth" to signify the positive changes that may arise from a traumatic experience. Thus one may learn to see oneself not as a victim but as a survivor.

Both illness and health, contagion and recovery depend upon the reader's identification with a fictional character. Identification, which may be a primitive form of empathy, is usually necessary to understand another character, real or imagined, but overidentification may lead to the loss of boundaries between self and other. To understand how this may occur, we may inquire into the process by which clinicians empathically glimpse their patients' lives. This process, described by psychoanalyst Theodor Reik and summarized by James Marcia, implies movement toward and then away from the patient:

1. *Identification*—paying attention to another and allowing oneself to become absorbed in contemplation of that person
2. *Incorporation*—making the other's experience one's own via internalizing the other
3. *Reverberation*—experiencing the other's experience while simultaneously attending to one's own cognitive and affective associations to that experience
4. *Detachment*—moving back from the merged inner relationship to a position of separate identity, which permits a response to be made that reflects both understanding of others as well as separateness from them. (Marcia 83)

Empathy involves both merging with another and a return to one's own self. It is not clear whether the movement toward and from the other is instantaneous or not, nor whether empathy can be so intense that certain people literally lose their sense of self. What is clear, however, is that those who cannot maintain boundaries between self and other become susceptible to contagion.

Toward the end of their book, Hatfield and her associates remark on a puzzling incongruity: "People seem capable of mimicking others' facial, vocal, and postural expressions with stunning rapidity and, consequently, are able to 'feel themselves into' others' emotional lives to a surprising extent; however, they also seem oblivious to the importance of emotional contagion in social encounters, and unaware of how swiftly and completely they are able to track the expressions of others" (183). The same incongruity appears in the classroom. I repeatedly ask my graduate students if they have heard of emotional contagion, and the answer is always in the negative, despite the fact that they have read a great deal of theory in their courses. The contagion effect has elicited little attention from literary scholars even though students often find themselves at risk when reading novels like *The Bell Jar, The Awakening*, and *Lolita*, all of which are canonical texts, taught at every major college in the country. Why the silence? I suspect the main reason teachers are not aware of the contagion effect is that they do not ask their students to tell them when they have become at risk as a result of a reading or writing assignment. "Don't ask, don't tell" seems to be the implicit message in the classroom. Most of my undergraduate and even graduate students are startled when I give them "permission" to write their formal essays in the first person. They tell me that I am one of the few teachers who allow them to discuss their feelings in a paper. Such a discussion can be as academically rigorous as any other scholarly topic. If students cannot write in the first person, they will not be able to express their affective responses to literature. Thus it should not be surprising that they are unable or unwilling to tell teachers when they are becoming anxious, depressed, or suicidal over a reading or writing assignment. Hence, teachers often have little understanding of the impact of literature on their students' lives.

If reading and writing assignments can be risky, how can teachers challenge their students without depressing them or shattering their identity? The answer is not to avoid emotionally challenging readings and writings, as some critics have suggested in their response to the contagion effect (see "Risky Teaching," the final chapter in *Empathic Teaching*). Nor is the answer to destabilize identity, to "make the student ill," as Gregory Jay urges in the effort to "dislocate fixed desires" (790). I agree with Mark Bracher's observation that the fundamental aim of education should be to "support and develop students' identities, those configurations of self that provide them with vitality, agency, and meaning, and give them a sense of themselves as a force that matters in the world" (11). Students value teachers who encourage them to explore vexing personal issues. Some assignments may unexpectedly create a crisis in students, but they usually have the resources and resiliency to venture into previously un-charted areas of their lives and return safely. Reading *Lolita* was "like a whirling vortex that sapped me of good feelings and plummeted me into blackness," Deanna wrote, but "I feel now that it was worth it."

Given the possibility that a reading or writing assignment may thrust students into a whirling vortex, teachers must have the fortitude to resist being pulled in themselves. They must have the confidence—but not over-confidence—that students will be able to emerge on their own from such tumultuous waters. They must believe in the value of transformational reading and writing and put into place the classroom protocols that will minimize the possibility that students will be harmed by reading or writing assignments. Teachers must know that their responsibility is not to rescue students but to create the educational conditions in which students rescue themselves. In psychoanalytic terms, teachers must be aware of their coun-tertransference so that they can maintain boundaries between self and other and avoid burdening students with their own fears and desires. Simi-larly, they must be aware of transference so that they can avoid becoming defensive when they become the recipient of their students' angry, scared, or aggressive emotions. And they must be able to lend a helping hand when students cannot find a way out of the vortex: to provide help in the form of extending the deadline for a paper, meeting with the student to discuss academic difficulties, or making a referral to the counseling center.

Although three-quarters of my writing students have found one or more of their essays painful to write, an even higher percentage have indicated in anonymous questionnaires that they were glad they wrote on painful topics. "They felt the experience was valuable because writing (in order of decreasing importance) made them feel better, brought them new insights, helped them to identify problems, helped them to master fears, and made them feel less isolated. Less than a quarter of students had ever written before on the topics assigned in class, including divorce, eating disorders, sexual conflicts, suicide, and binge drinking" (Berman, *Risky Writing* 235). Eighty-six percent stated that they experienced thera-peutic relief as a result of writing. Fourteen percent—15 students out of 105—became at risk as a result of a writing assignment; 3 percent became at risk as a result of reading their classmates' essays. Curiously, two-thirds of the students who became at risk as a result of a writing assignment believed there were adequate safeguards to prevent them from becoming at risk. How can we understand this paradox? "Writing is so painful for a small group of people that they may inevitably become at risk no matter how many safeguards are in place" (237). Just as life is often wrenching, so are reading and writing.

Avoiding Contagion

How, then, should teachers respond to the contagion effect? "They can alert their students to the possibility that some classroom assignments and texts may induce symptoms not unlike those experienced when receiving a flu vaccination. Generally these symptoms are mild to moderate in intensity and disappear in a few days, as students in my writing classes have reported" (*Risky Writing* 251). Alerting students in advance to the possibility of becoming at risk may have the opposite effect intended: the power of suggestion may by itself produce a change, as the well-documented placebo effect confirms. Nevertheless, teachers have an ethical duty toward full disclosure. "Just as physicians and pharmacists routinely inform their patients of possible adverse reactions to a drug, so might teachers alert their students to the untoward consequences of a novel or a writing assignment" (251–52). If reading and writing are as powerful as teachers claim, then educators must acknowledge that such power can be for good or ill.

Teachers who seek, in Deanna's words, to "create a bridge, a connection, between the student and the text" may find themselves inadvertently encouraging the contagion effect, but they may also, in Ultra's words, be helping to "inoculate" them against disease or depression. Indeed, many of the students who reacted most strongly to the contagion effect experienced the greatest benefits in their ability to work through conflicts that had previously burdened them. Deanna now believes that reading *Lolita* was "worth it" despite the pain and shame elicited by the novel. She still identifies with Dolores Haze and incorporates the fictional character's experience, but, in James Marcia's words, she has the detachment to move back from the "merged inner relationship to a position of separate identity" (83). In a later email, Deanna states that her confrontation with inner demons "has enabled me to have a greater understanding and empathy for others. I do believe that I am a good reader because I am empathic; your class allowed me to view my empathy as a tool in the classroom instead of as a hindrance." If, as Hatfield and associates suggest, depressed teachers may have a depressing effect on their students, so may hopeful teachers instill in their students the belief in the value of talking, reading, and writing. Reader-response diaries and personal essays help teachers to understand their students' reactions to literature, reactions that are as legitimate and, in many cases, as enlightened as their teachers' own reactions. These writings enable teachers to grasp and, as Deanna points out, to *validate* students' reactions to literature. This is what Deanna wanted most from me. *"This is why I feel the way I do. These are my reasons. Please understand me."*

My students believe they have benefitted from risky reading and risky writing. That is why I continue to give assignments that encourage students to write about important issues in their lives, including those often deemed too personal for the classroom. One cannot prevent the possibility of contagion, but one can reassure students that its effects can be lessened when anticipated and understood. Sometimes contagion can prove beneficial, strengthening the body's resistance to illness. My faith in the transformative power of reading and writing has enabled me to avoid feeling burdened by my students' self-disclosures. A diary or essay may sadden or distress me, but I never fail to be moved by my students' courage and strength in writing about their lives.

CHAPTER 8

Minimizing the Risks of Personal Writing
The Empathic Classroom

Teachers cannot eliminate the risks of personal writing, but they can minimize and manage these dangers by adopting the following classroom practices. (For an extended discussion of these protocols, see *Risky Writing* 29–48.) These practices help to create and maintain the "safe haven" that enables students like Patty to disclose painful or shameful experiences that are rarely discussed in the classroom.

Empathizing with Students

Empathy is the foundation of a self-disclosing classroom, and I encourage students to try to understand their classmates' feelings and thoughts. Heinz Kohut, a leading psychoanalyst who founded a new movement, self-psychology, based on the empathic-introspective stance, argues that "empathy is the mode by which one gathers psychological data about other people and . . . imagines their inner experience even though it is not open to direct observation" (262). So does Carl Rogers elevate empathy to the highest importance in psychotherapy and in education. "This attitude of standing in the other's shoes," he writes in *Freedom to Learn,* "of viewing the world through the student's eyes, is almost unheard of in the classroom. One could listen to thousands of ordinary classroom interactions without coming across one instance of clearly communicated, sensitively accurate, empathic understanding. But it has a tremendously releasing effect when it occurs" (112). The most striking description of empathic listening that I have come across appears in Rogers's book *A Way of Being*:

> Almost always, when a person realizes he has been deeply heard, his eyes moisten. I think in some real sense he is weeping for joy. It is as though he were saying, "Thank God, somebody heard me. Someone knows what it's like to be me." In such moments I have had the fantasy of a prisoner

in a dungeon, tapping out day after day a Morse code message, "Does anybody hear me? Is anybody here?" And finally one day he hears some faint tappings which spell out "Yes." By that one simple response he is released from his loneliness; he has become a human being again. There are many, many people living in private dungeons today, people who give no evidence of it whatsoever on the outside, where you have to listen very sharply to hear the faint messages from the dungeon. (10)

On the first day of the semester I give my writing students a handout called "Reading Empathically" (see the appendix) in which I tell them that the success of the course depends upon their ability to engage in empathic reading, listening, and speaking. Some people are more empathic than others, but empathy is an acquired art that can be developed, like other befriending skills.

I am not always successful in creating an empathic classroom. Sometimes I make statements that students experience as hurtful. As far as I know, this did not happen in Patty's class,, but it did occur in the same Age of Freud course that I taught two years later. Whenever students write essays in my literature courses, I ask them to agree with two of my in-class statements and to disagree with two other in-class statements. I do this so that students will listen attentively in class and develop their own critical thinking. "One repays a teacher badly if one remains only a pupil," Nietzsche observed wryly, and teachers who encourage students to disagree with them avoid creating discipleship. Sometimes a student's disagreement convinces me to modify an interpretation. I ask students to state their disagreements as I collect their essays, and generally I listen without defending my original statement. Louise, an education major, disagreed with my statement that Sylvia Plath was a famous poet whose suicide had contributed to her cult status. She said that she had never heard of Plath before my class and, to support her argument, stated that her Google search on Plath's name had turned up only 10 entries. I expressed surprise and said that probably every good library in the country had several books written by or about Plath. The following class I returned the essays to their authors, and I told Louise that my Google search on Plath's name yielded 675,000 entries—a statement that prompted her classmates' laughter. She also laughed, but it was mirthless laughter, as I discovered when I read her response to one of the final exam questions, "What is the single most important insight that you learned from this course?"

The single most important insight I have learned from this course is unintentional cruelty can hurt just as much, if not worse than, cruelty which is intended. My paper on The Bell Jar *inspired some comments and laughter from the class and Dr. Berman which cut me very deeply because I had tried my hardest and been found wanting in a public situation. The comment Dr. Berman made, "If you went to a library you would find shelves of books written on her" hurt but I knew it wasn't intended to. Still I wanted to cry, "Of course I go to libraries! They are educational ones, though, not English literature ones." Yet I held my tongue because it's not good to lose one's temper. Then the next class Dr. Berman announced his Google results contrary to mine in front of the entire class and they laughed. I know that the laughter was a reflex but that didn't stop my tears from falling or my desire to retaliate and hurt them as they had hurt me. If I had seen the comments as laughter coming maybe I could have braced myself but I didn't because they were unintentional.*

This insight counts in life because so often we are told in business classes to scold an employee privately and praise them publicly. In education classes we are told the same thing about students. Through this method authority figures inspire loyalty and trust. By public degradation of employees or students that trust is broken. Now that I have experienced that degradation I know it is all the more true and shall be careful to try my best not to cause others that pain born of public cruelty and humiliation.

In literature I believe this insight is important because it makes stories seem more real. Characters who misspeak and hurt their friends make themselves more human. Stories which try to create unintentional cruelty can in turn seem canned if they are poorly done.

The discovery of the pain caused by unintentional cruelty is an important one. It cost me to learn it but will stay with me a good, long time. I hope others do not have to learn this lesson the hard way, and I am thankful I learned it in a setting where I will likely never see anyone involved ever again.

I would not have made my class observations had I known they would be so upsetting to Louise, and I would have apologized to her in class had she expressed her feelings in a diary, which I would have read aloud had she given me permission to do so. So too did I unintentionally anger and humiliate Deanna in class. "Part of the reason that I became so angry with you in the Freud class when we were discussing *Lolita*," she wrote in an email, "was because of this: every time you addressed my reaction to the novel in front of the class, you constantly followed it with the word 'but' and then followed it up with something positive about the novel. I can understand that you enjoy the novel. It was the use of 'but' that seemed in fact to be invalidating my reading at the same time as you were trying to validate it."

Avoiding Harmful "Critique" in the Self-Disclosing Classroom

Deborah Tannen observes that we live in an "argument culture" where everything is contested and often litigated. Neither traditional "critique" nor contestation is conducive to self-disclosure. The fundamental principle in my writing classes is that everyone is entitled to his or her feelings. I avoid "interrogating" students who write personal essays, and I remind them that I am less interested in agreeing or disagreeing with their statements than I am in helping them find the best words to express themselves.

Critique, or critical thinking, as it is generally called, remains central to English studies, but it may be unbearable to authors of personal essays. Disclosing a wrenching experience often makes authors wish to hide or disappear when they read aloud their essays or when they hear me read them aloud. The pain or shame may be so intense that such writers cannot look at their classmates or teacher: they keep their eyes focused on the essay, trying to be invisible, or they consider walking out of the classroom. Such is the experience described by Samantha, who asked me to read aloud an essay describing her friend's suicide:

Writing about the actual events of that day was difficult. I had never written about it except once in a journal around the time it happened. I even remember then writing faint details because I became overwhelmed with emotion reliving that day. They were probably just a few short sentences saying what happened. In this essay [for class], I built the story from what I can remember now, five years later. Once I started to write, I could remember the weather that day, and exactly what I was doing when my brother came looking for me. Once I was at the point of my essay in which I first saw my friend's body I started to cry. I could remember the feelings of the day and they were brought back while writing the paper. I kept writing and then walked away from typing it. I didn't want to proofread it until the following morning because I was too emotion struck.

I brought copies to the class and was supposed to read my essay aloud. I did not realize when originally reading the assignment sheet that this essay would bring out this event. When I was in class, I looked over the essay again and felt like I was going to cry. I didn't think I would be able to read the essay aloud without becoming upset, so I asked Professor Berman to read it for me. As he read it, I kept my head down, staring blankly into my copy. I listened to him read it, and then started to hear the words describing my friend's suicide. At this point I contemplated walking out of the room, but remained in my chair and tried covering my eyes. I know my foot was tapping because I was nervous and wanted the story to be over. When he was done reading it, I lifted my head. My face was probably drained of color. I didn't look at my classmates because I knew I had tears in my eyes, so I didn't see any reactions. I know that Mr. Berman was inclined to share his story about his friend's suicide after reading my essay. It was comforting to hear him say that he had been through a suicide, but I also felt sympathy for him. The entire class seemed to have sympathy in their voices when they spoke, for my story and the professor's.

Their reactions were what I was expecting. The class listened intently and no one said anything negative about suicide. Our class has learned to listen empathically, and proved it with my essay. I was worried that if I had cried, someone else in the class might have as well. I am glad I did not cry much because then I would've cried more if someone else did because of my story. I am also glad that I stayed in the class to hear my story read by Professor Berman because the voice in which he spoke made it easier to hear the story. If I had read it, I would have been shaking and choking back tears.

I think that I had many strong sentences, especially when I would use short sentences while describing where I found my friend. I tried avoiding comma splices, but there was one at the end of my essay. I was not sure how to end the essay, but I don't think I did a bad job. Overall, this was one of my stronger essays in this course, and one of my most powerful.

Samantha's experience was so painful, five years after the suicide, that she could not trust herself to read her essay aloud. Only with the greatest difficulty could she listen to me read aloud the essay. Her vulnerability had two physical consequences: she describes the color draining from her face and her eyes welling up with tears. Turning white "as a ghost," like blushing, is a symptom of acute pain or shame, the body's involuntary response to that which is dreaded. Samantha's fear that if she cried, "someone else in the class might have as well," reveals her implicit knowledge of the contagion phenomenon and her desire to avoid infecting classmates with her own sorrow. An extended discussion of suicide following the essay would only have intensified her pain. In addition, it is likely that such a discussion would cause extreme discomfort to her classmates, who would empathize with her pain. Now imagine if Samantha were reading aloud an essay about her own suicide attempt. She would almost certainly feel shame as well as pain, along with increased vulnerability. Unlike protracted discussions of suicide, which might inadvertently produce statements that heighten the writer's discomfort, a balanced discussion of diction, grammar, tone, and style is safe and welcome. One can sense Samantha's pride that her essay was well written and powerful.

Maintaining Professional Boundaries

One of the many criticisms of risky writing is that teachers will be tempted to play the role of therapist and ignore helping students to improve their writing, which is the main goal of any writing course. Kathleen Pfeiffer's criticism of Carole Deletiner's article sympathetic to personal writing reveals the mistrust of many in the profession who believe that writing teachers will react as therapists when they receive emotionally charged essays. "What she teaches in this weepy world of confessions and revelations is a fundamentally egocentric sort of absorption. Such teeth-gnashing and soul-baring might help a student recover his or her lost inner child, but it will do little in the way of developing a sophisticated communicative ability, analytical skills, or a clear-sighted understanding of the world" (671). This criticism can be avoided if teachers focus their classroom discussions on the elements of writing: diction, grammar, tone, voice, and point of view. These are "safe" topics to discuss when reading gut-wrenching essays, and no matter how well written an essay is, it can be strengthened through revision. We don't avoid discussing the content of an essay, but we do avoid making judgmental observations that would make the writer feel uncomfortable. We are supportive of each other, but the class is not a "support group." Teachers are not clinicians and are not trained in diagnosis or treatment. I do not tell my students more about their lives than they already know. They do not ask me to play the role of therapist, nor do they ask me for advice about how to live their lives.

Sometimes students are frustrated when I do not offer solutions to problems that are at least partly psychological. I sympathize with those who, for one reason or another, find themselves unable to overcome a problem like writer's block, but I avoid giving them explanations for why they are blocked. Such explanations would be highly speculative at best and would lead literature teachers into clinical areas for which they are not trained. Nor do I try to persuade students to be self-disclosing: there is a fine line between "encouraging" and "pressuring" students to write about their lives, and I would rather err on the side of caution. The riskier the situation, the more cautious I become, as can be seen when Morgan came to my office seeking advice about whether she should be more personal in her writings. She was impressed with her classmates' self-disclosures but didn't know whether she could write with the same degree of openness about her life. I couldn't solve the problem for her, but I could suggest, as I did, that she might find it helpful to write about our conversation and identify the specific issues that were troubling her. A week later she turned in the following essay:

As the biographies ended, and the personal writing began, I started to become frustrated. I had thought for a long time that I was a great writer, one who could find almost all her grammatical and stylistic problems, as well as writing in such a way that people would be fascinated. But for the first time, in Expository Writing, I was incredibly jealous of other's writings. Other people in the class had superior stylistic and grammatical skill, and I felt I was lacking, especially when it came to writing about myself.

I was not terribly surprised by this revelation. For many years now, I've been suffering from depression and anxiety. That, and what I learned through therapy, to protect myself and not give too much away, has resulted in me revealing few details about myself. This is also a defense mechanism, as it keeps others from hurting me. But it also left me with a feeling that my writing was lacking, since I have such difficulty in revealing deeply personal aspects of myself. And even if I could write of such things, my emotions tended to take over, causing my writing to suffer greatly. I felt trapped, swinging from one extreme to the other, without finding a balance.

One assignment left me particularly jealous and frustrated. The assignment had been to write a letter to our parents, and write a response from our parents, imagining what they would say. This particular assignment was incredibly frustrating for me. I spent over seven hours struggling, venting out much of the anger and resentment I had toward my parents, and imagining a response that didn't come nearly close to the coldness that my mother would have written. And when it was done, I went over what I had written, trying to make the paper more cohesive, but it was no use. I was so emotionally vested in the writing that I couldn't think of any changes to the numerous problems the paper had. So I handed the paper in as is, knowing it was subpar for me at best.

Then in class several students either read their own letters, or Mr. Berman read the letters (sometimes anonymously). And two classmates just amazed me with their superior writing skills. Both wrote so passionately, yet their writing was so controlled. I was incredibly jealous of their ability to balance what seemed to be such opposites.

After class, I approached Mr. Berman, and asked to speak to him on the subject. He agreed, and I went to his office. There, I sat down, and began explaining my past history, and how I've been dealing with a writer's block, personal and otherwise, for the past several years, due mostly to my emotional issues. He was sympathetic, understanding how such weighty issues would make it difficult for me to write about myself. But he also stressed that I didn't have to write about such personal topics, that I could choose another, safer, topic instead. I became somewhat upset at that comment, declaring that it was necessary for me to get past this problem, since I wish to have a job in writing. Mr. Berman understood my feelings, and said I should just keep writing, that perhaps the problem could be worked through simply by writing. I became somewhat more upset. I wanted to find some sort of answer other than "to keep plugging at it." It soon became apparent that was the only answer I was going to receive. I kindly thanked Mr. Berman for his time, and left, still left with the original problem of how to balance emotions and controlled writing.

Perhaps I was seeking some sort of mystical answer; some book, or phrase, or comment that would make my writing problem go away. But that didn't happen, and I'm left with only one option—to keep writing in the hopes that I can work through my issue. Hopefully I can. Until then, the envy will most likely continue.

I couldn't offer a solution to Morgan's writer's block, but writing about the dilemma helped her to articulate the problem. She realized that she wanted to express dark emotions that may be associated with her earlier depression, but she feared that writing about these feelings might be like opening a floodgate that would sweep her away. One could feel her rising frustration toward me: my comments made her feel at first "somewhat upset," and then "somewhat more upset." I wasn't deliberately trying to upset her, but I did not want to *tell* her what to do. Had I done so, I suspect she would have become *very* upset with me.

Morgan was distressed by my refusal to give her the "sort of mystical answer" for which she was searching, but I helped her realize that she alone had to decide the comfort level of her writings. I was not try-ing to be a "blank screen" to her, as Freud urged psychoanalysts to be toward their analysands—advice, ironically, he never followed with his own patients. Rather, I was simply suggesting that she needed to evaluate the risks and benefits of opening up in the classroom. She knew that her teacher and classmates would remain empathic if she did decide to write about an emotionally charged issue. I had spoken in her class about the recent death of my wife and the sadness and loneliness in my life, and Morgan knew that her classmates had written about their own losses. She could do the same—or choose *not* to. Just as relational and intersubjective psychoanalysts reject Freud's blank screen approach to transference-countertransference dynamics, arguing instead for a more equal relationship between analysand and analyst, each influencing and being influenced by the other, so do psychoanalytic composition scholars affirm a dialogical relationship between student and teacher. As Dawn Skorczewski observes, "A teacher's autobiographical revelations can open up the world of the classroom, inviting students to be the complex and multifaceted individuals that they are" (142). Interestingly, Morgan's essay reveals the balance between emotions and control for which she was searching. She told me, a few weeks later, that she did not want to write her next essay on any of the "happy" topics that I had suggested to the class. In a later essay, she wrote about the devastation she felt upon being betrayed by a close friend, a betrayal that led to clinical depression and two suicide attempts.

Choosing Not to Write on a Topic

Students are not required to write on any topic that they find too per-sonal or threatening. I give students a list of alternative topics they can use whenever an assigned topic proves too self-disclosing. They always choose the degree of self-disclosure when writing on an assigned topic.

Grading Pass/Fail Whenever Possible

A pass/fail grading system works best for self-disclosing writing. Pass/fail grading minimizes the possibility that students will feel pressured into self-disclosure to receive a good grade. All the students who took my ex-pository writing courses from 1995 to 1999, and whose essays appear in

Risky Writing, were graded pass/fail. In 2003, the English Department at the University at Albany changed its policy, and writing courses are now letter graded. Surprisingly, this change has not been problematic for my students; no one has complained about feeling pressured into self-disclosure. I believe it is possible for teachers to grade personal essays and reader-response diaries on the quality of writing, as I do. Teachers who feel uncomfortable letter-grading a personal essay can usually give students the option of pass/fail grading for a particular paper.

Allowing Anonymity

Students who give me permission to read aloud their reader-response diaries always remain anonymous to their classmates. Such anonymity allows the freedom to self-disclose without the fear of having one's identity exposed. Masking their identities allows them to unmask their thoughts. Patty's final reader-response diary was a response not only to reading *Surviving Literary Suicide* but also to hearing me read aloud an anonymous classmate's diary on cutting. Students who write weekly essays in my expository writing courses generally sign their own names when they give copies to classmates, but a student can choose to remain anonymous. In that case, I read the essay aloud anonymously, and there is no discussion afterward.

Prescreening Essays

I try to prescreen essays in advance to make sure they are not too disturbing to read aloud or discuss. Students who are experiencing a crisis may find it too painful to read aloud an essay. Sometimes I will alert students in advance to an essay that may be difficult to hear. Prescreening is not always possible, however, especially in courses that meet only once a week. Students know that they have permission to leave class whenever they feel emotionally overwhelmed by an essay.

Protecting Self-Disclosures

I have never lost a diary or essay in more than thirty-five years of teaching. I take special precautions with self-disclosing essays: I never leave them in my office unless my door is locked, and I caution my students to be careful with their own writings. Losing a highly self-disclosing essay can be awkward or embarrassing, particularly if one's name is on it. I also remind students that they must use discretion when self-disclosing and that they should not disclose more than they wish. Discretion also implies a respect for classmates' self-disclosures.

Balancing Risky and Nonrisky Assignments

I try to balance "dark" topics with lighter ones so that class doesn't become depressing. Students sometimes cry during class, as I do, but there are always far more smiles than tears during the semester.

Having Conferences

I have at least two private conferences with each student in my writing classes. These conferences allow me to find out how my students feel about the course, how they are doing, and whether they have suggestions for improvement. I enjoy speaking with my students, and I give them both my office and home telephone numbers. Rarely do they phone me at home: they respect my privacy as much as I respect theirs.

Making Appropriate Referrals

Sometimes a teacher will read a diary or personal essay that indicates a student is experiencing a crisis, and it is important to know how to make a referral to the university counseling center. All teachers should be trained to do this, especially English teachers, who are often the first to suspect that a student is in a crisis. Perhaps once a semester a student will ask me to suggest a therapist. It is reassuring for students to know that many of their classmates have been helped by therapy, and I share with my students my own positive experiences with therapy when my wife was dying. (For a discussion of the signs of suicide and appropriate and inappropriate ways to respond to a person who is depressed or suicidal, see *Surviving Literary Suicide* 23–25.)

Avoiding Legal Problems

We live in a contentious age, and teachers, like other professionals (and nonprofessionals), worry about lawsuits. Risky writing implies risky teaching and perhaps a heightened fear of legal difficulties. I have never found myself in such a situation. No student, parent, colleague, or college administrator has complained about my emphasis on self-disclosing writing. Following the above protocols greatly reduces a teacher's risk of legal problems.

Finally, students may feel ambivalent about self-disclosure even if these classroom protocols have been followed. The riskier the self-disclosure, the more intense will be the self-discloser's ambivalence. For example, immediately after her presentation, Deanna felt that she had exposed too much of herself to a group of strangers:

> *Reading Vladimir Nabokov's novel,* Lolita, *was torture for me. My first reaction was very emotional and I found it extremely difficult to control. It came from my gut and raged out of me. My reader response diary was painful to write and even more so to read. I was filled with fear before I read it to the class and while I read it there was a sinking, sickening feeling in the pit of my stomach. Jeff asked me after I read it if I felt better and I said yes, but now I think that was a lie. I do not feel better. I feel that I announced the darkest, most painful secret of my life to a roomful of people that I know only as acquaintances. I feel shamed in a way; I fear that these people will now see me differently. Do I regret writing my response? Yes and no. While it did release my emotions, I feel that perhaps I did too much feeling and not enough thinking.*

Within a few days Deanna began to feel more positive about her class presentation, partly because several of her classmates told her how powerful it was. They wrote reader-response diaries in which they expressed admiration for her courage and strength during her oral presentation. Their empathy, as the following entry reveals, written by a middle-aged lawyer who was pursuing a lifelong passion for literature, did not necessarily imply agreement with her interpretation of the novel:

> *In writing about* Lolita, *I find it impossible to avoid responding to Deanna's moving disclosures about her life experience and how that life experience shaped her reactions to Nabokov's novel.*

I felt empathy for Deanna's presentation—both her grievous life experience and her experience reading Lolita. I cannot recall any presentation in any class or on any topic that moved me as much as Deanna's presentation moved me. While we read and hear about cases of sexual abuse, pedophilia, and more heinous crimes every day in the newspaper and on television, and sometimes have strong and even gut-wrenching reactions to those crimes, I never have been so profoundly and intimately touched by the reader of a novel, never have so clearly understood how a life experience like sexual abuse can profoundly affect both life and literature. By sharing her deeply personal and traumatic experiences, and allowing me to see how those experiences affected her reading of the novel, I learned firsthand what Professor Berman has been saying about the sometimes traumatizing effect reading a novel can have on certain readers—about "risky reading"—and about how self-disclosure of those effects—"risky writing"—can be cathartic for the writer and, at least when the writing is shared with other readers, disturbingly enlightening for those other readers.

While I felt empathy for, and understanding of, Deanna's reading of Lolita, I cannot say that I agree with her vilification of the novel and of its author, nor with her seeming conflation of the identities of Humbert and Nabokov. Of course, I have never been the young female victim of a sexually predatory older male, so I speak from a much different vantage point. I am, figuratively speaking, more like Humbert than Dolores, and seem to approach Humbert more closely with each reading of Lolita (I first read the novel thirty years ago, while a college student, and most recently—for this class—read Lolita for the fifth time at the Humbert-like age of fifty).

Deanna, in her presentation, alluded to the fact that the novel was particularly disturbing to her because it was so brilliantly written; Nabokov's linguistic alchemy elevates the despicable acts of a middle-age pedophile to literary delectation. Humbert-like, I can only confess that it is precisely this aspect of Lolita—the word play, the punning, the language, the vocabulary, the style—and Nabokov's unerring ability to capture the overworked, lustful imaginings of his middle-age narrator in a way that transmutes mere sexual titillation to literature, that so attracts me to this novel. While Lolita *brings a sensual stirring, Nabokov's genius—his style, structure, and imagery, among other things—successfully detracts me from my tepid lust.*

Nabokov, in his afterword, says the following: "Lolita has no moral in tow. For me, a work of fiction exists only insofar as it affords me what I shall bluntly call aesthetic bliss, that is a sense of being somehow, somewhere, connected with other states of being where art (curiosity, kindness, tenderness, ecstasy) is the norm" (Lolita 315). While I would not limit the category of worthwhile fiction to those that merely provide "aesthetic bliss," as Nabokov seems to do, I believe Lolita *does represent a remarkable aesthetic achievement and deservedly is considered one of the great works of twentieth-century American literature.*

While Humbert is not an admirable man, Humbert is not Nabokov. Character and author are confused only when the author of a work, or its reader, are too close to the fictional narrative because of their unique life experience: Sylvia Plath's writing in The Bell Jar *is a good example of the former, while Deanna's reading of* Lolita *is a good example of the latter. In saying this, I do not mean to denigrate Deanna's reading of* Lolita, *but to point out that a novel is more than just a novel for some writers and some readers: it is a work of cathartic release for some writers (as, perhaps, in the case of Plath) or a traumatic experience for some readers (as in the case of Deanna). For these writers and readers, their engagement with the work is overdetermined by their life experience; their writing and reading, accordingly, lacks distance from the narrative and, while profoundly enlightening for other writers and readers, is inherently unreliable in evaluating the text.*

Deanna may have felt that her presentation was more emotional than analytical, but she demonstrated in her formal essay on *Lolita* that she could write incisively about the ways in which Humbert seeks to appropriate Dolores's life. She showed that "disliking this text does not make one an unsophisticated reader." Risky self-disclosures like Deanna's are fraught with conflicting feelings—the desire for openness versus the need for continued secrecy, the wish to trust versus the fear of betrayal, the need for acceptance versus the fear of rejection. Students and teacher alike must be able to tolerate ambivalence in the self-disclosing classroom. Many students have told me that however painful it was to read a self-disclosing essay to their classmates, it would have been more painful had they *not* read their essay aloud. They would have been disappointed that they did not seize the opportunity to share a previously undisclosed aspect of their lives with teacher and classmates. As I report in *Risky Writing,* 87 percent of the students in five different expository writing courses indicated that they did not regret any of their self-disclosures; 5 percent indicated that they did regret a self-disclosure; and 8 percent indicated that they were not sure (235). One of the most notable findings is that 86 percent believed that the ability to disclose personal information about oneself contributes to health and well-being. F. Scott Fitzgerald's observation in *The Crack-Up* comes to mind: "The test of a first-rate intelligence is the ability to hold two opposed ideas in the mind at the same time and still retain the ability to function" (69). Self-disclosures like Deanna's contribute to what Daniel Goleman calls emotional intelligence, which includes self-awareness, self-control, zeal, and motivation. To write personally is to write with one's entire being, including the mind and the heart. Such writing is admittedly risky, because so much is at stake. And it is precisely because such writing is so important that students are motivated to do their best work.

CHAPTER 9

Attachment Theory and Self-Disclosure
Strengthening the Teacher-Student Bond

The protocols described in chapter 8 help not only to lessen the possibility that students will be harmed in the self-disclosing classroom but also to strengthen their attachment to classmates and teacher. The success of any pedagogy based on self-disclosure depends on the empathic bonds that permit students to reveal painful or shameful aspects of their lives without the fear of being criticized or attacked.

Attachment theory, formulated by the English psychoanalyst John Bowlby in his landmark three-volume work *Attachment and Loss*, implies that the longing for human connection is as instinctual as hunger or sexuality. Bowlby's research focused on the parent-child relationship, but it also has profound implications for psychotherapy. M. D. S. Ainsworth noted in her obituary on Bowlby in 1992 that attachment theory "has had a stronger impact on American psychology than any other theory of personality development since Sigmund Freud" (668). As Jeremy Holmes suggests, the best predictor of success in psychotherapy is a "positive therapeutic alliance, which can be understood as secure attachment" (118). Holmes demonstrates that secure attachment creates a paradoxical state of intimacy and autonomy: "Autonomy is possible on the basis of a secure inner world—we can go out on a limb, stand our ground, make our own choices, and tolerate aloneness if we can be sure that attachment and intimacy are available when needed. Conversely, intimacy is possible if the loved one can be allowed to be separate; we can allow ourselves to get close if we feel autonomous enough not to fear engulfment or attack, and also know that separation does not mean that our loved one will be lost forever" (19).

Attachment theory has no less relevance to education in that students' success depends upon their strong attachments to teachers. As I observe in *Empathic Teaching*, "Teachers who make a difference in their students' lives and who are regarded as supportive, dependable, and empathic become attachment figures, and they are the ones whom students regard as instrumental in their personal and professional lives" (109). If we extend the meaning of Holmes's reference to a "secure inner world" to the empathic classroom, we can see how students' autonomy derives from a feeling of security. They can make risky self-disclosures in their diaries and essays, revealing experiences they might otherwise be reluctant to share for fear of being viewed as different or, worse, as "sick" or "crazy." They can tolerate frightening feelings that are now being made public for the first time. They can begin to open up to their teacher and classmates, exposing aspects of their lives that in many cases they have never publicly revealed. And they can begin to discover that their own secrets may not be entirely different from those of their classmates. Insofar as self-disclosure begets self-disclosure, students who share secrets with classmates become the recipients of their classmates' secrets, resulting in heightened trust and understanding of everyone in the classroom.

Cutting Criticisms

Self-disclosures about cutting will not occur if students fear "cutting criticisms" from their classmates or teacher. Sometimes, as with Louise, teachers don't know they have made a caustic remark until students tell them. Prolonged exposure to biting critiques is a form of verbal abuse that may provoke people into cutting themselves. As Patty documents, one of the reasons people cut is that they fear exposing their pain and unhappiness to others. Such exposure would result in further stigmatization and rejection. Caroline Kettlewell makes a similar observation in *Skin Game.* "I kept my cutting so resolutely to myself not because I feared *its* discovery, per se, but rather because I knew it would be like the fatally ill-timed sneeze that gives the heroine away when she most needs to escape detection. It would be the signpost to a whole inner life I could neither justify nor explain, a life that was like one of those 'find the item that doesn't match' games" (94). This "inner life" is the opposite of the "secure inner world" that promotes autonomy and intimacy. Indeed, none of the fictional characters whom Patty discusses have a secure inner world, and none demonstrate genuine autonomy or intimacy.

Cutters experience relief during the act of cutting, but they derive little or no pleasure from receiving a cutting comment. Such comments are infectious, serving only to weaken the cutter's already fragile self-esteem and sense of self. I have never heard students say that they felt better when a relative, friend, or teacher made a cutting comment to them—though the author of the remark may derive sadistic pleasure from the act. Nothing could be further from the truth than the adage "sticks and stones may break my bones, but words will never hurt me." In many cases, verbal abuse is worse than physical abuse.

Many students have told me that they were so devastated by a teacher's or classmate's withering criticism in a fiction workshop that they no longer wished to write. Such criticisms are even more destructive in personal writing courses, when students write about their own lives, often with insufficient narrative distance separating the author from the first-person speaker. There is an art to criticism, and those who lack this art can damage a young writer's self-confidence. Examples of brutal criticisms abound. In a letter to the editor appearing in the "Book Section" of the *New York Times*, a reader attacked Joan Didion's award-winning *Year of Magical Thinking*, a memoir about the death of her husband, John Gregory Dunne, and the illness of her daughter, Quintana Roo, who died shortly after the book's publication. "This obsession with Didion's obsession with her loss on the part of the *Times* and other publications has become morbid and tiring. O, St. Joan of Didion, stop ye whining and complaining. Find some inner strength and stop crying a river in public. Want to mourn? Have the dignity of doing it in private. Enough!" (10 October 2005). If a mean-spirited comment like this can undercut a professional writer's morale, as reviews often do, imagine its effect on a beginning writer.

I am not suggesting that teachers avoid criticizing student writings. On the contrary. I comment on every grammatical and stylistic error in a diary or essay, regardless of whether the topic is happy or sad. I also suggest how an essay can be developed. Sometimes I ask classmates to raise questions they would like the author to explore further in a revision. These are constructive comments, motivated to help students find the best words to express themselves. But I avoid judgments like "whining" or "complaining" because they are so hurtful to the writer.

Peter Elbow has made a distinction between the "doubting game," which he associates with critical thinking, and the "believing game," which he identifies with Carl Rogers's advocacy of empathy. The believing game, Elbow writes, is particularly valuable for testimony: "First, speaker(s) are invited to tell stories of the experiences that led them to their points of view and to describe what it's like having or living with this view. Not only must the rest of us not answer or argue or disagree while they are speaking; even afterwards, we must refrain from answering or arguing. (This process is particularly useful when issues of race, gender, and sexual orientation are being discussed.)" (395). I agree with Elbow that both the "doubting game" and the "believing game" are necessary; I also agree that the "believing game," which Elbow acknowledges is little recognized or understood, has not received the attention it deserves.

An extreme example of the doubting game occurs when a teacher asks students whether they are "lying" in a self-disclosing essay. The question immediately puts them on the defensive. At least one composition teacher, Carra Leah Hood, has criticized me for accepting the truth claims in my students' personal writings. In her essay "Lying in Writing or the Vicissitudes of Testimony," she states that she would deliberately lie if she were one of my students. "I might have written about being molested, raped, or incested, in other words, but I would have written about one of these experiences to challenge the teacher. Knowing that my essay was motivated to mock his need to view my trauma, rather than to tell a truthful story, I would have written an essay that confessed too much, that confessed too conventionally, or that confessed the truth of an hypothetical other" (138). She then admits that she lied in her English assignments twenty years earlier when she was an undergraduate:

> I realized quite by accident, as a result of assignments like Berman's, that I did not always need to write the truth in essays for school. I only recognized the truth hiding in every untruth, the autobiographical facts disclosed in every choice of topic, the confession folded into every close reading, the trauma weighing down every insight, later on. By that time, however, lying in writing had become a habit, a survival skill. I learned from my various experiences lying in writing for school that there is more than one way to tell an untruth. There are avoiding lies, the kinds that elide the awful reality. There were also generic lies and hyperbolic lies, stories that do not represent my truth but reproduce a truth which appeared in a movie, book, or news story and stories that push a truth beyond credulity. (139)

I don't believe there are many students like Hood who intentionally and cynically lie in self-disclosing essays. This is not to suggest that anyone can capture the full truth of an experience, traumatic or otherwise: language can never fully reproduce or represent a complex experience. I agree with Hood that trauma survivors are resistant to unlocking painful secrets. I also agree with her that teachers must not pressure students into self-disclosure. Evidently she was pressured into self-disclosure two decades ago and still remains angry about it. But I disagree with her claim that it is an "impossible task" for students to write safely and accurately about traumatic experiences. Hood ignores the world of difference between encouraging students to write about traumatic experiences and coercing them. She also ignores or trivializes the many testimonies of students and nonstudents alike who have affirmed the value of writing about painful or shameful experiences.

For example, Hood focuses on my student Diane, whom I discuss at the beginning of *Risky Writing*. Diane had written two essays in her Expository Writing course, one about baking bread, the other about childhood molestation. She concludes the second essay with an observation that she has found it helpful to read about other students' disclosures of sexual abuse. "While my experience was not as dramatic as some of the stories presented in the book, it left an indelible mark on me at a vulnerable age. I am more fortunate than some people who have been molested or abused. I feel as if I am one of the lucky ones because I have become informed. I have a chance to get beyond these memories" (Risky Writing 9). Hood not only questions the student's honesty—"did Diane write a true story of being molested by a family friend when she was a child, or did she lie?" (139)—but also rejects Diane's conviction that she derived psychological benefit from writing the essay and reading other essays on the subject. In Hood's view, "writing trauma, especially for assignments in school, rather than healing, rather than symptomatic repetition, constitutes an exercise for students in pleasing the teacher. Real healing does not occur so simply, with this kind of objective in mind, when writing for a grade" (149).

Unlike Hood, I never call into question the truth claims in my students' self-disclosing diaries and essays. Nor do I contradict or dismiss their conclusions about whether a particular writing assignment was helpful or harmful to them. Why should teachers assume, as Hood does, that students tell the truth when they find a writing assignment offensive or intrusive but lie when they find an assignment empowering? Why should teachers assume, as Hood does, that students always lie to please them? Why does she assume that students tell teachers only what they want to hear rather than, as we can see with Deanna and Louise, what teachers do not want to hear? Why does she assume, as in the example of Diane, that a teacher such as herself can read students better than they can read themselves? And why does she assume that teachers who want to help their students achieve emotional as well as intellectual breakthroughs are motivated only by the desire to see others' trauma? Hood invokes certain theorists to prove that "theories of trauma and therapies to treat trauma fail precisely because they focus on the survivor rather than on the world to which the survivor returns" (146), but she ignores other theorists, such as Charles Anderson and Marian MacCurdy, coeditors of the influential volume *Writing and Healing*, who argue that the writing classroom can be a site for genuine psychological growth.

Hood's deconstructive approach to survival narratives prevents her from distinguishing between "lying in writing" and the unrepresentability of trauma. "Deflection, avoidance, elision, hyperbole, cliche are all among survivors' ways of writing an event that resists telling, or even sometimes recognition. A sort of lying, then, is not only a common feature of survivors' stories but also the truth. In other words, the traumatic experience cannot be represented as the survivor's trauma because the event characteristically appears as a trace, an incoherence or temporal disjuncture, in narrative" (139). Confronted by the "impossible task" of writing about trauma, she implies that silence is the only response.

In light of the dishonesty of memoirs like James Frey's *A Million Little Pieces*, it is understandable that a reader may be suspicious of autobiographical writing. It is also understandable, indeed crucial, to recognize the implicit risks of self-disclosing writing in the classroom. But to reduce *all* personal writing to "a sort of lying," as Hood does, is to rule out the possibility of posttraumatic growth and self-discovery. Rejecting the possibility that writing may be therapeutic, she implies that *all* writing, however sincere, is an acting out rather than a working through of trauma. And she concludes by suggesting that the instructor who encourages students to write about traumatic experiences is satisfying the "reader's/teacher's desire to see another's trauma and creating the opportunity for the writing teacher to feel instrumental in effecting student's healing" (149).

What would happen if I asked students whether they were lying in an essay? After reading Hood's essay, I posed this question to the students in one of my Expository Writing courses:

We are not yet at the midpoint of the semester, but many of you have written essays about traumatic experiences: severe depression or suicide attempts, conflicted parent-child relationships, drug or alcohol addiction, imprisonment, eating disorders, and sexual abuse. No one in the class—neither your classmates nor I—has challenged the truthfulness of these self-disclosures. Suppose, however, that I did raise the possibility in class, during a discussion of a highly self-disclosing essay, that the author might not be telling the truth. How would you feel if you were the writer whose truthfulness is being challenged? Would you be more or less likely to write another self-disclosing essay in the class? Would your feelings change about the course? Would you be inclined to feel more or less trust toward me? Please write down your responses to these questions. Remain anonymous. After I collect your responses, I'll tell you why I asked these questions.

The overwhelming majority of students stated that they would be upset and offended if I implied they were lying in an essay. "I would be furious if my truthfulness were to be challenged," wrote one person. "To me there is no point in being dishonest. If someone were to doubt me, I would definitely not want to write another self-disclosing essay. I would think anything I wrote from that point on would be called into question. My feelings would change about the course because I believed the aim of this course was to be critical about the writing and not the writer or content of one's writing. I would not trust you." Another observed that raising the question of honesty would shatter the empathic classroom atmosphere. "If I was challenged I would feel hurt and very vulnerable. I only disclose under the condition that I will have complete acceptance and empathy from my classmates and professor. I would be much less likely to write a self-disclosing essay. My feelings about the course would change because the empathic environment promised in the beginning [of the semester] would no longer stand. Other students would be less likely to disclose for fear of being [persecuted]. I would have lost trust completely in you. You would probably not gain it back within the semester." Another student's response was the *opposite* of Hood's: "If you said this while I was reading my essay and I actually was lying, I would confess. If I wasn't lying, however, I would be offended and feel like my emotions were trivial. I would feel less trust toward you and the class in general because I would feel like I always had to defend against the truthfulness of my essay. I would probably stop writing self-disclosing essays and lie to make my life seem less traumatic. I feel like an accusation about my truthfulness would force me to lie."

Playing the believing game does not guarantee that all students will tell the truth, as they see it, in their writings. In *Risky Writing* I report on the results of a questionnaire completed by 105 students who were members of five different sections of Expository Writing I taught from 1995 to 1999:

> Some of the most important questions I asked involved the honesty of students' writings. "How often were you honest in your writing? That is, how often did you tell the truth as you saw it?" Eighty-one percent indicated "all of the time," 18 percent "most of the time," and 1 percent "some of the time." Interestingly, when asked "how often do you think your classmates were honest in their writing?" the figures were much lower: 40 percent indicated "all of the time," 56 percent "most of the time," and 5 percent "some of the time." I reported the same phenomenon in *Diaries to an English Professor*, where close to 100 percent of the polled students reported that they were honest in their *own* diaries, whereas only between 60 to 70 percent of the polled students believed that their classmates were honest in *their* diaries" (233–34).

Sometimes students will acknowledge in a later essay that they were not entirely truthful in an earlier essay. This usually happens not because they wish to portray themselves as victims of trauma but because they are not yet ready to acknowledge the full extent of the trauma they experienced. This was true of Nick in *Risky Writing*, who wrote in an early essay about his twin brother's death in a car accident and then acknowledged in a later essay, which he read to the class, that there was no twin brother, car accident, or death. "There was only me and John, a family relative, who was also a child molester. I was the child" (188). For Nick, the lie covered up a more painful truth that he was ready to admit only at the end of the semester.

Classroom self-disclosure is a complex process, occurring only when students feel safely attached to their classmates and teacher. As we saw with Deanna, students are sometimes ambivalent about self-disclosure, wanting both to reveal and conceal the truth. Sometimes there is a subtle pressure to self-disclose, especially after others have done so. Some students may feel competition with their classmates to tell the most shocking story. Other students may feel guilty that, unlike their classmates, they have led happy, protected lives, not yet darkened by tragedy. I tell my students that self-disclosing writing can be about happy as well as sad experiences, and that they are in competition not with their classmates but with themselves.

English teachers are not therapists, but in *The Noonday Demon* Andrew Solomon refers to an important 1979 study in which researchers demonstrated that "any form of therapy could be effective if certain criteria were met: that both the therapist and the patient were acting in good faith; that the client believed that the therapist understood the technique; that the client liked and respected the therapist; and that the therapist had an ability to form understanding relationships. The experimenters chose English professors with this quality of human understanding and found that, on average, the English professors were able to help their patients as much as the professional therapists" (111). Solomon also points out that if people who suffer from depression feel better as a result of a particular treatment, even if it is only a placebo, then they *are* better: "Depression is a disease of thought processes and emotions, and if something changes your thought processes and emotions in the correct direction, that qualifies as a recovery" (137).

Far from mistrusting healing narratives, I believe that teachers should encourage them, always respecting students' right to refuse a writing assignment they deem too personal. Jeremy Holmes's observation is relevant here: "Recent attachment research supports the view that the development of a healing narrative—the Shakespearean injunction to 'give sorrow words'—is the key task of psychotherapy" (31)—and, I would add, of education as well.

Only rarely do we see secure attachment behavior in any of the cutting novels, and when we do, it is toward the end of the story, when recovery begins to take place for one or more characters. The anorexic Becca doesn't understand how her refusal to eat and her wasting away demoralize the other patients in McCormick's *Cut*. "It's not like I did anything to you guys," she exclaims, with a smile on her face. "'Yes,' says Tara. 'Yes, you did.' She looks down at her lap, cracks her knuckles. 'What you did affected all of us'" (113–14). Becca looks "hopefully and doubtfully" as the other adolescents in "Sick Minds" agree with Tara. "'We were scared,' says Sydney, all in a rush. 'We . . . you know, we want you to get better. That's why we're all here, isn't it? To get better?'" (114).

Fictional Therapists

The therapists who prove most effective in the cutting novels are those who are empathically attuned to their patients, encouraging them to speak about their problems without imposing their own judgments or theoretical explanatory systems on them. As Sharon Todd states, "viewed as an explicitly moral emotion, empathy is the very form of attachment seen to be necessary for living responsibly together, and it is this emphasis on what empathy brings to our sense of togetherness that, to my mind, has made it so prevalent within educational projects committed to social justice" (43). Throughout *Cut* Callie addresses her silent thoughts to an unnamed "you" who turns out to be her psychiatrist. The unusual narration, which recalls the mute Chief Bromden in Ken Kesey's antipsychiatric novel *One Flew over the Cuckoo's Nest*, is at first mystifying but highly effective, for the "you" may be viewed as both the psychiatrist and the reader. The psychiatrist knows how to speak and to listen. She asks openended questions, such as "What was it like seeing your family?" and "Is there anything you want to tell me?" (14). She responds to Callie's continued silence with the observation, "It must take a lot of energy. . . . Not talking" (25). Unlike Amanda, the psychiatrist never uses psychobabble; she uses simple English that is devoid of professional jargon, as when she states, "Sometimes when we're in situations where we feel we're not in control, we do things, especially things that take a lot of energy, as a way of making ourselves feel we have some power" (30). She gently tells Callie, who has remained mute for several sessions, that she cannot help her unless Callie is willing to help herself. Once the patient begins to speak, the psychiatrist promises her that "I'll never make you tell me anything you don't want to tell me" (56). In one of the most important scenes, she functions not only as an empathic therapist but also as a narrative device whose timely questions elicit her patient's story:

"[Amanda] does what I do."
  I watch for your expression to change, for there to be some slight shift from neutral to . . . to what? Disgusted? Disapproving? You wait calmly.
  "She showed everybody her scars."
  I bite my lip some more. That's it. I'm finished. I listen for the plane, but it's gone.
  "You think she should have kept them to herself?"
  "Huh?"
  "Do you think this new girl should have kept her scars hidden?"
  "I don't care." Then, right away, "They're gross."
  I pull on my sleeve, pinch the fabric tight, wrap it safely around my thumb.
  "What's wrong with letting people know what you're doing, or how you're feeling?" (83)

There is not a big difference between a cutter exposing her scars to others and a writer describing these scars to readers. Both involve risky self-disclosures that are likely to produce revulsion and rejection, increasing the distance between self and other. Both may further stigmatize the cutter, heightening her isolation, loneliness, and silence. And both may evoke pain and shame. This is precisely what Callie fears. In a later scene, as she discloses the details of her cutting, including the use of her mother's "Exacto knife" and embroidery scissors, Callie watches intently for any negative response from her psychiatrist. "I check for your reaction. You're expecting something, I can tell. Your normal, calm face shows a hint of waiting. Waiting, and something else, something like hope" (123). Callie then rolls up her sleeve and exposes her scars. She is immediately relieved. "You're not disgusted or frightened or any of the hundred wrong things you could be; you look like yourself, serious, curious, and maybe, maybe, just a little bit proud of me" (123). A few moments later, after the psychiatrist reassures Callie that the scars will fade, the latter exclaims, "I may not want to get rid of my scars," adding, "they tell a story," to which the psychiatrist responds, "Yes . . . they do" (125).

Cut may be a formulaic novel, as Patty suggests, but it provides a helpful guide to the dynamics of self-disclosure. After helping Callie to see that she was not to blame for her brother's illness and that she may have saved his life by performing CPR on him before she raced to her father for help, the psychiatrist urges her to expand her point of view. "Please try to see that day from a slightly different perspective. Try to imagine it as if you were on the outside looking in. Try to think of yourself in that situation as someone else, just a girl, a thirteen-year-old girl on her own, alone, with a sick little boy" (131). While it is unrealistic to believe that this advice can enable Callie to recover so quickly, it testifies to the importance of heightened self-understanding, which may arise from psychotherapy or literature—the talking cure or the reading cure, respectively. Whether literal or metaphorical, scars tell stories of injuries to the body or psyche, and recovery may depend, as in Callie's case, on memory, interpretation, and narration.

The positive image of the psychiatrist in *Cut* stands in sharp opposition to those in *Crosses, Skin Game,* and *Girl, Interrupted.* Each of these stories contains one or more therapist figures who are ineffectual or sadistic. Nancy, the first-person narrator in *Crosses,* sees a psychiatrist whom she refers to as "Dr. Pear-Buttock (a name affectionately given to him by my fellow loonies)" (Stoehr 131). But there is nothing affectionate in the portrait of a psychiatrist who pesters Nancy with harsh questions, including why she treats her friends and herself so cruelly. Nancy spends two hours a day for an entire month speaking with the psychiatrist, but she learns nothing about herself to help her stop cutting. Caroline Kettlewell refers positively to Armando Favazza's psychiatric textbook *Bodies under Siege*, which Patty also found insightful, but although Kettlewell cut herself for nearly twenty years, and "went through five therapists in as many years" (164), none prove helpful. "Perhaps you'll find it odd that never, in any of these successive rounds in the psychotherapeutic ring, did I go with the express intent of addressing the cutting. Instead, I went because—I don't know exactly why I went. I went because there's something fatally seductive about being granted license to talk about yourself virtually nonstop for an hour" (164). If Kettlewell does not know why she spent so much time in therapy, neither does the reader.

The most unsympathetic psychiatrist appears in *Girl, Interrupted* in the chapter titled "The Shadow of the Real." Everything about the analyst seems pathetic and foolish. "'You want to sleep with me,' he crowed" (116). He has the annoying habit of telling her what she is thinking. "Eventually he said so many wrong things about me that I had to set him right, which was what he had wanted in the first place" (117). He begins to badger her to go into analysis with him, telling her that she has a "fairly well integrated personality to be in analysis" (118), but his formulaic response to everything she tells him is "could you say more about that" (119). His interpretations are equally mechanical, as when he tells her that the hospital's tunnels, with which she seems to be obsessed, represent a "womb" (121). When she informs him that the tunnels probably represent the "shadows on the wall of the cave," and then elaborates on Plato's well-known metaphor of reality, he evinces no understanding. Kaysen ends the chapter on a note of wry irony. "He died young, of a stroke. I was his first analytic patient; I found that out after I quit analysis. A year after I got out of the hospital, I quit. I'd had it, finally, with all the messing about in the shadows" (122).

I Never Promised You a Rose Garden

Sometimes a patient's interpretation of self-mutilation differs from the clinician's interpretation. This may be seen in Joanne Greenberg's *I Never*

Promised You a Rose Garden, published in 1964 under the pseudonym of Hannah Green. The story is a fictionalized account of the author's battle against schizophrenia, for which she was treated for two years at Chestnut Lodge Sanitarium in Rockville, Maryland, and then treated for another two years as an ambulatory patient. The fictional Dr. Fried is based on the distinguished German-born psychiatrist Frieda Fromm-Reichmann, who pioneered the use of modified psychoanalysis for psychotic patients. *I Never Promised You a Rose Garden* is one of the most authentic portrayals of verbal therapy. Patient and doctor originally intended to write a story together about their collaboration, but the plan ended with the psychiatrist's death in 1957 at the age of sixty-seven. While writing *The Talking Cure*, I discovered that long before Greenberg published the novel, her psychiatrist had written about her, in a thinly disguised medical case study, in her two medical textbooks, *Principles of Intensive Psychotherapy*, published in 1950, and *Psychoanalysis and Psychotherapy*, published posthumously in 1959:

> One exuberant young patient, the daughter of indiscriminately "encouraging" parents, was warned against expecting life to become a garden of roses after her recovery. Treatment, she was told, should make her capable of handling the vicissitudes of life which were bound to occur, as well as to enjoy the gardens of roses which life would offer her at other times. When we reviewed her treatment history after her recovery, she volunteered that this statement had helped her a great deal, "not because I believed for a moment that you were right, Doctor, but because it was such a great sign of your confidence in me and your respect for me, that you thought you could say such a serious thing to me and that I would be able to take it." (Fromm-Reichmann, *Psychoanalysis and Psychotherapy* 204)

> "Look here," Furii said. "I never promised you a rose garden. I never promised you perfect justice . . . and I never promised you peace or happiness. My help is so that you can be free to fight for all of these things. The only reality I offer is challenge, and being well is being free to accept it or not at whatever level you are capable. I never promise lies, and the rose-garden world of perfection is a lie . . . and a bore, too!" (Greenberg 106)

One of the main differences between Joanne Greenberg's novel and Frieda Fromm-Reichmann's psychiatric case study is that the latter describes in far greater detail than the former interpretive disagreements over self-mutilation—disputes that the patient and doctor apparently never resolved. There is only a brief reference to Deborah Blau's skin-cutting in *Rose Garden*; her rejecting mother, who cannot accept the reality of her daughter's illness, regards it as "silly and theatrical wrist-cutting" (16). But Dr. Fried, also called "Furii," takes all her patient's symptoms seriously, believing they illuminate the causes of mental illness. Deborah does not begin burning her skin until Dr. Fried goes on vacation, which the patient experiences as an act of abandonment, and which stokes inner volcanic fires evocative of hell. In the narrator's words, "Deborah perceived that by burning she could set a backfire that would assuage the burn kiln of the volcano, all the doors and vents of which were closed and barricaded. And by this same burning she could prove to herself finally whether or not she was truly made of human substance" (161). Until Dr. Fried's return, this is the only way that Deborah can relieve herself of intolerable psychic pain. "For Deborah, the backfires became the only way of easing the pressure of the stifled volcano inside her. She continued to burn the same places over and over, setting layers of burns on top of one another" (166). Deborah disagrees with Dr. Fried's interpretation that the skin-burning is "most serious." " 'You are wrong,' Deborah said simply, hoping that the doctor really believed what she had so often said about the patient trusting her own deep beliefs. There were over forty burns, inflicted over and over again on flesh scraped raw to receive them, and yet they didn't seem worth the fuss that was being made about them" (174). As Deborah moves slowly toward cure and integration into society, the volcano subsides as does her need to set backfires.

The symbolism of the patient's self-mutilation is more complicated in the psychiatric case study. "The skin-pulling as a symptom similar to another self-mutilating act of burning herself, which she repeatedly committed while acutely ill, helped her to maintain her continuity. It made it possible to be ill and well at the same time, because it was only she who knew about the symptom which could be hidden from everybody else with whom she came in contact as a healthy person. After this discovery, the symptom eventually disappeared" (Fromm-Reichmann, *Psychoanalysis and Psychotherapy* 197). A few pages later the psychiatrist adds another interpretation of the patient's skin-pulling: resentment against the psychiatrist. "In her judgment, I misevaluated the other act of self-mutilation from which she suffered during her psychotic episodes, the compulsion to burn her skin. The patient thought of it as a means of relieving unbearable tension, whereas she felt that I thought of it only as a serious expression of tension. In maintaining the skin-pulling, while otherwise nearly recovered, she meant to demonstrate to me that skin injuring was not a severe sign of illness" (206).

We cannot say whose interpretation is more accurate, the patient's or the psychiatrist's. Perhaps both are accurate. It is to Frieda Fromm-Reichmann's credit that she urged therapists to listen carefully to their patients' words and to respect their interpretations. "Any interpretation which a patient is able to unearth for himself," she writes in *Principles of Intensive Psychotherapy*, "is more impressive to him, hence more likely to produce an immediate and lasting curative effect, than any interpretation offered by the therapist" (128). She believed, along with her mentor Harry Stack Sullivan, that "there is as much of a tendency toward health in the mentally or physically ill as there is a tendency toward intake of food and liquids in the hungry and thirsty. In some mental patients, a spontaneous wish for change and recovery is found. In others, such a wish can be aroused on the basis of their tendency toward health, unless life has so little in store for them that they cannot be expected to become interested in being able to cope with its vicissitudes" (*Psychoanalysis and Psychotherapy* 22). These wise and compassionate observations go unheeded by most of the therapists who appear in both real and fictional accounts of cutting.

The Teacher-Student Relationship

The sympathetic doctor-patient relationship in *Cut* and *I Never Promised You a Rose Garden* has intriguing implications for the teacher-student relationship. The psychiatrists in both novels never claim to be omniscient or omnipotent, never claim to be anything other than human. In one telling exchange in *Cut*, the psychiatrist tells Callie, "I can't keep you safe. . . . Only you can" (McCormick 126). The psychiatrists maintain appropriate distance from their patients, neither too close to them nor too distant. They listen attentively to their patients, never interrupting them or placing words in their mouths. They accept their patients' silence but encourage them to speak, reminding them that self-expression is vital to health. So too does the teacher listen empathically to students, urging them toward self-expression while at the same time acknowledging inevitable resistance to difficult knowledge. Sometimes the psychiatrists restate their patients' words, enabling them to explore the implications of their language. Teachers proceed in the same way with their students. And just as the two psychiatrists never fail to praise their patients for confronting painful material, so do teachers praise their students for hard work.

Teachers, no less than mental health professionals, must gain the trust and respect of those with whom they work, especially in the self-disclosing classroom. My self-disclosures encourage their own. I acknowledge my vulnerability without, I hope, implying that I am needy, dependent, or weak. As Harry Stack Sullivan observed often, "We are all much more simply human than otherwise." To be human is to be vulnerable, and I give permission to my students to write about their own vulnerability. They discover that it requires strength and courage to write about one's vulnerability and that they become *less* vulnerable in the process.

My vulnerability has not weakened my self-confidence in the self-disclosing classroom. My confidence is "infectious"—an example of positive contagion. My students discover from the first day of the semester that I value our attachment to each other. They know that I love teaching, that I would rather be in the classroom than anywhere else, and that I cannot imagine wanting to retire from what I consider a nearly perfect job. My passion, engagement, and commitment are obvious to everyone. Nearly any topic on which a student writes is fine with me: if it's important to one student, it's likely to be important to classmates and teacher. They quickly learn that I never criticize another person's emotions, that I limit my comments to helping them find the best words to express themselves, and that I attempt to practice the empathy that I expect from them.

I do everything possible to strengthen students' attachment bonds with each other. The first two assignments involve students writing each other's biographies; within a few weeks they know more about their classmates than they do about those in any other college course. Every week I divide them into groups of three to revise each other's sentences. They feel relaxed with each other and with me. As a result, they are willing to self-disclose secrets that in some cases they have not expressed to their closest friends.

I do not expect anything of my students that I do not expect of myself. I schedule two conferences a semester with my writing students each semester, and I tell them that if they miss an appointment without calling or emailing me in advance, they must write five additional pages, over the required forty pages. If I miss a conference, they subtract five pages from the minimum writing requirement. No one thinks this is unfair—and neither they nor I miss an appointment. I always come to class on time and end on time, which encourages them to be punctual. I always thank students after they read aloud their essays, and then I ask classmates to identify the best sentences in an essay, after which we discuss how to revise other sentences containing grammatical or stylistic errors. I return essays back to students within a week, filled with suggestions for revision.

I ask students on the first day of the semester for permission to call them by their first name, and then I tell them that since I believe in reciprocity, they can call me by my first name. Most do not, but they know they can if they want to. Sometimes when I discuss an esoteric grammatical question—such as, "Do I say 'I feel bad' or 'I feel badly'"—I bet students a dollar that they don't know which is correct and why. (The former is correct because "feel" is a linking verb.) Over the course of the semester I lose more dollars than I gain, but it doesn't matter because everyone has fun during these moments. I always crack jokes, usually at my own expense, which also contributes to the relaxed classroom atmosphere. I circle semicolons when used appropriately and write the word "sexy" next to it—despite Kurt Vonnegut's satirical warning in his book *A Man without a Country* that semicolons are "transvestite hermaphrodites representing absolutely nothing. All they do is show you've been to college" (23). At the beginning of the semester I tell students that several of them will probably cry during certain essays, but that the "smile-to-tear ratio" is at least twenty-to-one. They know that when I cry in class it is because I have been moved deeply by an essay.

Intimacy and autonomy: both occur in the self-disclosing classroom. As students feel closer to their teacher and classmates, they take greater risks in exposing the secrets of their lives. They convey in their writings the unique experiences that have made them who they are. They alone decide what to reveal and conceal to others. They alone decide on the degree of self-disclosure. Sometimes the question of what to reveal and conceal is difficult, and it may take weeks or months before they decide to write about certain experiences that they know will be startling to others in the classroom, including one of the most frightening of all—cutting.

CHAPTER 10

Cutting in the Classroom

Paula, Ralph, Judy, Christine, and Cordelia

"Suddenly[,] self-cutting, a clinical problem that evokes considerable anxiety, seems to be almost everywhere, bursting onto the cultural scene in very much the same way eating disorders exploded into our awareness twenty or thirty years ago. Both are hot topics now" (Farber xxiii). So states Sharon Klayman Farber in the introduction to her book *When the Body Is the Target*, published in 2000. Eating disorders have long been rampant among college students, as my colleagues Mary Valentis and Anne Devane report in their 1994 book *Female Rage*. "It's no wonder that today's little girls are aware of body image at age two and three, that by fourth grade 80 percent of them are on self-imposed diets, and at twelve most girls are into serious dieting. As college professors, we know that one out of eight of our female students is using laxatives or vomiting to control her weight" (77). There is a close relationship between eating disorders and self-mutilation, as Caroline Kettlewell suggests. "I learned, just a few years ago, that among self-mutilators, as many as sixty percent report a parallel history of eating disorders: a statistic that didn't surprise me. From the outside, their shared theme might appear to be self-destruction, but from where I've stood, what they have in common is something altogether different. I subdued hunger, overcame the animal self's blind instinct for self-preservation, in search of a perfect silence" (84).

Despite this link between cutting and eating disorders, many more of my students have written about the latter than the former. Is this due to the "Dodge Viper" effect? With the exception of Maryann and Paige, whom I discuss in the next chapter, I could recall only two students who wrote about cutting, Christine and Cordelia. But once I read Patty's master's thesis and then reread *Diaries to an English Professor*, I was surprised to find that three others, Paula, Ralph, and Judy, also wrote long entries about cutting. Paula's entry appeared in the chapter "Hunger Artists," a study of eating disorders, and Ralph's and Judy's appeared in "Suicide

Survivors." The five undergraduates offer insights into why people cut themselves, how relatives and friends react to cutting, and how they feel about their self-disclosures. The writings confirm that people cut themselves mainly because they feel psychological relief and, secondarily, to receive attention from others.

Paula: "Why Does This Kind of Pain Give Me Pleasure?"

Paula, a junior, began to cut herself because of her unhappiness over her parents' divorce and her desire to gain attention from her father and boyfriend:

> I wonder, is masochism uncommon? Not masochism in the context of deriving sexual pleasure from self-inflicted pain, but just plain old pleasure from experiencing pain one purposefully inflicts on oneself. I am a masochist. There is sometimes an ulterior motive for my masochistic tendencies—attention. It's strange to admit this, but I have before, and probably will again, hurt myself to gain the attention of someone else.
>
> The first time I did it was when I was in high school, and I remember being angry at my dad for spending too much time with his wife, with whom I did not get along. It wasn't so much the time he spent with her, it was the time he didn't spend with me, and the fact that he was in some ways becoming very much like her and seemed to want to push me away.
>
> While I was at work one afternoon during a weekend I was visiting him, I picked up a single-edged razor blade and started slicing up the backs of my hands. Nothing worthy of stitches, but I did draw blood. My dad did eventually notice at some point during the weekend, and I shrugged it off as being bored over work. Funny, I don't remember if I achieved the desired effect—more attention from my dad.
>
> I repeated this hand-slashing action a few times during high school and my first year of college, primarily as an attention getter from my parents. Sophomore year, I remember trying to cut myself with a plastic knife, which didn't work too well as far as breaking the skin, but it was painful, and the pain made me feel better about whatever it was that was troubling me.
>
> Another time I cut myself was when I thought my boyfriend was becoming attracted again to his old girlfriend, who was in one of his classes. Her presence most certainly threatened me, and I needed reassurance that he loved me and not her. One afternoon at work, where I have access to single-edged razor blades, I decided that cuts on my arms would make me feel better and command attention from my boyfriend. This time it worked—not only did

the pain make me feel better, but my boyfriend became very concerned and
started to show all the things he said he felt about me. Why does this kind of
pain give me pleasure? If it were just the guilt I meant to impose on others, it
would not be as difficult to understand. At any rate, it would be interesting
to see what Sigmund Freud would make of this case study. (112–13)

Freud would have endorsed Paula's interpretation, for he saw a close link between femininity and masochism. "The suppression of women's aggressiveness," he writes in *New Introductory Lectures on Psycho-Analysis*, "which is prescribed for them constitutionally and imposed on them socially favours the development of powerful masochistic impulses, which succeed, as we know, in binding erotically the destructive trends which have been diverted inwards" (116). Most feminist scholars would dismiss this interpretation as another example of Freud's misogyny; instead, they would emphasize the self-destructive consequences of women's efforts to conform to an impossible patriarchal standard of female beauty. In her other diaries, Paula wrote about feeling depressed about her weight and appearance. "Sure, I've had an eating disorder—I always ate too much. I binged and binged but never quite made it to the purge." Like Patty and the adolescent protagonists of cutting novels, she felt better after cutting herself, more in control, though she realized, like them, that cutting and starving herself were short-term solutions to potentially long-term problems. "All the time I knew that in the long run I was actually avoiding my problem by taking the easy way out, but it was the only thing that I felt I could do to make me mentally stable and not on the verge of being suicidal" (114).

Much of the value of psychoanalytic diaries derives from students' efforts to reach their own interpretations and conclusions about their experiences. It is the student, not the teacher, who facilitates this self-analysis. Hearing classmates' introspective diaries aids in the process of self-discovery. Paula felt uncomfortable hearing classmates' entries on eating disorders because they hit too close to home. "I have essentially been poking fun at something that should not be taken lightly. I can certainly relate to the feeling of containing a 'deep secret' about their disorder, for I did the same thing, except my secret was that I was eating almost whatever I could but pretending that I wasn't" (115).

Ralph: "Writing This, I Am Almost in a State of Panic"

Ralph was the second student in *Diaries to an English Professor* who wrote an extended entry on cutting. His diary reveals the fear and helplessness of those who witness a relative or friend's cutting:

> *What I am about to write is very distressing to me, but I haven't been able to think about anything else.*
>
> *My ex-girlfriend and I are talking for the first time after a messy breakup. I am glad that we are able to be friends again because I still care about her very much and very deeply. The details of why we broke up aren't important, but let's just say that it was a very intense relationship and seemed to run out of control of all reason and sense. She had been abused for her whole life—emotionally abused by her parents, sexually abused by a neighbor, emotionally and sexually abused by so-called boyfriends.*
>
> *When she was going out with me, it was the first time she had ever had a relationship where the other person thought of "us" before "me." She didn't know how to handle it. She was always looking for some other reason for my behavior; for instance, if I bought her flowers, she wouldn't think that I was buying her flowers simply to buy her flowers, but instead thought that I must be buying them because I expected something in return—sex, in other words. I was amazed at this because I did things for her innocently. I never had a relationship like the abusive ones she had experienced in the past, so I couldn't even fathom the idea.*
>
> *Anyway, that has all passed for me. Now we are talking again, and it looks like we will be friends. I really enjoy her company, and I love talking to her and just being with her. I realize that she can't handle an emotional relationship because she has to come to terms with her abusive past. I am proud to have her as a friend. She is a very special person.*
>
> *This next part will be difficult.*
>
> *Thursday we went to a movie and then back to her apartment. We were sitting on the couch when I noticed a red, irritated mark on her wrist. I immediately became concerned because I had a cousin who was suicidal and have seen those marks before.*
>
> *I asked her what the mark was.*
>
> *"Just a scratch," she said.*
>
> *"A scratch from what?" I asked.*
>
> *"I scraped it on the table."*
>
> *Although I knew damn well what the mark really was, I left it at that— partly because I could tell she didn't want to tell me, and partly because I*

really didn't want to know the truth. I really wanted to believe that she had scraped her wrist on the table.

About half an hour later she suddenly told me that she was lying before about scraping her wrist. What really happened was that in a fit of depression she started to dig at her wrist with a key until it started to bleed. When she saw how upset I got when she said this, she said not to worry, she would never really do anything, she wasn't stupid enough to commit suicide. She is always telling me not to worry about her.

Right now I am very frightened for her. She said that she would never do anything, and the attempt did not cause serious damage except for a few dig marks in her wrist, but what if she has a more serious fit of depression and tries to do something more permanent to herself?

I am very confused. I have emotions swimming around inside of me that I do not know how to deal with. Writing this, I am almost in a state of panic. Sometimes I wish I could just make all of her pain disappear with the wave of a wand, but I know it's not that easy. She's abusing herself because all she has ever known is abuse. I wish I could show her that there is something else out there, that love doesn't have to be abusive—in fact, it shouldn't be abusive. I wish I could be there so that she doesn't attempt it again, but it's impossible to be with her every minute, and that wouldn't be good for either of us anyway.

A part of me knows that she would never commit suicide. Is that part just denying the obvious? What if leaving her to work out her problems is the wrong thing to do—then what? What will I do if she does the unspeakable?

I wish I had the answers. (141–43)

I find Ralph's entry remarkable not only in its sympathy and empathy but also in its insight into his friend's situation. With the exception of Callie's psychiatrist, no character in any of the cutting novels displays the compassion that Ralph does here. Unlike Susanna Kaysen, who asserts that there's "always a touch of fascination in repulsion" (124), there is nothing lurid or melodramatic in his description of his friend's cutting. Nor is he like "rubberneckers at a train wreck" (5), Caroline Kettlewell's characterization of those who witness cutting. I can't recall what I wrote on his diary entry, which he submitted fifteen years ago, but perhaps he would have been less frightened if he knew that cutting often prevents more serious self-destructive behavior. And in the unlikely event that he showed his entry to her, perhaps she was able to see how much he cared for her.

Judy: "Although He Chose to Kill Himself, He Also Killed Her in So Many Ways"

Judy was the third student in *Diaries to an English Professor* who wrote about cutting. Her diary was a response to my discussion of the suicide of Len Port, my mentor and best friend:

Hearing your story about your friend this week brought back memories of a few years ago when my best friend's boyfriend committed suicide. I have known Myra since high school, and we are very close. Jason was also from our high school, and he and Myra continued to be boyfriend and girlfriend until college, when they were separated for the first time. He was nice enough, but he drank a lot and smoked pot. He was nice to Myra, it seemed. I truly believed she loved him and he loved her. In their freshman year of college they began having problems. She wanted more freedom, and he wanted to get married. They broke up, and Myra began dating many other guys. Jason kept in touch with me, and I knew at the time he was partying more and more. During summer Jason began following Myra around and said he wanted her back. She was reluctant. She missed him but felt she needed more time to herself.

In September, one day before Myra was to leave for college, Jason shot himself in the head. He and Myra had just had a big fight, and he was really drunk. He first cut himself with a razor and wrote in blood the words "I love you" in a letter which he sent to her. Obviously he had been planning this—Myra received the note two days after his death. He added "ed" to verbs so that they would be in past tense. In accordance with your discussion of suicide in class, I believed then and believe now still that he killed himself instead of killing her.

Myra was devastated. Still is devastated. She left home immediately and went to college. She felt great hurt and anger. She did blame herself, as Jason had wanted. Although he chose to kill himself, he also killed her in so many ways. When she came back home during Thanksgiving, she was a mess. She wore black and covered her room with memories of Jason, gifts he had given her, pictures of him, etc. I felt so uncomfortable in her bedroom. I never knew what to say, so mostly I said nothing but, "Myra, I understand." I didn't really understand, but I grieved his loss. I told her not to blame herself that Jason was just really wasted at the time and couldn't handle things.

None of this helped her really. I felt sorry for her—exactly what she didn't want. This was such a great strain on our relationship. I watched her losing control and suggested she seek professional help. This really pissed her off.

The next year I shall never forget. The emotions she felt were so intense and even scary at times. I was afraid she might kill herself. She must have sensed this as she kept telling me she would never do that. Myra is still haunted by Jason's death. She couldn't return to college the following year—it was too much for her. This year she has started again. She still has an ominous way about her, though. She will probably never be able to retain a mental state as before Jason's death.

What has plagued me, as well as Myra, is what could have been done to stop Jason—if anything at all. In a sense, Myra feels as if she failed him, and so do I. I feel anger toward Jason for changing my relationship with her forever. Myra's recovery or reconciliation with Jason's suicide is a day-to-day thing with her and with me also. We are still in touch regularly. Part of Myra has died with Jason. I hope she can live with the rest. (146–47)

Jason's cutting is unusual in that it directly preceded self-inflicted death rather than serving as a substitute for it. Maggie Turp points out that although self-harm is generally not motivated by the desire to commit suicide, "statistics suggest that 10 per cent of people who harm themselves eventually go on to commit suicide" (218). Jason's cutting apparently produced pain without psychological relief. Nor was there anything private or secret about his self-mutilation: he wanted the entire world to know why he was killing himself. Just as I felt that Len's suicide had killed part of me, so did Judy believe that Jason's suicide killed part of Myra. As I write in *Diaries to an English Professor*, "The subtle verbal ambiguity in Judy's last paragraph reveals the psychological ambiguities of suicide. 'In a sense, Myra feels as if she failed him, and so do I.' Does Judy share Myra's belief that Myra has failed Jason, or does Judy believe that she too has failed them? Jason is the one who pulled the trigger, yet both women seem to believe that they should have been able to stop him. Myra ended her relationship with Jason because she sought more freedom, but now she seems wedded to a dead past, married to suffering" (147).

Christine: "Seeing This in Writing Is Very Disturbing Somehow"

Apart from these three entries in *Diaries to an English Professor*, two female students wrote about cutting themselves. Christine, a member of a course called Literature and the Healing Arts that I taught in 2002, turned in a reader-response diary about her reactions to Primo Levi's memoir

Survival in Auschwitz. Just as Patty's high school students identify closely with Elie Wiesel's *Night*, sometimes so closely that they lose sight of the distinction between self and other, the same problem affects Christine, leading to emotional contagion. She found the story so unsettling that she began having nightmares and found herself returning to an action that she had not performed in years. She allowed me to use her entry in *Empathic Teaching*:

> *Last night I was up until five something in the morning, afraid to fall asleep because I know that then I will be there, in Auschwitz. I am unable to get the horrible images and thoughts out of my mind; I cannot stop thinking about it. I awoke from the nightmares and went into the kitchen late last night. I saw a sharp knife and I thought, maybe if I cut myself a little, it would make the pain stop. I made a small nick on my arm, just a few drops of blood, and I thought that maybe I felt a tiny bit better. Yes, I thought, it feels better. I looked in horror at what I had done and dropped the knife to the floor. I cried so hard after that, for over an hour, until my eyes were swollen and red, and my head ached. I thought, I deserved to be there, not Primo Levi, not all of those innocent people.* (337–38)

Like Patty and the fictional characters she discusses, Christine feels better after cutting herself, though she also feels horror when she sees the cuts on her arm. She gave me permission to read her reader-response diary to her classmates, but I chose not to do so because I didn't know how she would react to hearing her words read aloud. Rarely do I read aloud writings of students who strike me as severely anxious or depressed. Writing about a past conflict, by contrast, is less risky. One cannot tell from Christine's writings whether her identification with Primo Levi leads to catharsis or traumatization. As I suggest in *Empathic Teaching*, "She identifies not with Primo Levi's survival but with his suffering, and unconsciously she suffers along *with* him, or perhaps *instead* of him. Her discovery that he committed suicide years after being released from Auschwitz is even more unnerving to her" (339). In her diary on William Styron's *Darkness Visible*, she revealed "tormenting" a friend who later committed suicide, an act that almost led to her own. "I began to think that dying was my secret life. I would climb high up, to the tops of tall buildings, and frighten myself senseless. Walk midway on bridges, in freezing weather, crying and trying to convince myself to jump, to not be such a pussy, to do it already. I would cut myself with razors, long thin ones, for relief to pay for my sins" (340). Perhaps this statement explains her wish to exchange places with Primo Levi.

Christine told me during a conference near the end of the semester that she was feeling better and went on to describe how years earlier she had cut herself during a time when she was suicidal immediately following her friend's suicide. She also asked me for the name of a therapist. In her last diary, she describes how William Styron's decision in *Darkness Visible* to seek psychological help for suicidal depression inspired her to make an appointment at the university counseling center, though shame prevented her from going there. "Seeing all of this in writing is very disturbing somehow," she wrote in her final diary. "I mean I am not really crazy. I get all my responsibilities accomplished. I work hard. I try. I fight the sadness every step of the way; I refuse to give in to it. That is why I am taking your class. I am trying to heal myself. I hope it works" (340).

Cordelia: "I Was a Different Person Then"

Like Myra after Jason's suicide, Cordelia also wore dark clothes during her troubled adolescence. A member of the Expository Writing course I taught during the spring of 2004, when my wife died—it was the class in which I read my eulogy of Barbara—Cordelia was about Patty's age. Writing about herself in the third person, she describes with uncommon insight and detachment the loneliness, isolation, confusion, and hopelessness she felt when she cut herself:

I have been to dark places; I have seen dark things. There were days that the darkness was so thick and dank, that the slightest flicker of light was blinding and painful to my eyes. Stepping into lightness of any kind was to subject myself to the unpredictability of the world, and the harsh scrutiny of its inhabitants. The thought was unbearable. As I reflect, I wonder how I survived it. I was a different person then.

She was fourteen when the darkness first descended upon her. She, the me that was, always dressed in black, and adorned herself with strange jewelry depicting snakes or eyes or bearing crystals. She associated with few people, and those she chose to spend time with were as odd as she. One of her friends chose a hearse in place of the more traditional limousine for the prom, and was suspended for putting a hex on another student. She was well known for her brutal honesty. Truth-telling does not win you friends in high school. No one but a brave and understanding minority dared ask her opinion of anything.

At home, she stayed in her bedroom, emerging for nourishment only. This room, though painted cheerfully white and blue, was wall-papered with posters and littered with dirty clothes and dishes. The only organized space in the entire room was around her stereo and cassette rack, which were carefully ordered alphabetically by artist and date of album release. Here, in this dimly lit, filthy room, she sat every day listening to music her parents wouldn't have approved of and reading books. She read a perverse amount of Shakespeare and Vonnegut. There is no faster way to warp an already disturbed mind.

This pattern continued throughout high school. Some days were worse than others. There were nights she spent hours stabbing herself in the arm with sewing needles just to see if she could feel it. Would it bleed? She was sure that she could not be human, but over and over again, she could feel the sting of the needle and a little droplet of blood would form on the surface of her skin. She wrote poems, hundreds of them, about death and dying. She would scribble out a poem on whatever paper was handy; maybe she would show it to whoever was standing near, but often she immediately threw it away. Once the poem was born, she didn't need it anymore.

One summer, she began losing weight. It was not through any conscious effort. She didn't feel like eating. She wanted to sleep, and to forget that this horrible existence was real. Her mother became convinced that her daughter was bulimic, and took her to the doctor in spite of angry protests. The doctor could find nothing wrong, *aside from a probable caffeine addiction. Thus satisfied, her mother returned the girl to the sanctity of her dungeon.*

She spent hours contemplating novel ways of committing suicide. Death seemed so alluring, but she would never kill herself in any mundane way. It would have to be spectacular. She contemplated how reliably death could be induced by electrocution. Her mother's first husband was electrocuted. The irony would have been poetic. Who would come to her funeral? Her family would certainly be there, as would her teachers. Who else would feign to have cared for her? The vision was perfectly clear in her mind. The church was standing room only, but only a third of the people there actually knew her. The rest were there to gawk at the specter of suicide. All of the people attending would claim that they never saw it coming. She always laughed at the thought of this. They never saw it coming. They didn't notice a horribly withdrawn girl who was preoccupied with death.

After high school, she began college at the University at Albany. She found a sense of solace among the tall gray buildings. The tons of cold concrete and hideous sharp angles resonated with the discord in her soul. She vacillated between acceptance and loathing for the anonymity that this new setting afforded her. She spent all of her time before, after, and often during her classes in Lecture Center 4. She found comfort and companionship there. The socially inept are attracted to the way computers can help them communicate. She loved watching the amber letters fill up the black screen as she typed. She began to think that there could be hope for happiness in her.

Then there was a failed relationship with a disturbed individual that sent her spinning back into the chasm from whence she came. Her emails to her friends became disjointed and erratic. She wrote letters that started out normally but would then begin to lose structure. first, she forgot the capitalization at the beginning of sentences. Shortly thereafter all of the punctuation would disappear Finally, the spaces wereomittedbetweenwords until the page was filled with jumbled incoherent letters like some sort of encrypted code. But what was the message? She couldn't breathe. She could not walk from the humanities building to social sciences without collapsing. She felt some unseen force compressing her chest, and restricting airflow to her lungs; she was suffocating.

Sometimes she heard voices. It might be a sinister sounding voice from over her shoulder beckoning to her. "Hey! Come here." She would spin around frightened, and find no one in sight. Sometimes when someone was speaking to her, the voice would change suddenly into something incomprehensible, sounding as though the person were speaking in some foreign tongue, underwater. Or was it she who was drowning? She was terrified. She felt horribly isolated and confused, but mostly she was tired. She was tired of fighting herself to get out of bed in the morning. She was tired of being miserable. She was tired of being afraid.

In a poetry class her junior year, she discovered a poem in an anthology. It wasn't assigned. She happened upon it while flipping haphazardly through the pages. The poem, written by Philip Whalen, is titled "Further Notice." It's about a man who can't live in this world yet who refuses to commit suicide or allow another person to kill him. It ends with his decision to be himself, "Free, a genius, an embarrassment / Like the Indian, the buffalo / Like Yellowstone National Park." She never fully understood the reference to Yellowstone, but the rest of the poem vibrated her very being. She would not be kept prisoner any longer. The change was immediate. She ended the relationship she was in at the time. She explained to the man when they broke up that she was on the verge of something wonderful, or terrible: she wasn't sure which. She told him that she was full of grotesque jagged pieces of herself that were so sharp that she couldn't imagine how they had kept from slicing open her flesh from the inside out. She told him she was capable of happiness but she needed to hatch first. She needed to be alone in order to force out the demons within her and become the whole person she knew she could be. She needed to break free of this shell. Somehow, he understood.

I started trying harder to be cheerful. I focused on goodness as much as possible. I changed my perspective from that of a defeatist to that of an optimist. It required significant effort to retrain my thought processes against the negative. I concentrated on living. At first it was exhausting, but it became easier with time. Is it possible to be happy just by choosing happiness? It is. I stand in evidence of it. My joy is contagious; I hope that my misery wasn't. I have moved on, and left my pain, that numbing throbbing melancholy, in the void that used to consume me. I remember the past only as a means for appreciating the present. I have found spirituality in the mountains, love in my companion, delight in the company of dogs, and joy in the very air I breathe. I have made myself whole again. I follow my bliss wherever it takes me, and always move forward. As Mark Strand observes in his poem "Keeping Things Whole," "We all have reasons / for moving. I move / to keep things whole."

After the semester ended, I asked Cordelia to describe how she felt in a self-disclosing classroom:

How do you describe a course that has shattered long-held beliefs about higher education? I had come to expect a comfortable amount of anonymity and indifference in my courses. I expected to blend into the background. I expected to be surrounded by people with similar expectations. On the first day of class we had a discussion about what our expectations were for the course and the professor. The professor commented on people trying to avoid being singled out, just before calling on me for an answer. Where was my anonymity? It was gone in that instant on the first day.

This course was vastly different from any other courses that I have taken at this university over the past ten years. There are not many courses that could broach the topics discussed here while still adhering to the curriculum. It was different partially because it could be. A course on British literature would have little room for discussion about personal experiences. However, the most unusual aspect of this class was that I learned the names of almost every student in it. I don't talk to people in my classes. I never have. But, I chatted with other students of this class.

The most interesting moment of the semester was every class. It seemed like something quirky happened daily; there were people weeping, or odd papers, or some other situation that left me scratching my head in disbelief. I was never certain what to expect walking into that room, and sometimes the anticipation made me nauseous.

Every time I finished a writing assignment and asked my husband to proofread it for me, he would comment on the assignment being peculiar. He would say that when he took Expository Writing (in 1997) there were not assignments like this. He would say with good-natured skepticism, "Did I pay for this course? It's so odd." I told him that an upper level writing course was the last obstacle between graduation and me; I reminded him that I attended exactly one class of Expository Writing with a different professor during the fall semester and was so intimidated that I never went back. This class was more comfortable, most likely because of the openness and tolerance required to foster discussions on the topics we covered.

I will likely remember my classmates, in the same way that I remember classmates from other classes. I probably won't remember them at all after a year. Ideally, I would have them remember me as a genius with immense writing talent, but they will likely remember me as I remember them—not at all.

The course is great just the way it is, but if an improvement is necessary, I would suggest trying to minimize the invisible pressure to outperform your classmates. I'm not referring to writing ability so much as shock value. I felt a need to outdo my fellow students. "Maybe your mom was a drunk, but my whole family was drunk." I know that it sounds stupid, but peer pressure exists on so many levels. Even though I knew that the pressure didn't

*exist except in my mind, I still felt it. What can I say to astonish
people?*

*I began this class knowing that every person has a unique story
to tell, and that some of them would be tragic and some triumphant.
I knew that I would encounter awkward moments and situations.
There were certainly uncomfortable moments, but both the professor and the class behaved respectfully and admirably. I thought that
college students were incapable of proper respect, but they proved
me wrong and reminded me to judge others less critically. More
significantly, they reminded me to be less critical of myself.*

Cordelia appears to have little difficulty in finding the words to express
her feelings of isolation and withdrawal during her troubled adolescence.
The aesthetic power of her first essay is palpable. She *shows* instead of
merely tells how her writings began to reflect her breakdown: first she
fails to capitalize a sentence, then she omits punctuation, and finally
she disregards the spacing between words. Readers can almost feel the
unseen force compressing her chest and shutting down her lungs. She in-
duces in the reader the violence against her body. We can almost hear the
terrifying voices beckoning her to death, as we can in *I Never Promised
You a Rose Garden*.

Cordelia's fantasy of her funeral recalls Holden Caulfield's daydream in
J. D. Salinger's *Catcher in the Rye*. "I hope to hell when I *do* die," Holden
confesses, with typical mordant humor, "somebody has sense enough to
just dump me in the river or something. Anything except sticking me in a
goddam cemetery. People coming and putting a bunch of flowers on your
stomach on Sunday, and all that crap. Who wants flowers when you're
dead? Nobody" (155). Like Holden, Cordelia assumes that most people
will be indifferent to her death, attending her funeral only "to gawk at
the specter of suicide." Unlike Holden, at the end of her story she is able
to look upon her earlier life with sympathetic detachment, changing
her perspective "from that of a defeatist to that of an optimist." Interestingly, she ends the final essay by expressing affection for her classmates,
with whom she has shared confessional and transformational stories—a
statement that recalls Holden's final words in the novel: "Don't ever tell
anybody anything. If you do, you start missing them" (214). She also af-

firms the positive value of communicating emotions to others: "My joy is contagious." She implies that reading Philip Whalen's poem "Further Notice" was like hearing a wake-up call. She identifies with the speaker, who can neither live in the world, commit suicide, nor allow another to end his or her life, and she credits the poem for ending an unsatisfying relationship and turning around her life. Such examples of bibliotherapy are not uncommon.

Cordelia was one of several students whom I contacted several months after the course ended. I asked her to describe how she felt when she wrote the essay and how she now felt rereading it. Responses to these questions help us to understand the value of the pedagogy of self-disclosure and the possibility of posttraumatic growth. She believed that the essay was "extraordinarily easy" to write. "It was merely a matter of putting onto paper all of the things that I had often thought about but never verbalized. I recall that the first paragraph was difficult, but once I was beyond it the rest of the essay seemed to write itself. It was the first time that I had written about death and/or suicide, except for some dark, poorly written poetry when I was in high school."

It was much more challenging for Cordelia to read the essay aloud. "I was nervous. I wanted to make sure I didn't stumble over my words because I felt that the delivery was important. I did well in spite of the trembling." She felt that her classmates responded positively to the essay. "There were several students who empathized with its content, having been through similar experiences themselves." So too did I respond positively to her essay: I recall telling her that I felt it was her best writing of the semester. My main criticism was that I thought she should have maintained the third-person narration throughout the essay, a recommendation with which she initially disagreed. "I resisted this suggestion at first, partially because the first paragraph was so arduous to write, but in retrospect a consistent third-person perspective would probably strengthen the essay."

Did Cordelia learn anything about herself or her family as a result of writing the essay? Her first response, she said, was an emphatic no. "I prefer to think that I am completely self-aware. However, it isn't true. By writing the essay, I discovered how much I have grown. I am a stronger, happier, more well-rounded person now, and writing that essay helped me realize how far I have come." After completing the essay, she showed it to her husband, who became alarmed. "He thought it was well written, but it frightened him. He spent a week asking me if I still think about suicide." She also sent the essay to an old friend who had known her during that time in her life, and he too was surprised by its dark content. "He said that he had no idea what I had been going through, and that it 'explained a lot'—his words, not mine." The essay, she added, "cleared up a few unresolved issues that he had with our relationship."

Paradoxically, it was easier for Cordelia to share her writings with classmates than with her husband, an observation that was also true for Patty. So too would Patty agree with Cordelia's statement that sometimes former cutters do not remember the person they were decades earlier when they cut themselves. Writing helps to recall this former identity, but the writer may feel understandably ambivalent about showing the writing to others. It is often easier to self-disclose to a stranger than to a relative or close friend. Cordelia's husband learned something about her past that he had not known previously, and the knowledge troubled him. Sometimes risky writing becomes risky reading—both writer and reader may find themselves disturbed by a communication, a form of emotional contagion. Self-disclosing writers must be careful about whom they share their writings with, for such writings often expose aspects of one's dark past. For this reason, James Pennebaker advises his students not to share their self-disclosing writings with others. It is obviously risky to share personal writings with relatives and friends, but there are advantages in doing so. Showing our self-disclosing writings to other people may help them to understand us better and to forge closer relationships. Others may also reciprocate with their own self-disclosing writings. In addition, survival narratives instill hope and confidence in others, affirming that they can survive their own crises. Cordelia is one of many students who commented on the value of sharing a self-disclosing essay with other people.

Cordelia had not reread the essay until I asked her to, and the only change she would now make is to maintain the third-person point of view. "There isn't anything that I would omit. I am not ashamed of a single word in that essay. I recall that immediately after I submitted the essay, I thought of several additional ideas that I would have liked to explore, to flesh it out more, but presently I don't remember what they were." She did not know whether she would have written it had I not read my eulogy of Barbara to the class. Nor was she certain how readers would respond to it. "After reading my essay, some of your readers will likely think that

I require professional help, and the rest of them will recognize some of the feelings and scenarios that I have related. I would like to think that some of them would consider it powerfully written." She believed that she would have responded positively to the essay had a classmate written it. "I imagine that I would empathize with the writer. How could I not? I might also feel relieved that there are other people who survived struggles similar to my own."

Cordelia felt that writing about cutting and death is an appropriate assignment for college students as long as they have the option not to write on any topic they deem too personal. "It was appropriate for me. It was appropriate for some other members of my class. It might not be appropriate for everyone. My classmates and I were given the opportunity to opt out of this topic. I am certain that there are some who did. If Professor Berman had mandated that everyone write about suicide, then it would most certainly be an unfair and inappropriate topic. However, the assignment was presented in such a way that gently encouraged willing students to write on this topic, without condemning students who chose not to."

I sent Cordelia a copy of the present book in manuscript form and invited her to offer her impressions after reading it. She was happy to comply:

You were correct. I did find the book very interesting, on multiple levels. Probably the most startling is that I never actually considered myself a "cutter" until I read it. The connection with OCD is fascinating and perhaps underacknowledged. All of Patty's research and background made me realize how much I omitted (consciously or subconsciously, I'm not sure) from my essay. Rose Garden was one of my favorite books in high school; I did an oral report on it, shortly before a research paper on teen suicide and during the time I was reading everything I could get my hands on by or about Plath, Sexton, Woolf, and to a lesser extent Hemingway. Somehow when I wrote that essay [for you], I only suggested reading Vonnegut and Shakespeare (which is also true). Curious isn't it? . . . Thank you for giving me the opportunity to read the MS and if there's anything specifically that you are interested in knowing about my response to it, please ask. As always, I will help in any way that I can.

I can't recall whether I read aloud Paula's, Ralph's, or Judy's diary entries and, if so, their impact on classmates. I did not share Christine's essay with the class because it described an ongoing conflict. Cordelia read aloud her essay on cutting, but she described a problem that occurred several years earlier. Suppose, however, a teacher reads aloud an essay about a past problem only to discover that it is ongoing. What should the teacher do?

CHAPTER 11

"Falling in Love with Cutting"

Maryann and Paige

How should a teacher react to a student's ongoing medical or psychological problem? This question arose in an expository writing course I taught in the spring of 2005. In an effort to encourage students to write on a "light" topic that would balance the preceding darker topics, I asked them to write an essay on either falling in or out of love. The assignment came exactly at the midpoint of the semester:

> For your next assignment, please write an essay about falling in or out of love. Try to capture the experience of love: the passion, excitement, confusion, and mystery. You may describe falling in love with a person, a pet, a religion, an ideal, or a hobby. Try to evoke the special qualities that you love or loved about the love object. Remember that the reader of your essay does not know the object of your love—nor does the reader know you. See if you can characterize both yourself and your love object.
>
> Try to describe how your feelings of love changed over time, either becoming stronger or weaker. What specific events occurred to strengthen or weaken your love? What did the experience of falling in or out of love teach you?
>
> I would like eight volunteers to bring 26 copies of this assignment. You may choose to remain anonymous.

Most of the students wrote about falling in or out of love with another person. Some of the essays were intense, describing high school relationships that ended in pain or in disappointment, but most were lighthearted and playful, affirming the transformative power of love, however short-lived it may be. I was stunned, however, when I read Maryann's graphic essay, written only for me, on a subject that I never imagined one could "love":

Maryann: "I Can Remember Feeling the Sting in My Wrist and the Shame in My Heart"

I have never experienced falling in love with a person. I have always put up my guard when it comes to other people and emotional attachments. I will have rendezvous with men who have girlfriends or are otherwise unavailable, but I never allow myself to fall in love with them. There is emptiness in my heart. There is a void that love should fill, but I don't allow it to. Unfortunately, I have filled this void with unhealthy habits. Drinking and smoking have shown their love for me; however, the one habit that I truly fell in love with took me years to control.

In tenth grade I remember watching an episode of 7th Heaven. This show dealt with controversial issues, such as teen pregnancy, alcohol and drug addiction, as well as the trials of everyday life. The episode I am referring to dealt with self-mutilation. Throughout my entire high school career I was depressed. I hated life; I wanted to die. In the 7th Heaven episode, there was a girl who cut herself to feel better. The show's purpose was to create awareness for the problem and how to deal with it. Rather than listen to the show's message that self-mutilation was horrible, I thought, "I should try that. Maybe I'll feel better." It was one of the biggest mistakes of my life because I fell in love with it.

I remember sitting next to the computer in my basement with tears streaming down my face. I was miserable. Life and school were becoming unbearable. The scissors were shiny with blue handles, and I quickly dragged the blade across my wrist. While the place I chose to cut was questionable, I was never trying to kill myself. Suicide is a permanent solution to a temporary problem; I wanted a temporary solution to a temporary problem. Cutting allowed myself this. The first time I cut myself, the cuts were shallow, offering tiny beads of blood. I can remember feeling the sting in my wrist and the shame in my heart. I bandaged myself and went to bed. I never thought I would continue to do [this] on and off for over four years.

At first I cut myself on a situational basis. If I had a rough day, before I went to bed I would make myself bleed. I should have known better though because I have an easily addictive personality. I became a guru at learning how to hide my pain on my wrist and but appearing to wear my heart on my sleeve. To everyone I was the same happy girl they had always known and loved, but inside I was killing myself. Soon the little scratches on my wrist weren't enough and I had to do something more drastic. I wore a watch to hide the cuts on my wrist and soon used it to do more than conceal. I would loosen my watch and bring it up to my forearm where I would tighten it again. As the veins popped in my wrist, I would cut myself. I stole a Leatherman pocketknife from my father. This became my instrument of choice. The more I bled, the better I felt. I was in love.

I loved cutting myself so much because I never allowed the people around me to see the pain they inflicted upon me. I was always happy; I never cried. To me, cutting was proof of the pain other people unconsciously inflicted upon me, and the pain I was inflicting upon myself. When my parents yelled at me, I'd cut myself; when I got a bad grade, I'd cut myself; when a friend was upset with me, I'd cut myself. I always had a smile on throughout my ordeal. Sometimes when people would comment about how happy I always was, I wanted to take my watch off and show them my battle scars. I wanted to scream at them, "Happy?! Happy?! Look! Look at what you're doing to me!" However, in the back of my mind, I always knew I was doing it to myself.

Work was always a stressful place during my adolescence. My love for cutting caused me to cut myself before every shift at work. Sometimes I'd be running late and would cut myself as I drove. Cutting myself revolved around two strong feelings. The first feeling was despair, hopelessness, and sadness. As soon as I made the cuts and watched my blood collect on my wrist, I instantly felt better. I was in love with feeling better. Over time, this feeling wasn't enough. I had to make more cuts, but never any deeper cuts. As I have said, I never hoped to cut deep enough to result in my death. I just loved seeing my blood and how it made me feel.

At one point, my wrist was too mutilated to further cut. I would never drag my knife through already open cuts; I always cut in an area that had already healed. After one particularly hellish week, my wrist was in shambles. Red lines covered the half-inch section of my wrist that was hidden by my watch. I thought, "What should I do? I can't live without cutting myself. I need it." That's when I realized how much I loved it and what the power of love makes a person feel. You need it. Love is like a drug and sometimes people cannot get enough of it. Thankfully it was winter and long sleeves were in style. Cutting myself was always harder in the spring because short sleeves exposed too much skin that was perfect for mutilation. I cut myself close to my elbow; it was a single perfect line. I wanted more. Five minutes and 3 paper towels later, I had 45 or 50 cuts that decorated my forearm. It felt wonderful.

I knew my love for cutting myself wasn't healthy. At the time, I had developed confidants in two seniors, a guy and a girl, who both knew what I was going through. I could call them at any time if I needed to talk, and they would tell me that they understood what I felt. They didn't understand; they betrayed me. The last day of school my sophomore year, I was called down to the nurse's office. It was last period and I had the global regents to take the next day. I was incredibly nervous for it, and when I was called down to the nurse's office, the nervousness translated to fear. My heart dropped. I knew what was to come.

The school psychologist and nurse asked me to show them my wrist. Hoping they wouldn't press, I showed them my right wrist which was unmarked by any cutting; I had always cut on my left. They asked me to show them the other wrist, which I did. My watch covered the cuts and I thought I was safe. I wasn't. The nurse asked me to take my watch off. As soon as my watch left my wrist, I began to panic. I sputtered excuses, saying I was stressed out about finals and that I had only cut myself one time, and it happened to be the night before. They had to call one of my parents, and I knew that my mom would not handle my situation well. They called my dad. After talking to him for a few minutes, they put me on the phone with him. I tried to keep calm and composed, figuring that if I pretended it wasn't a big deal they would all believe me. They didn't.

My dad came to school and took me to a psychiatric clinic specifically for teenagers. I felt sick the whole way there. Why was this happening to me? Why was everyone trying to take away the one thing in my life that made me feel good? Why rob me of the one thing that I loved and loved me back? At the clinic my acting skills were in full force. The girl who was always smiling to mask her pain was able to do the same with the doctor there. I said I had cut myself because of finals and stress and that I had never done it before. They bought it. They declared me "normal" and sent me home with my dad. I knew what I was doing wasn't normal.

While I never gave up cutting completely, I don't do it with the same frequency I once did. After the first "episode" (as my parents love to call them) my parents kept a close eye on me. What they didn't know was that I resorted to cutting my hip, a place they never saw. I never had the same satisfaction that I felt when I cut my wrist, but at least it was something. I had my second "episode" in the beginning of my junior year. I wasn't taken to a clinic this time. They called my dad again and he had to come pick me up from school. The nurse and my guidance counselor were going to let my parents deal with me at their discretion. I'll never forget the confusion I felt when I talked to my dad on the phone the second time. He was upset he had to leave work early to deal with this again. He told me, "Well, you're not in that much trouble." I was going to be punished for this? From then on, I knew that the only person I would be able to rely on was myself. If anyone was going to make me better, it would be me.

Cutting myself was my first love, and as the saying goes, you never forget your first love. I have gone months without cutting only to succumb to it for a weeklong rendezvous with a pair of scissors. As a result of counseling, I haven't cut my wrist in over a year, and haven't cut myself at all in 7 months. I now have a therapist I can talk to whenever I feel sad, and she always knows when I cut myself and why; it's part of our agreement. I stay away from cutting my wrist because I still have the scars from years ago. A pain comes to my heart when I think of what my children will ask me when they see my scars. In church, I always examined my mother's hands; I would pretend to paint her nails, take off her rings and put them on my own fingers, as well as mull over every line, vein, and surface area. Whenever I saw an uncommon mark on her hand, I always asked her, "What's that?" Usually it was a birthmark, or a scar from gardening or something benign like riding her bike as a child. What am I supposed to say to my children when they see my scar?

I feel like an alcoholic in rehab sometimes. I can remember exactly how long it's been since I've had my "last cut" as they know exactly how long it's been since they've had their last drink. I loved cutting myself because it made me feel better; that's why people fall in love; it makes them feel better. I now feel better when I talk about my problems with my therapist. I am no longer a threat to myself, because I have learned how to handle my emotions without returning to the comfort of my first love. While I am ashamed of what I used to do, I can't say that I am upset that I resorted to self-mutilation. More people cut themselves than you think. In our class alone I can imagine that there are about 8 people who have cut themselves in the past. My experiences haven't weakened me, they have made me stronger. I'm even talking to my school nurse about incorporated self-mutilation into the curriculum in health classes. I want everyone to know that cutting yourself is wrong. It may make you feel better instantly, but what about when your "high" wears off? You are left in the same emotional status in which you entered.

I have replaced my love for cutting with a love for talking. I love talks that occur at 3am and last till 6 am. At hours like these, people feel their confessions are safer than if they were to occur at 1 pm.

I have learned a lot from my experience with love. I fell in love hard, and fell out of love hard. Most importantly, I have learned how to love myself. While I'm sure there will be a boyfriend in my future who I can share love with, right now, I'm content with being in love with life.

Unlike Christine's and Cordelia's brief references to cutting themselves, Maryann focuses unflinchingly on the details. She begins by describing the "emptiness" in her heart and the effort to fill it with "unhealthy habits." She knows that cutting herself was a mistake, one of the "biggest mistakes" of her life, but she is irresistibly drawn to it. She records in detail how and when she started to cut herself, noting that over time she had to cut herself more frequently though not more deeply to receive the same gratification from the act. Using simple, powerful language, she contrasts the superficial happiness conveyed by the forced smile on her face with the deeper anguish of her heart, affirming pleasure-in-pain: "The more I bled, the better I felt. I was in love."

Maryann's reasons for cutting resemble Patty's and those of the protagonists of adolescent cutting novels. They write about a period in their adolescence when they felt anguished, isolated, and misunderstood. Maryann's arms and wrists were a more accurate indication of her inner life than the smiling expression on her face. The women's scars were thus a physical marker of their unhappiness, revealing the truth that they were unable to express publicly. Both Maryann and Patty turned to cutting as a way to feel better: they never doubt that cutting prevented them from inflicting more serious injuries. Indeed, cutting was apparently the only way they could maintain a degree of control over their lives, which were spinning out of control. As the protagonist of Shelley Stoehr's novel *Crosses* says, "When we cut, we're in control—we make our own pain, and we can stop it whenever we want. Physical pain relieves mental anguish. For a brief moment, the pain of the cutting is the only thing in the cutter's mind, and when that stops and the other comes back, it's weaker. Drugs do that too, and sex, but not like cutting. Nothing is like cutting" (33–34).

Both Maryann and Patty sought to keep their cutting private—though the former was unable to do so. Both imply attachment problems during their adolescence, resulting in isolation and alienation. Both implicate parents in their unhappiness but do not imply radically defective or cruel parenting. Both suggest that cutting is largely a problem of the past. Maryann is in her early twenties and thus not as detached from cutting as is Patty, who is a decade older, but she seems to write about a past problem. However untypical cutting may be, they both write about their lives as generally "normal," and most readers would be able to identify with their situations. Although Maryann is a striking example of the contagion effect, infected by watching a television program, she is always able to "differentiate between make-believe and reality," as Patty puts it. And both are now motivated to disclose their histories as cutters in order to warn others not to make the same mistakes they did.

Unlike Patty, Maryann evokes the details of cutting. Indeed, her descriptions are as aesthetically powerful and convincing as those in the cutting novels. She is as articulate as any of the narrators in *The Skin Game*, *Crosses*, *Cut*, *Girl, Interrupted*, or *Thin Skin*, and more insightful than some of them in understanding the reasons for her cutting. She is also probably more successful than any of them in maintaining reader identification and suspense. I was especially moved by her ability to peer into the future to imagine the difficulty in explaining the scars to her children. Unlike the fictional cutters, she is determined to tell everyone about the dangers of cutting—though she doesn't explain how she will be able to do so without inadvertently awakening this dark love in younger versions of herself.

Was Maryann correct in suggesting that as many as eight of her classmates had also cut themselves? The figure struck me as far too high at the time—but this was before the publication of the Whitlock, Eckenrode, and Silverman study indicating that 17 percent of college students engage in self-injurious behaviors. But Caroline Kettlewell would have agreed with Maryann: "I can tell you that on a global human scale, ritualized self-mutilation is surprisingly common. What in Western culture is pathologized as an indicator of profound dysfunction is in other cultures the very vehicle, the visible sign of a society's claim upon that body—in scarification, in tattoos, and in measures more drastic than anything I ever considered" (58–59).

Maryann's essay was not only her best of the semester but one of the most memorable submitted by anyone in her class. It is technically strong, containing only a few grammatical ("it's instead of "it has," "who I can share" instead of "whom I can share"), stylistic (the colloquialism "big deal"), and typographical ("incorporated" instead of "incorporating") errors. The essay is also balanced and nuanced. She has little trouble in maintaining a sympathetic yet critical attitude toward her former "love," and she uses effective parallelisms, as when she writes, "I can remember feeling the sting in my wrist and the shame in my heart." She never minimalizes the physical problems caused by cutting. Throughout most of the essay she shows rather than tells: thus she reveals how at first her watch covered the cuts on her wrist, but later she is forced to cut other parts of her body to escape detection. She makes us feel her growing panic when she is sent to the school nurse, and we feel her shame when she is finally caught.

"Shame," notes Francis Broucek, "makes us want to hide; we avert our gaze and hang our head in shame. Shame is so painful that we hope it ends quickly; we have no particular desire to reflect on it or talk about it, because to do so is to run the risk of reexperiencing it" (4). Yet to write about shame, as Maryann does here, is not only *not* to run and hide but also to linger and reflect on it. To acknowledge one's shame is to adopt a "countershame" technique—shaming shame, so to speak, so that it no longer paralyzes the self.

What type of writing should we call Maryann's essay? It is certainly personal writing, and it is also *risky* writing, filled with admissions that result in heightened vulnerability. Compositionists would call this *expressive* writing. "Some expressive teachers," Richard Fulkerson observes, "are interested in helping students mature and become self-aware, more reflective. Others are interested in writing as healing or therapy. Some are most interested in creative self-expression. Some have students choose their own topics; others have concerns they want students to address" (667–68). Fulkerson quotes Chris Burnham's description of expressive pedagogy: "Expressionism places the writer in the center, articulates its theory, and develops its pedagogical system by assigning highest value to the writer and her imaginative, psychological, social, and spiritual development and how that development influences individual consciousness and social behavior" (667).

I agree with these characterizations, but I find the word "expressive" misleading and dismissive. As Carolyn Ericksen Hill remarks in *Writing from the Margins*, expressive writing "carries with it a negative value judgment nowadays for some people in composition studies: expressive writing as opposed to the more serious expository. To express oneself has been associated with pressing something out from an inside (often, an emotion-full subject presumably needing to release pressure), as opposed to indicating to others something 'objective' which is already outside oneself" (109). As I point out in *Risky Writing*, "Many of the most visible opponents of personal writing are staunch foes of capitalism and believe that writing teachers should train their students to critique and 'resist' society" (24).

Louise Kaplan suggests in *Female Perversions* that the self-cutter is "unable to communicate her anxiety and rage and longing in words" (385). Cutting is thus a form of communication. So is writing about cutting. A pen becomes the alternative to a knife, allowing one to express anxiety, rage, and longing on paper instead of on the skin. Cutting provides relief by carving violent emotions into the flesh, where they draw blood and fester. By contrast, writing is a way to express and release these emotions on paper, where they can be read by everyone. Writing may seem as dangerous as cutting, as Sylvia Plath observes in the poem "Kindness": "The blood jet is poetry / There is no stopping it" (270). Nevertheless, writing, unlike cutting, rarely poses a literal danger to one's health. Females who write about cutting are part of the tradition of women who write about anger and (self-)victimization: "rage and savage indignation sear the hearts of female poets and female critics" (Marcus 94).

Maryann's essay is as analytical as it is emotional. She uses many insight verbs, including "thought," "realized," "knew," "understand," and "learned," which appears four times. These insight verbs suggest she sees the past in a new way that is associated with emotional and cognitive processing. As James Pennebaker and M. E. Francis have demonstrated, the category of words most predictive of improved health is cognitive word use—words denoting cause and insight. Maryann's essay also reveals an interest in cultural studies as well as personal development. She doesn't mention feminism, yet her writing would be of interest to feminist scholars. Her essay is an example of "women's writing," exposing violence against the female body. She doesn't use the word "liberation," but her essay dramatizes the liberatory impulse that is central to feminism. The essay demonstrates the feminist belief that the personal is the political while at the same time affirming the Socratic injunction that knowledge is power.

Maryann implies that she was self-destructive during this time, yet cutting made her feel better and prevented her from greater self-harm. According to mental health professionals, this phenomenon is true of most cutters, including Patty, Cordelia, and Christine. Maryann conveys the pleasure and relief associated with cutting without letting us forget the damage she was doing to her body. Her voice takes on an ironic quality when she refers to herself as a "guru" at learning how to hide the pain on her wrist. Her description of "falling in love" with cutting is more powerful than "falling out of love," but she never loses sight of the fact that she is writing a cautionary tale, hoping to convince her readers not to make the same terrible mistake that she did.

Does Maryann romanticize cutting? I wasn't sure. She knows that good writing involves showing rather than telling, and she gives us the concrete details that enable us to visualize the experience of cutting. Thus she describes the pair of scissors with shiny blue handles, the watch that she wore to conceal the cuts, the veins popping in her wrist, the red lines signifying cuts on her flesh, and the paper towels used to absorb the blood. The reference to the "popped veins" in her wrist recalls Armando Favazza's observation about the dramatic reduction of tension people feel after cutting themselves. "When tense patients cut themselves, they in fact often describe the result in words such as, 'It's like lancing a boil' or, 'It's like popping a balloon.' The implied metaphor is clear: in cutting their skin they provide an opening through which the tension and badness in their bodies rapidly escape" (194). Maryann's details authenticate the essay and contribute to its aesthetic power. To the extent that the essay conveys the writer's passion for cutting, it might be viewed as glorifying cutting, especially since she spends more time describing "falling in" rather than "out of" love. Nevertheless, I did not feel that she dwelled excessively or morbidly on the details of cutting. Nor did I doubt that she succeeded in describing why she fell out of love with this destructive activity.

Was Maryann in imminent danger of further harming herself? I didn't think so, and for that reason I decided not to contact the university counseling center. She writes in the third paragraph that suicide is a "permanent solution to a temporary problem," adding that she hasn't cut herself in seven months. She succeeds in conveying the intoxicating emotions associated with cutting, but she always reminds us that she knew what she was doing to her body was harmful. She mentions using her "acting skills" when she was required to attend a psychiatric clinic for teenagers, but I did not feel that she was deceiving the reader. She recognizes that she is still tempted to cut herself—"I feel like an alcoholic in rehab sometimes"—but she has a realistic understanding of her "addictive personality" and seems to be making good progress in her recovery. Psychotherapy has apparently helped her to understand why she cut herself in the past, though she doesn't share these reasons with the reader. She ends the essay on a note of convincing resolution: "I am no longer a threat to myself, because I have learned how to handle my emotions without returning to the comfort of my first love." Indeed, she now wishes to use her experiences to educate others about the dangers of cutting, an education that may be seen in the writing of her essay.

I didn't know how hard it was for Maryann to write the paper or to turn it in to me. She trusted me to read it empathically, which I did. She remarks in the first paragraph that she has "always put up my guard when it comes to other people and emotional attachments." Now she was lowering her guard by submitting the essay to me. To write about the emptiness in one's heart and the effort to fill the void with a "love" as dangerous as cutting requires both strength and trust—in herself and in her reader.

How did I comment on Maryann's essay? Since she knew that cutting was harmful, I did not feel a need to repeat that observation in my comments. There was little that I could tell her about self-mutilation that she did not already know. Nor did I want her to feel heightened stigma or shame as a result of my comments. Instead, I began by praising the essay, noting in my comments that it was "beautifully written" and "deeply moving." I always commend students who write on risky topics, and I affirm their efforts to discover solutions to difficult problems. Risky essays tend to be well written, probably because students know they are writing on important topics and want to express themselves as well as possible. Nearly all of my comments focused on grammatical and stylistic revisions. I raised one substantive question. After telling the reader in the third paragraph that she was never trying to commit suicide, she states in the next paragraph that "inside I was killing myself," to which I responded: "do you want to use the expression 'killing myself' immediately after telling us that you were not suicidal?"

Only one statement in Maryann's essay did I find worrisome—the reference to the two "confidants" who "betrayed" her to the school nurse because they were concerned about her welfare. She assumes that they didn't "understand" her, but perhaps they knew what she was doing was harmful and were trying to be helpful. Perhaps they were being good friends and not traitors by sharing their concerns with the nurse. And perhaps she would have been worse off had they *not* sought counsel from the nurse. Toward the end of the essay she raises the possibility that she will talk to her former school nurse about incorporating self-mutilation into the health class curriculum; should she do so, she might note that friends can help by urging a cutter to speak to a parent, teacher, nurse, or counselor.

Maryann wrote the essay only for me, but I felt that it would be important for her classmates to hear it. Her essay not only creates awareness of self-cutting but also offers ways to overcome this problem. I knew there was the possibility that reading the essay aloud might inadvertently encourage classmates to "fall in love" with the same harmful habit. This was indeed how Maryann started to cut herself. Contrary to the intention of the television program *7th Heaven* to warn viewers *not* to cut themselves, she had reached the opposite conclusion. She was thus infected by the show's content. Teachers remain generally unaware of the emotional contagion phenomenon, either because they don't ask students to report such reactions or because students do not feel comfortable acknowledging that a story may trigger anxiety, depression, or panic, or encourage copycat behavior. By reading Maryann's essay on self-injurious behavior, would I reinforce what Ronni Stefl calls the "extrinsic sources of positive reinforcement such as attention" (2)? I didn't know.

I emailed Maryann for permission to read her essay anonymously, to which she agreed. Toward the end of the next class I announced that I was going to read aloud a graphic and disturbing essay written by a member of the class. Anyone who wished to leave before hearing the essay could do so, I said, adding that as with all anonymous essays, there would be no discussion afterward. I then read the essay in a quiet, measured voice, not wishing to make it more emotionally charged than it was. Afterward, everyone filed silently out of the room. I suspected that some students might wish to comment on this essay in their next assignment, which involved an oral presentation:

> For your oral presentation, I would like you to discuss a paper that you or a classmate has written in this course. This assignment should be written and thus will count toward the required forty pages, but it will also serve

as your oral presentation. You can occasionally refer to your paper during the oral presentation, but don't read it word for word.

Begin by summarizing the essay in one paragraph: what is the essay about, and for which assignment was it written? Was it hard or easy to write? How did you feel when you were reading the essay aloud? How would you judge the strengths and weaknesses of the essay? How did your classmates and teacher react to it? Were you pleased or displeased with their responses?

If you are writing about a classmates's essay, begin by summarizing it and then discuss how it affected you. Did the essay surprise you? What were its strengths and weaknesses? Have you continued to think about it? Has it influenced your own thinking and writing?

Paige: "I Too Had the Same Love"

Paige was the first to give her oral presentation. To put it in context, I must first cite an earlier essay that she read aloud. Of all the assignments that I give in Expository Writing, probably the most important and challenging is "A Letter to a Parent and His or Her Letter to You." I ask students to write two letters: in the first they describe their feelings toward one or both of their parents; in the second they imagine how one or both of their parents would respond. (The full assignment appears in the appendix to *Risky Writing*.) These letters are often the most emotionally charged writings of the semester. Students express powerful feelings—love, hate, gratitude, anger, joy, sadness. Many students come from divorced families and write letters to parents whom they haven't seen for months or years. Some students later show these letters to their parents, who are sometimes surprised by their children's feelings toward them. The assignment is valuable for several reasons. Writing helps students to understand how they feel about the people who have raised them—and how they are both similar to and different from their mother and father. Students often say that writing helps them to appreciate the people whom they usually take for granted. Imagining their parents' points of view is instructive: they discover the difficulty of imagining a (m)other who is not simply a version of themselves. They also learn about classmates' feelings toward their parents. Oscar Wilde's aphorism in *The Picture of Dorian Gray*—"Children begin by loving their parents; as they grow older they judge them; sometimes they forgive them" (20)—is true of some students. For others, like Paige, the parent-child relationship constitutes the vital center of life:

My Mommy,

We haven't talked in a while. I don't call you enough while I'm at school and even when I do we hardly converse. I talk, you try to respond, we interrupt each other and I know I should be better. So I'm writing this letter to you to make up for all the conversations we have not had. Besides, I think there are some things we need to discuss.

I've had the opportunity to learn a bit about a variety of people lately, and I've noticed many similarities, and also several differences. Everybody has had tragedy in his or her life, whether through friends or family. But even though all of this is the same, nobody seems to have quite the same relationship with their parents that I have with you. For that, I am so immensely grateful. I know that others view our relationship as slightly odd, and I know it even makes some people uncomfortable—I'm sure Gregory Santini wasn't too comfortable with the fact that I told you his . . . umm . . . size. But even if the way we relate is confusing to some, it works for me, and I wouldn't trade it for anything. This might seem like an inappropriate thing to say, but in a way I'm glad that Veronica was such a pain and treated you so horribly all those years. If she hadn't been so vile and anti-our-family, you and I would never have gotten as close as we did. Do you remember the day we stood at the kitchen counter and you asked me if I would start calling you Mommy again? I was 13, in seventh grade. You are my Mommy, and you always will be. Even when I'm forty-five and a woman with my own life and you're seventy-six and have no more children in your house I will still call you Mommy. I will still come to you to ask for back massages and tell you about my job, my husband, my gossipy coworkers, and my sex life. And you'll sit in your rocking chair and sip tea and listen. It sounds dorky, but I think of you as my best friend. Of course, as you know, I don't really have many friends, but even if I did you'd still be at the top. There is no one else who I feel I can go to with as much as I do to you. There is nobody else who I would wake up at

5:00 am with to go running. There is no one else who I know will literally knock food out of my hand for me when I'm on a diet. Obviously there are secrets that I keep from you, but you know about all that and I know you accept it too. And while I'm on that topic, there's something exceedingly important I need you to understand.

In light of what happened this past November, with me going to the hospital and everything, I think you deserve for me to explain some significant details to you. I'm tired of glossing the truth about what happened. I'm weary from lying. I don't care if it hurts you to hear it; we can't continue to mask this, or mask me. So I'm going to say it. I put myself in the hospital, knowingly and purposely. I wanted to die. I am so sorry, because I can see how much you and Dad were hurt by my actions, and you need to understand that at the time I didn't care. I refused to think about that aspect of what I was doing. I was so deep in my own mist of melancholy that I simply couldn't recognize anything but my own disappointment and ache. What happened was not your fault. You've lived with me for the past six years. You know I've been depressed. You've witnessed my slumps and falls and you were right here with me during my nervous breakdown. Remember that night? It was the end of summer; it was hot out. I had been shut up in my bedroom all night when suddenly, I came out and ran into the kitchen sobbing and screaming, and you were right there. You caught me when I collapsed and carried me to the couch. You stayed there the whole night, tried to talk to me, as scared as you were, and then you called my doctor the very next morning. You handled everything perfectly. Since then, you've driven me to therapy regularly and reminded me to take my pills every day. Now, when it's most important, you need to remember that what's wrong with me is something inside me, something internal and enduring. I don't know or understand what it is within me that's broken, but I do know for sure that it's nothing that you caused to crack. When I look back to when I was younger, and as I was maturing, I can only think of what amazing parents I had.

You were strict when you needed to be and lenient where it applied. You have always allowed me to make my own decisions about my life. Instead of telling me what to do all the time, you gave me your advice about what you thought was best and healthiest for me, but in the end you always told me it was my decision. I know you worry, but I wish you wouldn't, that if you had only been harder on me, if you hadn't left so much up to my own devising, that things would be different. They wouldn't. You did everything right. You found the ideal balance between parent and friend and I thank you eternally for that.

I couldn't ask for a better mother than you, and I want to be the best daughter I can be. I don't know what's going to happen in the years ahead, but no matter what happens, you will always be my favorite mommy, and I will always love you.

Love,

Paige

*   *   *   *   *

Oh Paige—my—Paige,

Reading your letter made me cry, but not tears of sadness. They were tears of joy and pride. I am always blown away by your ability to be so straightforward with me. You have an ability to be so very honest with your feelings, even when I try to hide my own thoughts and emotions. You have been through more than I could ever imagine in your life. Many obstacles have been thrown your way, and I have tried to be there for you through all of it. It is hard for me not to wonder if I could have done something to keep you from falling so far that you felt you had no other option than what you did. Through my doubt though, I do trust you in saying that it was not your father's or my fault. You have absolutely no idea how upset your dad and I were the day we got the call from Albany Med saying you had been brought into the emergency room. I had never made it to Albany in less than four hours before, but that day it couldn't have taken longer than three to get to you. We were so scared we'd lose you. I couldn't imagine my life without you, Paige. You are the bright spot in my day. I look forward to hearing your voice all week until you call me. I miss every weekday when I used to pick you up from school, and even two years later every time I'm on my way home all I can think about is you. I still remember all those nights we stayed up late together watching movies, baking cookies, and just talking. I miss you so much while you are away at school. I wish sometimes that I had forced you to go to school in Rochester, just so I could keep you home all to myself.

You and your brothers mean so much to me, regardless of the difficulties we all had with each other. I got something special and unique from my relationship with each one of my children, and I wouldn't be able to get along without each piece of that puzzle. You are the one I can open up to the most. You are the one who I know will come to me with anything and everything. Just like you said all those years ago, I am your chalkboard. You can confide in me any time you need to, and I will never pass judgment on you. You can say anything to me and come back just an hour later and erase it. I love you and respect your thoughts and feelings. I may not always agree with you or even understand you, but I will always listen to you and support you in your decisions.

You are a wonderful and intelligent girl, and you are becoming an even more amazing and impressive young woman. I look forward to many more years of girl talk and back rubs and stories about boyfriends as well as breakups. I hope you know I am here for whenever you need me. Through the good and the bad I am always your mother and I will always hold you dear in my heart. I love you, Paige, please don't ever forget that.

Love always,
Mother

The first two paragraphs of Paige's letter describe a mother-daughter relationship so intimate and lighthearted that we may need to read the third paragraph more than once to grasp what happened to her less than four months earlier. As close as she is to her mother, Paige has—until now—withheld the reasons she "put" herself in the hospital. She never uses the word, but we infer a suicide attempt resulting in hospitalization. She now recognizes, as presumably she did not before, that her actions were devastating to her parents. And she is now filled with guilt and sadness over the pain she has caused them. Through writing, she needs to reassure her parents that they were not the reason she became depressed and suffered a breakdown. She cannot explain what exactly happened to her: the use of the present tense implies an ongoing problem, something that is still "broken." She ends the letter on a note of uncertainty, though she implies that she will always love her mother.

Paige imagines her mother responding lovingly, devotingly, nonjudgmentally. It is easy to forget that the daughter, not the mother, pens the letter. I've never seen a chalkboard used to describe the communication between a parent and child, but the metaphor conveys the belief that words can be withdrawn as if they have never been expressed. She might have used another metaphor, a palimpsest, to suggest that previously erased words may still leave a trace.

It was understandably difficult for Paige to read aloud these two letters—and even more difficult for her to give her oral presentation. Walking to the front of the classroom, she was visibly distressed and on the verge of tears. She began by saying that she hoped her comments would not offend the anonymous author of the cutting essay, with which she identified closely. Emotionally charged, Paige's oral presentation was based on the following essay, from which she paraphrased as she spoke:

When I first received this assignment I thought I knew exactly what I wanted to write about. I have only read one paper to the class and I figured I didn't have much of a selection to choose from. Then, just this past class, something happened that completely changed my mind about this oral essay.

On Monday, Jeff read an anonymous essay about a student who had fallen in love with cutting. I was hit so hard by this essay that I almost had to get up in the middle of the reading and leave class. I was not shocked by the frankness of the subject matter, nor was I upset by the idea of someone being in so much pain. I was simply struck dumb because I myself almost wrote that exact same paper. The words that Jeff spoke were so much my own that I actually wondered to myself if I had somehow written the paper and forgotten about it—blocked it out of my mind in a fit of frantic repression. It was not so. There were a few differences in the essay that made it abundantly clear to me that what was being read was not in fact my story, but this did not make hearing it any easier.

Throughout the time that Jeff was reading it, my eyes looked up every once in a while to scan the class. I could not help but try to guess who had written the paper about being in love with self-mutilation. As I glanced from student to student I noticed something distressing. My peers were looking back at me, some of them with suspicious looks plastered on their faces. They thought I was the one who had written the essay. They had good reason to. I do cut myself. I have for over four years. I am usually very careful to wear long sleeves and never expose my arms, but there was one occasion in the beginning of the semester when it was simply too hot to keep my sleeves down, and I know for a fact that at least two students noticed my scars. I was infuriated. But that was not the only emotion that coursed rabidly through my veins.

Along with being incensed that I would be an immediate suspect as the writer of the essay I was jealous that I didn't write it myself! I was pissed off that someone else got credit for such an addiction. I know it sounds horribly sick, but it was how I felt. I wanted to figure out the real author and talk to them. I wanted to tell them I too had the same love. I know how she felt. I understood. The part in the essay in which the author described how she felt when people told her she always seemed so happy nearly made me cry. The only way I held back was by reminding myself that if I burst out in tears there would be no way anybody in the class would not think I was the anonymous addict. But the line that read something like, "I wanted to scream, 'happy? Happy?!? You think I'm happy?' and take off my watch and show them the cuts" hit me so hard I felt I'd get the *wind knocked out of me. The whole essay was powerful. It is possible that I liked it in large part simply because I identified with it. It was an interesting experience to be able to compare my own experiences and my own techniques with those of one of my classmates. There was a sense of camaraderie between myself and this nameless person. It almost made me happy. Interestingly enough, there was a feeling of being cheated too. In my own disturbing way, I felt that if I ever chose to write about my own struggles with self-mutilation, it would seem like I was simply copying whoever wrote about it first. Regardless of all these intense emotions, the feeling that effected me most of all was desire.*

I very recently gave up cutting myself (for the third time). Just five days ago I gave all my boxes of razor blades, my refills for my Exacto knife, both of my scalpels and my precious, authentic Swiss army knife to my boyfriend and vowed not to cut myself anymore. Already, since then I have wanted to cut several times. I was struck by the craving once again during class. There is no other way to describe it other than to say I was pissed off that I couldn't go back to my empty room after class and slice open my own skin. All I can do now is pick at my more recent scabs and watch them bleed their old blood. But it's not the same. I don't get the same rush from it and it is not exactly nearly as satisfying as creating new gashes.

Even now, I am getting carried away by my own addiction to this sick activity. I am going off on a tangent about the exhilaration and calm that washes over me when I open up a new cut. The important thing is, out of all the essays we have heard in class, this one affected me the most. It is a close race between this piece and one or two others that were read in the beginning of the semester. Based on the fact that I almost could not make it through the entire period though, I have to say that this essay was the most influential. Even now, hours and days after hearing it, I have still been thinking about who may have written such an intense piece. Who feels the same way I do? Who shares such a love for watching their own blood gush down their arms? Who knows what it feels like to love the pain? Who understands me?

The most powerful section of Paige's essay for me is the ending, where she raises four questions that affirm kinship to an unknown classmate. Each of the questions is simple and direct, evoking mystery and urgency. These questions convey a startling recognition of being understood by another person, a classmate who is able to read her mind and understand her violent passion. She challenges her anonymous classmate to reveal herself while at the same time she knows that the author may not feel safe enough to unmask herself. Nor does she feel entirely safe.

Paige seems to identify with Maryann's description of falling in rather than out of love with cutting. An essay that I hoped would be a cautionary tale had the opposite effect, reawakening Paige's "craving" to resume an action that she had ended only recently. Maryann's response to the cutting episode on *7th Heaven* and Paige's response to her classmate's essay both reveal the contagion effect, where viewers or readers find themselves infected with virulent emotions that threaten to undermine their health. Maryann's essay evoked in Paige what Hatfield and her colleagues call a complementary response. As if to demonstrate unconsciously this virulent contagion, Paige refers to the emotions that "coursed rabidly" (instead of "rapidly") through her veins, a typographical error that may be a Freudian slip. She was susceptible to emotional contagion, according to Hatfield and associates, presumably because her attention was riveted on Maryann's essay, with which she identified so closely, and also because she was able to understand the "dark love" described by her classmate. She identified with the cutter's need for secrecy, which was now being exposed by her classmates' stares.

Paige felt that writing an essay on cutting would be "simply copying" the author of the anonymous essay, and on one level, her oral presentation may be viewed as an example of copycat behavior. She would not have spoken or written about cutting had it not been for Maryann's essay. But on another and, I believe, deeper level, Maryann's essay may be seen as having inspired Paige's self-disclosure. We generally use the word "copycat" to describe harmful behavior, and it is evident that Paige's presentation is not a destructive but a constructive self-disclosure, intended to illuminate a serious problem that demands immediate attention. If

Maryann's essay reawakens Paige's craving to cut herself, it also shows that such craving can be resisted. To return to Ultra's metaphor, an essay or story may be an inoculation that heightens our resistance to illness.

Paige's response confirms an observation I made in *Diaries to an English Professor*: students identify so strongly with an anonymous diary that they may wonder for a moment whether they actually wrote it:

> Some students have told me that when I began reading a particular diary to the class, it seemed at first to be their own—until they realized that the entry was written by another classmate. They identified so closely with the contents of the diary that they actually thought I was reading their own writing. It was an uncanny feeling, they said, as if they had recognized the existence of a doppelganger in the class. Other students have told me about having the opposite experience, not realizing for several seconds that I was reading their own entry aloud. For these students, the initial feeling of detachment from their diary suddenly gave way to a recognition of involvement. In both cases, the students experienced an epiphanic repositioning of self and other. (229–30)

Paige's realization that she did not write the essay led first to self-consciousness—she feared that her classmates would think she was the author—then to disappointment and regret, followed by envy: "I was pissed off that someone else got credit for such an addiction."

Competition exists in most if not all classrooms, and it can be healthy or harmful. Competition can motivate students to improve their writing skills, but it can also lead them to outdo each other in stories of suffering. Recall Cordelia's recommendation that I attempt to minimize students' pressure to outperform their classmates: "I felt a need to outdo my fellow students. 'Maybe your mom was a drunk, but my whole family was drunk.'" Paige refers to the same implicit competition with Maryann. "I was pissed off that someone else got credit for such an addiction. I know it sounds horribly sick, but it was how I felt." Interestingly, Kafka's hunger artist feels similar competition, wishing to break his own record of fasting, and both wanting and not wanting others to admire him for an act that he cannot stop.

The protocols that I put into place to prevent students from becoming at risk were now being tested as never before. Paige feared that her classmates believed that she was the author of the anonymous essay, and the fear was generating extreme anxiety. The belief that she would involuntarily disclose her secret identity as a cutter reminded me of one of

Freud's most suggestive statements: "He that has eyes to see and ears to hear may convince himself that no mortal can keep a secret. If his lips are silent, he chatters with his finger-tips; betrayal oozes out of him at every pore" (*Fragment of an Analysis* 77–78). Students have the option not to write on any topic that they deem too personal or threatening, but Paige now seemed to be pressured to disclose her experience with cutting to dispel her classmates' erroneous belief that she was the author of the anonymous essay. Maryann's self-disclosure created a catch-22 situation for her.

Maryann may have overestimated the number of cutters in her class, but here was a striking confirmation that at least one person shared her illicit love. Paige felt a close bond with her unknown classmate, whom she regarded as a silent comrade despite feelings of competition with her. She ends the essay by addressing her secret sharer, who has demonstrated, through an anonymous essay, an uncanny ability to understand Paige's own hidden passion.

The 1960s was the formative decade for me, both personally and educationally, and the rallying cry of college students then was the demand for "relevance." Paige's essay was far more relevant than I could have imagined. And it was more honest in its acknowledgment of unruly emotions than one might have expected in an essay that seeks to distance itself from newly repudiated behavior. The powerful verbs in her writing attest to the anonymous essay's impact on her. She was "struck dumb" by the paper; she felt that the wind was "knocked out" of her; she feared that she would "burst into tears"; she found herself "getting carried away"; and she was "struck by the craving" to resume cutting herself. She knows that she is getting carried away by her addiction, "going off on a tangent about the exhilaration and calm that washes over me when I open up a new cut." Nevertheless, she seems scarcely able to help herself. The images and metaphors suggest not simply a passive contagion effect but being actively swept away, rendered unconscious. She makes no effort to hold back her anger toward classmates who, she fears, are gazing at her cut arms. They "infuriate" her.

"There's always a touch of fascination in revulsion," Susanna Kaysen writes in *Girl, Interrupted* (124). Perhaps so, but I found nothing lurid in Paige's essay. I did not feel then, nor do I feel now, that she was writing mainly for attention. I found nothing "crazy" or "sick" about her essay or Maryann's. Nor did I feel like a voyeur when listening to Paige's presentation or reading her essay. Voyeurs gaze at forbidden sights; I was looking at what the author wanted me to read. I was moved by her efforts to overcome her addiction, and I was struck by her empathy for an anonymous classmate.

"This is a moving and heartfelt essay," I wrote in my comments on Paige's paper, "and except for a few colloquialisms, it is well written." I made several grammatical and stylistic revisions, changing "pissed off" to "angry," "got credit" to "received credit," "effected me" to "affected me," "rabidly" to "rapidly," "between myself and this nameless person" to "between this nameless person and me," and "exhilaration and calm that washes over me" to "exhilaration and calm that wash over me." I suggested two other revisions, using a comma after the introductory clause on which she begins the essay and changing the second sentence so that she didn't end on a preposition. These are the types of technical criticisms that I make on all student writings, criticisms that are generally appreciated and helpful. I avoided any comments that might have caused Paige to regret her self-disclosure.

Did I make a mistake in reading aloud Maryann's essay? Did hearing the essay reawaken Paige's craving to cut herself? There is certainly evidence to reach this conclusion. Any writing that incites a reader to (self-)violence may be considered too dangerous to share with classmates. For this reason most high school teachers would be reluctant to share Maryann's essay with the class. But should college teachers practice the same restraint—or censorship? However disturbing the essay was to Paige, however self-conscious and exposed she felt on hearing it, and however it reawakened her craving to cut herself, she does acknowledge the value of knowing that she has something important in common with at least one classmate. "There was a sense of camaraderie between myself and this nameless person. It almost made me happy." This camaraderie, or attachment bond, enables Paige to feel less isolated and misunderstood, even if the identity of her fellow student remains unknown.

The contagion effect implies the "catching" of other people's emotions. We can see this when Paige refers to the feeling of exhilaration and calm associated with cutting. Such contagions are obviously countertherapeutic. But the anonymous essay also has an anticontagion or therapeutic influence on Paige, for she implies that she now feels less isolated, misunderstood, and stigmatized. Her willingness to write and speak openly about a problem that presumably she has shared with few people shows her desire to overcome it. She was not only identifying with an anonymous classmate's unhealthy addiction but also showing how, like her classmate, she has attempted to end what she knows is harmful behavior.

Just as Paige was moved by a classmate's anonymous essay, so were her classmates affected by her own self-disclosure. Ronna empathized with Paige despite feeling "envy" that her classmate had a supportive boyfriend to help her.

Ronna: "I Am Glad that I Can Empathize with a Classmate So Strongly"

I probably don't need to remind you that I choked up while I was reading my letter to my father in class. I was uncharacteristically open in that letter, and I didn't realize this until I attempted to share it with 20 strangers. However, it was not my own letter that evoked my most biting emotional response during that round of presentations; due to a single line in her letter to her mother, I found Paige's letter to her mother to be harder for me to swallow than even my own.

Paige presented an exceptionally honest, open, and eloquent letter that dealt with depression, an issue many people are uncomfortable disclosing and discussing. I certainly was. It also happened to be an issue that I was dealing with at the time, so her letter held particular significance to me. I sympathized, and more importantly, empathized with her deeply as she read her letter; when she read the sentence that discussed the incident in which she revealed her depression to her mother, I completely lost my composure. Not two weeks before, I had conducted a similar conversation with my own mother. It was among the most difficult conversations I had ever had. I knew exactly why Paige started crying when she read that sentence; I cried too. I cried for her; I cried for myself; I cried for everybody who has ever had to have that conversation.

When I came back to school at the beginning of the semester, I quickly found myself at an all-time emotional low. Due to a variety of factors, I found myself spending two or three hours sobbing myself to sleep every night. I didn't tell my friends or my ex-boyfriend about these sessions because, in large part, I felt they were to blame. I felt as though I had befallen on the most unfortunate circumstances of my life, and now, when I needed them most, they were distancing themselves from me. It was twofold anxiety, and it consumed me. One night I reached for the phone at two-thirty; I thought I had reached my breaking point. I didn't think I could handle this alone anymore. I wanted to call my mom. I wanted to cry to her. I wanted her to make me feel better, because I knew only she could or would. However, I ultimately decided against it, reasoning that I was tired and exhausted and I was overreacting. I resolved that I would call her in the morning if I was still so upset. I awoke in the morning still discontent; but, as my sobs had subsided, I decided I must be improving, and better not to burden Mom with worries for me.

Ordinarily, while I am away at school, I talk to my mom on a daily basis. On many levels, I am closer to her than to many of my friends. I didn't call her once during the first week I was back. I didn't want to tell her how I was feeling, but I was in such a state that I knew I wouldn't be able to convey contrary feelings convincingly. She started leaving me worried voicemails, but I couldn't return them. I finally answered one of her calls because I knew she was worried that I had been kidnaped or murdered. She greeted me, and asked how everything was going. I tried to say "fine," but I couldn't even muster the word. I started crying, and I cried for a solid three minutes before I could finally respond, "I am so . . . sad." This was perhaps the most difficult thing I have ever said to my mother. My mother has spent my entire life enslaved by devotion to my happiness. Heretofore, she had been extremely successful; for most of my life, I had never been a morose individual or even a content individual. I had always been a markedly happy individual. I didn't know what it was like to be sad for an extended period of time, and I certainly didn't know how to handle feelings of mild depression. I was a mess. Though it was no fault of her own, I knew my mother would assume responsibility. I couldn't bear for her to think she had failed me in any way when that was so far from the truth. Of course, I felt better after talking to her, but I felt guilty for laying my problems upon her shoulders. She doesn't deserve it.

This incident was still fresh in my mind when Paige read her letter to the class. So fresh that the wound wasn't reopened; it hadn't yet had time to heal. I found Paige's letter to her mother to be among the most well written from any in the class; yet this one sentence was all that was necessary to evoke my complete empathy.

When Paige stood in front of the class and conducted her oral presentation in response to the essay on cutting, I found myself once again strongly empathizing with her, yet this time in a different way. When she revealed herself to be a cutter, I was filled with sympathy and regret. I sympathized with the fact that she could be so unhappy so as to be driven to self-mutilation; I regretted how destructive the very real repercussions of this habit could be, because I have been impressed with everything Paige has read to us and I hate to think she could choose to be self-destructive when she is so clearly intelligent.

However, my deepest empathy came with Paige's comment that she had a twisted envy of the anonymous writer of the original cutting essay, for that writer had "stolen her thunder" and, in Paige's mind, devalued anything Paige may have written in the future about her similar experience. I didn't empathize with her because I felt another member of the class had "stolen my thunder"; I rather empathized to the general feeling of twisted envy, and my envy was directed at Paige. She mentioned that after she had heard the original cutting essay, she called her boyfriend and met him outside of the Humanities building because she couldn't stand to be alone. Though I was sincerely relieved that Paige had such a person in her life to support her through this ordeal, I was envious that I do not. I harkened back to the beginning of the semester, when I spent every *second wanting not to be alone, and the more I made this apparent to my boyfriend at the time, the more alone he left me. When I finally confronted the issue, he admitted that I was more of an emotional load than he was willing to carry. Paige's acknowledgment of her boyfriend's supportiveness brought to my mind the reminder that when I needed support, I was devoid. I was jealous.*

A year ago, even six months ago, Paige's writings would not have had nearly as much impact on me. I am glad I took this class when I did. I am glad that I am able to empathize with a classmate so strongly. I am glad that I am able to read a classmate's work and think "I know exactly what that feels like." And though I don't really talk to her and she will probably never even know this, I am glad Paige has someone who empathizes with her.

Shall we say that Ronna caught Paige's envy and jealousy, as she herself says? Perhaps, but the dominant feeling is one of sympathy and concern for a vulnerable classmate—*two* vulnerable classmates. As Ronna's essay demonstrates, a student's empathy for a classmate may exist despite feelings of envy or jealousy. Ronna empathized with Paige's pain and loneliness, just as Paige empathized with her anonymous classmate's self-mutilation. The students' connection with each other derived in large part from the self-disclosing essays they heard every week. One can see the attachment among the three students, who have become connected by a recognition of shared vulnerability. Nor is this a sentimental connection, since Paige and Ronna acknowledge feeling "twisted envy." They are not telling their teacher what they think he wants to hear. They are writing about the complexity of their feelings. They are writing on risky topics that require emotional intelligence to understand and articulate. Sharing these writings with each other heightened their attachment to classmates and teacher. Over time trust develops, and they begin to disclose experiences and feelings that they have concealed from all but a handful of people. A striking example of this trust occurred the following week when Maryann, the next-to-last person to volunteer for the oral presentation, walked to the front of the classroom and revealed, with a characteristic wry smile on her face, that she was the author of the anonymous essay.

Maryann: "I Felt an Obligation to Expose Myself to the Class in the Same Manner Paige Did"

Writing the essay about falling in love has been the most challenging essay to write for this class. As I mentioned, I have never been "in love" with a person. My first thought was to pick a hobby or a habit that was important to me. I have no time for hobbies, so I automatically thought of the "habits" that I loved. Cutting myself seemed like the natural choice. I've had a relationship with it for over 4 years. It has been a tumultuous relationship; sometimes I love it and sometimes I hate it.

When writing the essay, I simply began with the beginning: the first time I cut myself. As my words and emotions spilled on to the page, I had a nagging fear in the back of my mind. "What if I have to read this essay out loud? Everyone will think I'm crazy. I don't know if I can be this honest about myself with my classmates," I thought. I decided to continue writing; whether this essay was read out loud or not was irrelevant. The essay needed to be written because I never reflected on this habit that consumed my high school career. I needed to sit back and think about what I had done in the past, why I had done it, and what made me subdue my tendency.

Once the essay was handed in, I didn't think about it. As quickly as I had relived my past, I had buried it again. Then I received an email from Jeff asking me if he could read my essay out loud. At first, I agreed to my essay being read anonymously without qualms. However, the more I thought about what my essay detailed, the more anxious I became. Walking to class on the day my essay was to be read was nerve wracking. "Maybe I shouldn't have said yes," I thought. "What if there are identifying factors in the essay that will expose me?" I never thought I would choose to expose myself by writing about this essay for my oral presentation.

As my essay was being read to the class my mind was racing. "Focus on Jeff, don't look around, don't make any sudden move-

ments, keep it together, and don't get red." These thoughts raced through my mind. I was scared I would expose myself as the author, but would never get a chance to defend myself or my actions to my classmates. After my essay was read and class was over, I again tried to push it to the back of my mind. It didn't work this time.

Paige chose to write her oral presentation on my essay. Before she began talking, she made a "disclaimer," stating that she hoped she didn't offend the author. She didn't. The fact that my essay stirred her emotions, stirred my own emotions. I felt horrible that the timing of my essay was so off. She had given up cutting only days before and she was subjected to relive her cutting by my cutting being described to the class. She opened up to the class and her emotions were clearly evident throughout her presentation. As soon as she was finished, I knew what I was going to write my oral presentation about. It was going to be about my anonymous essay.

The entire [spring] vacation I wrestled with the idea of exposing myself to my classmates. Was it a good idea? Would I ultimately regret it? I felt an obligation to expose myself to the class in the same manner Paige did. I've thought about my history of cutting myself every day this vacation and have subsequently thought about my oral presentation. I never thought that one simple essay would awaken so many emotions within me. I knew why I cut myself, but I never gave serious thought as to why I cut myself less frequently. Suddenly, I realized why I had stopped cutting myself so much. I stopped cutting myself on a regular basis when I came to college; when I came to college, I started smoking more pot. I smoke pot every night that I spend at college. I hadn't quit cutting, I had replaced it. I replaced something that made me feel pain with something that didn't make me feel anything.

When I'm home, I rarely smoke. None of my home friends smoke and I'm usually too busy to take time out at night to get stoned. This break, the haze that I live with was lifted. The numb feeling I had grown accustomed to had disappeared. I felt the same way

I did when I was in high school; I wanted something sharp all the time. Knowing that I would be exposing myself to my classmates prevented me from indulging in my previous habit. Even if they didn't say it, I knew that they would be looking at my wrists and my arms for scars and markings. Part of me wanted to write about my letter to my parents and to be able to remain anonymous. I wanted to be able to cut myself when I wanted to.

The essay forced me to reevaluate my relationship with my parents. I was in high school and I was scared when I was cutting myself. They only reached out to me once and even then they quickly accepted my assurance that I was okay. Never underestimate the power of denial. I love my parents so much, but I still can't figure out why they didn't try to help me. Should I love them less? I also thought about two people who had betrayed me. One of them goes to school here and I haven't spoken to her in over 3 years. Should I forgive her for betraying me? Should I forgive my parents for betraying me and not taking care of me? To this day I can't trust people the same way I used to. It's hard for me to trust people because of their betrayals.

My lack of trust caused me to lie in my anonymous essay. I'm not in therapy and it hasn't been 7 months since I've cut myself. I wrote those sentences because I'm afraid someone will say something to an authoritative figure who would inform my parents, or who would send me to a mental hospital. I thought that I needed to convince Jeff that I was completely taken care of and that this was a problem that lives in the past. It's not in the past; it's still in my life. I am more mature now, and I can deal with my emotions appropriately. I will compare a cutter to an alcoholic again, as an alcoholic may slip and have a drink after they haven't drank in two months. Just because they have slipped once doesn't mean they are going to drink an entire bottle of Jack Daniels every night again. The alcoholic needs the comfort of something that made them feel safe and secure at one point. They have an itch to drink, and having one drink may *satisfy the itch and help calm it. The same goes for cutting. As I write this paragraph, I realize how off-topic I have strayed. I will never trust people the same way I used to. This paragraph was supposed to be about my lack of trust, and I displayed that by going off on a tangent about how I have my cutting under control. I can't bluntly state what I want to say without trying to cover my tracks. That is what betrayal has done to me; I feel as though I always need to smile and laugh to convince everyone I'm okay.*

Writing the essay about falling in love made me realize that a lot of the issues I used to have are still there. After I came to college, I thought all the sad feelings I had experienced in high school had dissipated. They haven't; I've masked my feelings by indulging in other habits. Writing this essay was one of the most therapeutic events of my adult life. It forced me to sit back and reflect on different aspects of my life, the good and the bad. While I understand that I still have many issues to work out, writing this essay helped me to identify them. Rather than pretend my past isn't real, writing this essay made me realize I have to accept what happened and learn from my experiences.

These student writings reveal an ethics of caring. It is unlikely that Maryann could have known that her essay would distress Paige; as I suggested earlier, Maryann wrote the essay only for me and did not expect that I would ask her for permission to read it anonymously to the class. (Hers was the second anonymous essay that I read aloud that semester.) Despite the statement that many of her classmates may have also cut themselves, Maryann sat at the opposite side of the room from Paige and thus could not have seen the scars on her arms. And so although Maryann did not intend to make Paige feel self-conscious, this was exactly what happened, and she empathized with her classmate. If I had not read the anonymous essay aloud, it is not likely that Paige would have disclosed her secret history as a cutter. Nor is it likely that Maryann would have revealed her identity if Paige had not focused her oral presentation on the anonymous essay. These self-disclosures were interconnected, suggesting not only an element of chance or serendipity but also an element of caring for another person. Maryann and Paige were concerned with each other's welfare, even if it meant acknowledging something in public about which they were deeply ashamed. Each student exposed and was exposed by the other. Ironically, Maryann talks about "falling in love" with cutting, an unforgiving, self-destructive love, but the decision to reveal her identity may also be viewed as "falling in love" with Paige, not a romantic or sexual love, but a love based on a definition that appears in the *Oxford English Dictionary*, "that disposition or state of feeling with regard to a person which . . . manifests itself in solicitude for the welfare of the object."

I have seen this ethics of caring in every personal writing course I have taught. It makes little difference whether students read their essays aloud or ask me to read them anonymously. If, as Paige suggests, she feared that her classmates would incorrectly assume she was the author of the anonymous essay, one of the reasons they wanted to know the writer's identity was to express support for her. Such support is evident in the following comment made by a student in a different writing course. "Listening to my classmates' experiences with depression was difficult. I must admit, when I hear anonymous papers, I often want to know the author. When I listened to the anonymous depression papers, I wanted to know the authors. I do not know why I wanted to know. I think I wanted to know because I would have hugged them."

An Ethical Dilemma

I was not surprised that Maryann had disclosed her identity to the class. This happens often, especially toward the end of the semester, when students feel greater trust in their classmates than earlier in the term. Nor was I surprised that she was so moved by Paige's response to her essay. I *was* surprised—and disturbed—to hear Maryann admit that she had not given up cutting but had simply replaced it with another habit, smoking pot. At least two discernible motives lay behind her lie: she wanted to convince me that I did not need to worry about her, and she wanted to make sure that I would not "betray" her to the authorities, as her two "confidants" had done in high school. Maryann's class presentation confronted me with an ethical dilemma. If I felt that she was likely to harm herself, I was compelled to notify the counseling center; and if I knew that she was engaging in illegal activity, I was required to notify the campus police.

I also reflected on my relationship to Maryann and to other students, specifically, the transference-countertransference dynamics of teaching. She saw me as a trusted authority figure, one to whom she could disclose her feelings and experiences without the fear of rejection or betrayal. But she was also testing me; I would, from her point of view, fail the test if I acted the way her high school nurse did. Doing nothing might render me into a parent figure: "Should I forgive my parents for betraying me and not taking care of me?" Doing nothing might be irresponsible, as well as leave me open to criticism from the university community, especially if I decided later to write about Maryann's two cutting essays. Only the students in her class would know about my ethical dilemma—unless I decided to "go public," in which case hundreds or thousands of readers, many of whom are educators, would then evaluate my actions or nonactions. To write about one's teaching is to expose oneself to public scrutiny—and to acknowledge that one engages in risky teaching is to call attention to vexing ethical ambiguities.

I try to be as good a teacher as I can in all of my courses, the "risky" and "nonrisky" ones, and students who have taken several courses with me indicate that I am the "same person" in each class. Yet there is no denying that I feel different in my personal writing courses—and act differently, too. In my literature courses I analyze and, no doubt, overanalyze; little harm is done if my psychoanalytic interpretations are wrong. I tell my students that my "psychoanalytic practice" is limited to conflicted imaginary characters and that, consequently, my malpractice insurance is low. By contrast, it is far riskier to analyze living characters, especially students. Consequently, I do far more listening than speaking in my writing courses; nearly all of my class comments are limited to grammatical and stylistic suggestions for revision. I seldom think twice about a student leaving early in a literature course, but I am more concerned when a student leaves a writing class before it is over. Was he or she upset? Was the student infected by a classmate's essay? Has a student become at risk as a result of my class? I cannot help wondering about these questions. In my literature courses we talk about Edna Pontellier's suicide in Kate Chopin's *The Awakening* or Sylvia Plath's suicide immediately following the completion of *The Bell Jar*, but in my expository writing courses students write about their *own* suicide attempts. Far more is at stake when students write about their own lives. That is why I have two conferences a semester with my writing students: to make sure they are not emotionally overwhelmed by the course. I get to know all of my students, at least superficially, but since my writing students reveal hidden aspects of their lives to me, I know more about them than do their other teachers.

I rarely have boundary problems with students. Many of my colleagues make it a practice to leave their office doors open when speaking with a student; they fear that a closed door might compromise their safety or reputation. By contrast, some of my students request that they close my door so that they can discuss more freely an academic problem. I can understand my colleagues' anxiety. Anyone who has seen David Mamet's controversial 1992 play *Oleana* will recognize the ways in which a closed office door can imperil a male professor or a female student. Generally it is the student who is disadvantaged by a closed door, though sometimes it is the teacher. I allow students to close my office door if they wish. I am as trusting of my students as they are of me. My faith in the process of empathic teaching and the pedagogy of self-disclosure is evident to my students. My faith heightens their own.

This faith has been tested many times. It is never easy for a teacher to see a student crying or weeping in class. Nor is it easy when teachers cry in class. It took me several years to realize that tears can be as appropriate in a classroom as are smiles. How can one avoid feeling sorrowful when writing or reading about sorrow? How can a teacher not well up with tears when hearing a student read an essay about a parent's or grandparent's death? Students have told me that I become less of a teacher and more of a "person" to them when I become teary-eyed during the reading of an essay. My tears confirm that I have been moved deeply by the essay. Though educators have expressed criticism of my use of reader-response diaries and personal essays, those who are in the best position to evaluate my teaching—namely, my students—have been overwhelmingly positive.

What would happen, however, if one of my students committed suicide? This is a psychotherapist's worst nightmare—and mine, too. Or suppose one of my students suffered a breakdown and attributed it to the course writings or readings. Or suppose other teachers who experiment with the pedagogy of self-disclosure find these chilling scenarios coming true. Would my faith in the process of self-disclosure remain unshaken? I cannot answer these questions. That these problems have not arisen in the past is no guarantee that they will not arise in the future. A retired professor said to me, when I told her that I was coauthoring a book on cutting, that I was going "where angels fear to tread." Was Maryann's essay implicating me in an ethical problem from which I could not extricate myself?

As I pondered these questions, I read carefully the paper on which Maryann based her oral presentation. Her two essays on cutting were an opportunity to reflect on one of the major problems in her life, one that had "consumed" her throughout high school. Writing was a form of problem-solving for her. "I needed to sit back and think about what I had done in the past, why I had done it, and what made me subdue my tendency." She felt a strong bond with her classmate Paige: "The fact that my essay stirred her emotions, stirred my own emotions." Maryann notes her "obligation" to expose herself to her classmates, presumably to allay Paige's fear that her oral presentation had offended an anonymous classmate. Paige had "opened up to the class," and Maryann felt that she should do no less. Self-disclosure begets self-disclosure; nowhere is this more true than in these three essays. Rather than being offended by Paige's remarks, Maryann implies that she felt validated, though she was also saddened by the unfortunate timing of her essay, which she feared may have weakened Paige's resolve to end her cutting. Concern for a classmate prompts Maryann to disclose her identity to the class.

Maryann concedes that she was not truthful about being in therapy, yet she was trying to construct a healing narrative that would help her end self-mutilation. She lied not because she wanted to "mock" her teacher's need "to view [her] trauma," as Carra Leah Hood apparently did, but to tell her story. This healing narrative was written in part to assure me that she was not at risk for serious self-injury. Perhaps she felt the need to protect me from worrying about her, as Caroline Kettlewell tried to shield others from the disturbing knowledge of her cutting. "For some reason, I believed that I had above all else an obligation to protect everyone—my teachers, my family—from the knowledge of my cutting. What they did not know would not cause them pain" (68). Kettlewell also explains how easy it was for her to conceal the autobiographical nature of her gloomy writings from a young English teacher who was concerned about her. Along with other gifted students, the thirteen-year-old was invited to participate in a new enrichment program called Quest that encouraged creative writing. "Can't you write something more *cheerful?*" a teacher-in-training asked her. One of her stories involved an unhappy teenage girl who, rejected and misunderstood by her family, commits suicide by swallowing a bottle of pills. "It's just a story," Kettlewell reassures her alarmed teacher, and she makes the same observation to her parents "to throw them off the scent" lest they become similarly alarmed. At the same time she was writing these morbid stories, she was reading books about suicide and madness, such as *Lisa, Bright and Dark, The Bell Jar* (which she read three times in ninth grade), and *I Never Promised You a Rose Garden.* "What is it about insanity and untimely death that so captivates the imagination of young girls?" (92–94).

I mention Kettlewell here because it is easy for a troubled student to deceive a teacher, as Maryann deceived me. This should not discourage teachers from trying to help troubled students, but it does indicate that students can easily reject the help of authority figures such as teachers who are reaching out to help them. Kettlewell's memoir also demonstrates how difficult it may be for a teacher to help students who cannot help themselves.

Maryann must have felt that she was telling me what I wanted to hear in the anonymous essay, but she also knew that I would be displeased to learn that she was not entirely truthful in that essay. Did she now trust me enough to know that I would not "betray" her? She criticizes her friends for helping her too much and criticizes her parents for helping her too little. She never states what she would have *wanted* them to do. I felt implicated in an impossible situation. If I contacted the authorities, which would have been the safe and professional course of action, almost certainly she would have regretted her self-disclosure and mistrusted even further those who are trying to help her. If I did *not* contact the authorities, I would be condoning illegal and psychologically unhealthy behavior.

As I contemplated my dilemma, I recalled a story a colleague told me. Less than a week after his daughter began college, she called him to say—with pride in her voice—that she had acquired a fake ID so that she could drink illegally. She had rarely consumed alcohol in high school, but she was eager to enjoy her new freedom now that she was in college. My colleague found himself in a difficult situation. If he scolded her, as he was inclined to do, he feared that she would no longer trust him enough to confide in him. If he remained silent, he would be tacitly approving her illegal behavior. Avoiding a choice between Scylla and Charybdis, he decided on a third strategy—to extract a promise from her that she would never drive while intoxicated or allow herself to be driven by someone whose judgment was impaired by alcohol. He knew that his advice to his daughter was not perfect, but it was the best he could think of at the time.

Students often casually refer to underage drinking, which is one of the most serious problems on and off college campuses, but instead of calling the police, I suggest that they write about their experiences. One of the chapters in *Risky Writing*, "Writing under the Influence," explores how such writing may help students to recognize that they have a drinking problem and to reach potentially life-saving insights into how they can reduce their alcohol consumption. "Of all the topics on which they wrote, binge drinking provoked the most lively discussions inside and outside the classroom" (230). To date, despite colleges' efforts to confront the problem, more than 40 percent of college students engage in high-risk drinking. As James Schaefer, the SUNY director of alcohol and other drug prevention has noted, most people would be "shocked to learn that a significant percentage of first-year college students are already accomplished drinkers—veteran weekend warriors—extending risky behaviors into the 13th grade" (*Albany Times-Union*, 21 November 2005). Their "weekend," I might add, often begins on Thursday and ends on Wednesday.

After much thought, I decided not to contact the counseling service. I believed then, as I believe now, that Maryann was not likely to harm herself. Nor did I call the campus police. If I had to contact the police every time a student reports underage drinking or smoking pot, I would spend more time on the telephone than in the classroom. That would also be the end of students' willingness to write about their lives.

I saw Maryann at a book-signing party after the semester ended, and I told her that I had debated with myself whether to contact the counseling center for advice but decided against it. She told me that she was glad that I had not done so. I couldn't resist saying that many of my students have been helped by the counseling center, a free service that is a valuable campus resource. Afterward I did contact the counseling center, and I was told that students in Maryann's situation are encouraged but not required to speak to a counselor. Only if a student was in a crisis would the counseling center intervene. Recall the finding that among repeated self-injurers, only 5.4 percent disclose their actions to a physician and only 25.7 percent to a mental health professional (Whitlock, Eckenrode, and Silverman 1943).

I should add that at no time did any of the students in the class ask me for clinical advice about cutting. They knew I am not a therapist. They also knew that I would comment not on their lives or personalities but on their writings. Our class was supportive of each other but was not a support group—no one offered or asked for clinical advice on any topic. Yet in one important way I did function as a therapist. I created a safe, empathic classroom atmosphere in which students could self-disclose without the fear of being attacked or reprimanded. It is true that in one class Paige worried that her classmates might think she was the author of the anonymous essay, and this fear may have led to her own self-disclosure. But her trust in her classmates proved to be stronger than her mistrust.

I also trusted the class. Despite Maryann's admission that her "lack of trust" caused her to lie in her anonymous essay, I never questioned the truthfulness of any of the students in the class. I still don't. It is possible that parts of her oral presentation essay contain fabrications. For example, she may have told me what she thought I wanted to hear when she states that writing the cutting essay helped her to realize many of the "issues" about why she mutilates her body. Or she may have overstated the truth when she concludes that the essay was "one of the most therapeutic" events of her adult life. As I suggested earlier, I make it a practice not to question the truth claims in my students' personal writings. I'm a teacher, not a police officer or a jury, and I am willing to incur the risk that I may occasionally be misled by a student.

Geoffrey Hartman remarks in *Scars of the Spirit* that "autobiography, whether it deals with private acts and feelings or a life of public service, cannot escape suspicion. . . . Stories about oneself, whether performed within the 'public square' of encomium, funeral oration, and sanctioned self-praise, or outside of it, never quite detach from narrative fiction" (17). Hartman implies that although the writer may strive for "transparency—a standard of honesty that would allow us to discern truth freed of manipulation and deception" (12)—"no one is so naive as to think all masks can be removed, all memories unified, all shadows dissolved. Shadows may be deliberately added, in fact, and often to reveal rather than conceal" (9). I agree with Hartman, and in my literature classes I explore with my students the masks of "fictional" and "real" characters. I do not call into question, however, the authenticity of my students' personal writings, not because I believe the writings are perfectly transparent, an impossibility, but because I believe that students would become defensive if a teacher or classmate challenged the truthfulness of their essays.

Sarah: "This Essay I Shall Never Forget"

Several of Maryann's classmates found her anonymous essay moving, and they referred to it in their class presentations. Here is Sarah's response:

> One of the essays that most affected me during the course of this class was the anonymous essay about cutting. The topic made me most uncomfortable. I appreciate the people who can write about serious issues with which they may be embarrassed. My own work regarding the darker things in life, I replay within my mind. However, this essay I shall never forget. Cutting, as this person tried to convey, was about power and control. The control to make one feel better: create release. Cutting was also about love. This person fell in love with cutting; could not live without cutting, needed [it] to continue breathing. She would go to lengths to hide her "lovely" wounds: the wounds that made her love. She had a watch with which she would cover her lesions. Although she didn't want to die, she would cut and cut, sometimes fifty times to release her pain. People didn't know. Her parent's didn't know. No one knew they were maltreating her in such a way. When betrayed by one of her friends, when her cutting was discovered, she misleads doctors by pretending she was healthy. She was released and continued to cut herself. She would cut in different places, such as her hip, though this did not afford her the same satisfaction. Today, she no longer cuts. She has been free of this burden for seven months, and hopefully will remain forever free from this burden. She is content to "be in love with life," a topic which I myself want more people to accept and experience.
>
> This anonymous essay did surprise me. The topic was incredibly dark, and off-putting. Although I did not cry, I wanted to; I wanted to cry for every ounce of pain that person had felt or still feels. I wanted to bear away some of the pain upon myself. I even wanted to shake the poor girl that this person once was. Shake her to tell her that cutting was not the way to fix one's life. Most shocking to me was when the author expressed that eight or nine people within the class could be, or had at one time been cutters. More people cut

than is expected. I have never been a cutter, and I never could have imagined anyone in the class being so. This is my own naivety. The essay was incredibly strong. On a sensitive topic such as this, it is difficult to say something is weak, principally if it has such a strong effect on the audience. An incredible strength of this essay was the ability to be dark: unapologetically dark. This effect I shall try to re-create in my own works. This is a quality that is impenitent and striking. In the future, when I write about such topics as my father, I will attempt to harness this darkness that lurks inside me each day. Harness it and put it on the page, so that my writings too, may affect someone in such a profound way as this essay has me.

I assumed, when I first read Sarah's essay, that she meant to write "important" instead of "impenitent," but upon closer examination, I now believe that she chose the correct word. She admires the anonymous essay because of its unapologetically dark, impenitent quality. Maryann's essay inspired Sarah to write about her tangled feelings toward her father, who had died the previous summer. Sarah had written in an earlier essay about her father's death, but after hearing the anonymous essay, she wrote another essay in which she described her mother's anger toward her for not spending more time home. In her mother's view, Sarah was a "bad daughter," a judgment that she explored in depth in a powerful essay.

Baxter: "I Was Riveted by the Essay"

Maryann's essay also affected the men in the class. The essay helped Baxter to understand why his sister cut herself:

I was riveted by the essay. I was rocked into a trance at the idea that a person could fall in love with cutting herself. My mind was filled with questions about how she could truly feel this way. The account was so vivid. In my mind, I watched with wonder and sadness as a beautiful girl longed to bring a scissor across her arm. I say beautiful because the essay was beautiful, and so too the author. Masterfully crafted, it had a tremendous capability to show, not just tell.

I am easily distracted. Therefore, nearly all the other essays I heard in this class left my mind by the time I left the Humanities building. If I ever thought about someone's reading of his or her essay (which I did, there were many moving essays), it was only within the context of this class. Except this one.

Making eye contact is difficult because I don't know about whose paper I am speaking. I can't directly compliment and honor you for your essay. I struggled with wondering who wrote this. As I'm guessing we all did. When it was being read aloud, I couldn't look at anyone. I did not want to be distracted by reactions. Even if the reaction was like mine: an anxious stare fixed upon Professor Berman. Mostly I didn't want to look around and start to guess. I needed to be honest with this assignment; I could not choose any other essay. No other essay moved me like this one. However, responding to this essay made me nervous. I thought it maybe a disservice to bring up this essay. Clearly the author struggled with this. To rehash it seemed for a moment rude. Nevertheless, hearing this essay made me think and feel things I had never thought before. So I had to talk about it.

I need to summarize the essay but I do not remember many details. Without the text in front of me I can only cite the fragments that I remember. However, the impression of the essay supercedes the few details I can recall. As I try to remember details, I am overwhelmed with this essay's decimation of what I thought I knew about cutting. The first time she cut there were many tiny drops of blood. She spoke of not allowing herself to get emotionally close to boys or men, but referred to rendezvous. She spoke about the fear of being discovered and a trip to the doctor's office. I remember there was a watch that shielded eyes from the lines on her wrist, lines that were made with no intention of a permanent solution. After being discovered, she decided on her hip, a less satisfying, but a securely remote place to cut. Finally, we were informed that along with counseling the perpetual cutting has ceased.

I have not been able to stop thinking about this essay on falling in love. This essay made me again consider the definition of love. I'd like to believe that there was some sensationalism in the essay. That calling it love was taking artistic license. I'd like to believe that. But I am more inclined to take the author at her words and that there was no sensationalism at all. It made me again think about what love has become for our generation. I came to no conclusions. I was frustrated. I wanted to ask every girl in the class if she wrote the essay and ask for a copy. I was so moved by this essay that I regret how much I will forget. It was only until I spoke with my sister that I became disgusted with my lack of sensitivity. My sister made it clear, "If you haven't gone through it then you cannot understand it. You'll never know." I acknowledge that the mystery of authorship sparked my initial interest. After it was read, there was greater significance in the author's anonymity. She became every girl, the voice of every woman who suffers similar memories and habits. Certainly this account is unique in many aspects, but it is familiar as well. I am not suggesting that all people who cut are in love with it. However, the ideas in the essay transcended the author's experience.

I still have difficulty believing she loved cutting herself, only because I do not and cannot understand it. At first I assumed that the author must have undergone many intensely traumatic experiences to do and think and feel as she did. This idea was reinforced by a friend. She was fiercely abused and cut herself. She trusted me and would call me before, during and after she attacked her arm. So I thought I knew something about cutting. How wrong I was. And still must be. The words of my sister rang in my ears, "If you haven't gone through it then you cannot understand it. You'll never know."

This essay followed me as I went home for spring break. I had a mind to speak with my nineteen-year-old sister. I know that she had struggled with self-mutilation. We have never spoken about the scars she has from wrist to elbow. I did not know how to broach the topic. I spoke of the assignment and the essay that was read aloud. She showed the 30 lines and seven cigarette burns on her

arms and said, "If you haven't gone through it then you can't under-
stand. You'll never know." She was very gracious as I muddled my
way through a few questions. I could never bring myself to ask her
if she ever loved it.

That's what's so mystifying, the idea of loving the cutting. When
my friend would call me before she would cut herself she was dis-
tressed but sounded sadly hopeful about how she would feel better if
she cut her arm. If she called me afterward, she was not glad she did
it. She sounded in greater distress than when we first spoke. Within
a half hour of seriously cutting herself, she would tell me she's going
to do it again soon. Is it something like a battered woman returning
to her husband or boyfriend because he says he loves her and the sex
is good? I am going in circles, unable to understand how someone
could love this. I didn't understand the author's lack of distress in
the action of cutting.

I think that anyone can experience the temporary alleviation
from cutting. I've been told there is euphoria; localized physical
pain causes emotional distress to dissipate. Frustrated, powerless
and feeling defeated in my ignorance, I would resign myself to be
a listener. This essay reminded me how even as a listener I failed.
I suppose that's why I was so moved by the essay. The author re-
minded me of a troubled friend I once had.

Given the topic of the assignment, it should be no surprise that I
was surprised. I probably would not have selected this essay were it
not for the fact that it was written for assignment, falling in love.

I could not think of one weakness in the essay. The prose was
as beautiful as it was powerful. If I had the essay in front of me,
I doubt that I would have been able to find a small weakness. I
certainly would not have mentioned it. The magnificence of the
essay would have dwarfed any supposed weakness. I would not con-
sider this a weakness, but I wished the essay was longer. It was such
an overwhelming narrative that I was left wanting to know more.
The expression of loving cutting left an undeniable eeriness. It is

an intense human experience filled with emotions and impulses for which my mind has no sounding board.

I am grateful to the brave and generous author of this essay.

Empathic Listening

Baxter's opening statement, "I was riveted by the essay," is no overstatement. He doesn't use the word, but hearing the anonymous essay was nothing short of an epiphany, just as hearing Maryann's essay was a revelation to Paige. He refers to being overwhelmed by the essay's details about cutting, but instead of using the word "description," which he almost certainly intended, he uses "decimation." Is it reading too much into this unusual word choice to suggest that the essay has "decimated" him? It is scarcely possible to imagine a more intense response to a class presentation. He states in the beginning that he was "rocked into a trance at the idea that a person could fall in love with cutting herself," and then he suggests enigmatically that the paper made him "think and feel things" he had never thought about before. His language suggests that he could not help but be affected by the writing: "I could not choose any other essay," he states, implying loss of agency. The essay haunts him, rendering him unable to forget it, and it "followed" him home during spring break, where it compels him to question his sister about her own cutting experiences. Twice he repeats her statement to him: "If you haven't gone through it then you cannot understand it. You'll never know." One suspects that the essay is so powerful that it *almost* gives him personal experience. The essay has expanded his knowledge of self-mutilation, leaving him with the desire to know more. The essay also enables him to begin a dialogue with his sister on an issue they had never discussed before, one invested with both secrecy and shame.

Paige's and Baxter's responses are emotionally charged but in different ways. Paige's identification with cutting reawakens the craving to mutilate her body, and she is astonished that she has so much in common with an anonymous classmate, whose identity she needs to unmask. Emotional contagion has not spared Baxter, for he writes like a man in a trance. He stared at me during my reading so that he would not succumb to the temptation to locate the anonymous author's identity. Despite being "easily distracted," he accurately recalls several details in the essay and realizes that the writer could be "every girl, the voice of every woman who suffers similar memories and habits." The essay forces him to think about not only his sister but also his friend, who had cut herself. Empathy requires him to suspend judgment that the essay might be sensationalistic. Toward the end he reproaches himself for being a poor listener, yet his own essay shows how attentively he has listened to the anonymous essay.

Indeed, few readers would agree with Baxter's conclusion that he "failed" as a listener. The opposite is true. He not only records accurately many concrete details in the anonymous essay but also relates these specifics to conversations with his sister. He is intensely aware of others' suffering. If, as Sharon Todd suggests, listening is the "learning event par excellence" (131), how teachers and students listen to each other becomes an essential pedagogical task. "If we consider that stories of suffering invoke certain affective responses, then our responsibility as teachers turns upon our capacity to listen to those responses in ways that are for the Other, in ways that display our ignorance, that communicate to students 'tell me, for I do not know'" (137). Todd quotes a statement by Deborah Britzman about the risks of listening. "The paradox is that because learning from another's pain requires noticing what one has not experienced and the capacity to be touched by what one has not noticed, identifying with pain requires a self capable of wounding her or his own ego boundaries, the very boundaries that serve as a defense against pain" (138). Such empathic listening on the part of teachers and students alike produces change, not only in the form of increased self-knowledge but also in the desire to alleviate suffering.

Empathic listening, like empathic reading, heightens our sensitivity to suffering. As Chekhov observes in his haunting short story "Gooseberries," "Behind the door of every contented, happy man there ought to be someone standing with a little hammer and continually reminding him with a knock that there are unhappy people, that however happy he may be, life will sooner or later show him its claws, and trouble will come to him—illness, poverty, losses, and then no one will see or hear him, just as now he neither sees nor hears others" (381). Maryann's anonymous essay was like Chekhov's hammer, reminding us of the existence of human suffering. Readers can tolerate only so much pain before they become angry, depressed, or bored: as with everything, there are limits to empathy and sympathy. If, as Maggie Turp states, professionals are often terrified by self-injury—"Their normal empathy with others' distress and their confidence in their ability to help often desert them when faced with someone who persistently hurts herself" (209)—how do academics react? A retired colleague at another university told me about an undergraduate in his creative writing course who not only wrote several stories about cutting herself but also came to class with blood sometimes oozing through her bandaged arms. The sight was so distressing to the teacher and students that her presence proved disruptive to learning; he asked her finally to withdraw from the course.

Fortunately, this was not our class situation. Maryann and Paige wore long sleeves and did not expose their scarred arms (except, as Paige notes, on one occasion). They were discreet about their scars, not wishing to upset their classmates. Equally important, they were both describing situations of ongoing recovery. Witness Paige's email to me two months after the course ended, when I asked her for permission to read part of her essay to my summer school students, with whom I was discussing the contagion effect: "No, I wouldn't mind at all if you read my essay. If you want, you can feel free to mention that I still have not cut myself at all since I quit those few months ago (it was right before I gave the oral presentation, actually). I hope that helps." She sent me another email the following semester, telling me she was now taking a graduate workshop in writing. "It's funny, but in my writing class I was actually called 'frighteningly bright' by my professor the other day because I know all the answers to the grammar and punctuation questions because of your class last year. Hahahaha. So thank you for that." And Maryann told me after the course ended that cutters can be helped only when they are ready. "I fooled people because I wasn't ready to stop cutting and deal with the issues that were making me cut. Eventually I dealt with these issues myself and stopped cutting."

At no time during the semester did anyone express a "cutting" remark—either in class or in an essay—to a classmate's paper. The students followed my lead in responding sympathetically to each essay. We limited class discussions to reading aloud essays, identifying the best-written sentences, and revising sentences that contained a grammatical or stylistic error. At no time did we discuss cutting as a psychological, cultural, or medical problem—largely because I did not want Maryann or Paige to feel self-conscious or threatened, and also because of my emphasis on writing. There is, of course, value to such discussion in individual and group therapy as well as in traditional academic courses, but we were a writing class. Paradoxically, the empathic classroom helped to diminish much of the toxic shame that Maryann and Paige felt about cutting, for they could see how moved their classmates and teacher were about the problems that were now made public for the first time.

If education is "what you remember after you forget everything you've been taught," as the father of one of my students says, education is also what you remember when you leave the college campus and return home. From this point of view, the essays on cutting will be an unforgettable educational experience for many, if not most, of the students in my writing class. Maryann and Paige enlightened their classmates about a topic that is seldom discussed in the classroom. They put a human face to a practice surrounded by fear and stigma. They wrote about experiences of which they are not proud but that are part of the human condition. As the Roman playwright Terence observed more than two thousand years ago, "I am human; nothing human is alien to me." Maryann and Paige demonstrated that "cutters" have far more in common with "noncutters" than most people imagine. They demonstrated that cutters are not "crazy" or "sick" but searching for a way to regain their health and self-control. And they demonstrated that a pedagogy based on self-disclosure can heighten students' understanding of and empathy for their classmates. Teachers who encourage their students to write about cutting are not glorifying or "rewarding" problematic behavior but enabling them to engage in constructive problem-solving. Thus Baxter displays his newly acquired education about cutting by his willingness to talk with his sister about the anonymous essay. We see classroom education literally brought home, where it gives him a new insight into his sister's unhappiness. He was so moved by Maryann's anonymous essay that on the last day of the semester, when we had a party, he played a song he had just written. Imagining himself as Maryann, he captures many of the ambiguities of cutting:

> The first time I met love
> I remember it clearly
> What a great idea
> I got from the t.v.

> With miserable tears
> From an unbearable school
> Found a blue-handled scissor
> To be my love's tool.

Now know if you help me, you would just hurt me
Had best you let me and my love alone.
And don't dare you seek
To take away my peace
Leave for me my love and my release.
Surely not healthy but
I love it so much
I am always happy I never cry

OK I lied
But you can't replace the way
Bitter drops of pain
Freely escape me through my veins

Are you listening?
You think I like what I am doing?
This is no solution
Each cut's a chain
Causing greater and greater . . .
But it felt so much like love.

CHAPTER 12

Conclusion
Writing about Cutting—Contagion or Inoculation?

After the semester ended, Maryann and Paige gave me permission to read their essays anonymously to my next section of Expository Writing, which I taught in the fall of 2005. The two essays evoked strong identificatory responses from male and female students alike. Three women and three men wrote about their own cutting experiences, and a fourth woman wrote about her sister's cutting. Each implied that cutting was a response to low self-esteem and depression. Most of these essays were in response to the following assignment, given one week before the end of the semester:

> Many of the students in *Risky Writing* have written about depression or suicide, and several of you have also hinted at this in an essay. No doubt all of you know a relative or friend who was seriously depressed or suicidal. Write an essay in which you discuss your own or another person's experience with depression or suicide. Try to re-create the feelings associated with depression or suicide, and draw a contrast between sickness and health. Indicate whether the depression or suicidal thinking is ongoing. What if anything did you learn from this experience?
>
> A related essay topic: write an essay about what can be done to help those who suffer from depression or suicidal thinking. Try to be as specific as possible. Another essay topic: discuss what you have learned about depression or suicide from reading *Risky Writing*. Or what you have learned from hearing a classmate's essay on this topic. If you wish, you can write a letter to a student in *Risky Writing* in which you discuss how his or her essay has affected you.
>
> Another essay topic: As I mentioned in class, I am coauthoring a book (with a former graduate student) on cutting. Feel free to write about cutting and its relationship to depression or suicide.
>
> If you have not brought in copies of an essay in the last two assignments, please bring 25 copies of this assignment. You can exercise the anonymity option.

I have used a version of this assignment in every personal writing course I have taught in the last decade, and it, along with the letter to and from a parent assignment, has produced the most powerful essays of the semester. Past students have told me that their essays on depression and suicide have been the most painful—and most therapeutic—of all their writings. The fall 2005 class, however, was the first time I encouraged students to write about cutting. I intended to ask them, upon completing the assignment, whether they felt infected when they heard these essays read aloud.

I focus in this chapter on Francesca, Lea, Rosemary, Isabelle, Aaron, Greg, and Eric, all of whom wrote about depression and cutting. Many offer reasons for cutting themselves and reveal their present attitude toward past cutting. Most implied that they no longer cut themselves. I begin, however, with a noncutter. In every personal writing class there is one essay that "opens the floodgates," allowing students to overcome resistance to self-disclosure and release pent-up feelings. Becky wrote the "breakthrough" essay on depression, which arose from her mother's death in a car accident.

Becky: "Being a 15-Year-Old Female Is Hard Enough without Having to Deal with Such a Monumental Loss"

Before my mother died, depression was just another word in my vocabulary; the only encounter I had with it was the vague drug commercials with the bouncing ball. When I heard the words "your mother has gone to heaven," I was wrenched from the life I had known into the unfamiliar world of depression. In an instant, I went from a 15-year-old who worried about my hair, to one who worried about what my mother was thinking in her final moments.

During the first few months following her death, I was irrational and unpredictable. I couldn't even stand to be around me, imagine how my brother and father felt. Some days I wouldn't stop crying, others I had looks on my face that surely would have taken down the strongest man. My emotions were flying from one extreme to another, seemingly from minute to minute. Being a 15-year-old

female is hard enough without having to deal with such a monu-
mental loss. After my father had about enough of my mood swings
and increasingly violent temper, he suggested "I talk to someone."
I retorted with, "I talk to my friends every day"—a typical smug
teenage response. He was less than pleased.

Several weeks later, after doing some online research, I was sitting
in the office of Smyrna or Syrla; I don't remember her name. All
I do recall is thinking, wow, this lady is one of those quacks that
I hear about. She had a soothing voice and soothing comments,
all portrayed in a less than genuine manner. I felt as though I was
being placated and put down when I was on her couch. She merely
validated my own behaviors to me, making me want to act even
more unabashedly. Our hour-long sessions were split in half: 30 min-
utes alone, 30 together with my father. The second half was always
what I dreaded more. I was afraid to hear what my father was going
through. More than that, I was afraid that maybe he would cry. At
15 I was still daddy's little girl, and was not ready to see him in tears.
We spoke about our relationship and how to improve it, but, not to
my surprise, as soon as we left that office, it was as if we hadn't been
there. After 4 visits, I decided that therapy was not for me.

My mood swings increased, my temper grew more and more vio-
lent, and there didn't seem to be any end. Once the summer was
over and I was back in school, my life began to improve. I was in
a social setting, and wasn't being treated as the girl whose mother
died, which is what I feared the most. When my time was being
spent doing schoolwork or in the company of friends, I had less time
to dwell on my unfortunate circumstances. I began to realize that
maybe therapy wouldn't be such a bad idea. A large factor in that
decision was my best friend and her mother. I spent a good deal of
time with them, both before and after my mother's death. After the
accident, I resented the relationship they had. It showed me daily
all the wonderful moments I would never be able to share with my
mother. This caused me to withdraw from our friendship, leaving

me with no "shoulder to cry on." I approached my father and told him I would like to find another therapist. If his back were healthy, he would have leapt ten feet into the air. The next step was finding the antithesis of Smarma.

Ding-Dong! The doorbell rang and I raced to answer it. I didn't recognize the woman, and when I opened the door she asked to speak to my father. Local elections were fast approaching, and I recognized her face from campaign posters on neighbors' lawns. Once my father arrived, I returned to an enthralling television show. Several minutes later, I went down to the kitchen to ask him what the woman wanted. A smile stretched from ear to ear as he explained their conversation. She started by rattling off her goals should she be elected, and all of the other standard political rhetoric. My father, being a naturally outgoing person, introduced himself. After my mother died, he developed an annoying habit of telling every person he met that his wife was killed in a car accident however many months ago. He did not spare Maria the story, but for once it was beneficial that he mentioned the tragedy. Maria was a psychologist, specializing in children. He took her number, promising to call soon. He spoke with her the following day, and set up my first of hundreds of visits with Maria.

For the next three years, I was in and out of Maria's home. I at first saw her three times a week, after a year I was down to twice a week, and in the final year I saw her between once and twice every two weeks. Although my mother's death was the catalyst for therapy, I soon found out that was not the only reason why I should be there. I had issues with my father that hadn't manifested yet, and never did, since we worked through them together. She helped me through the days when I could barely hold my head up, and cheered me on those days when I walked in with a smile. She taught me to utilize "worst case scenario," where you prepare yourself for the worst, that way, when it did or did not happen, you were ready. By the end of my senior year, I was a changed person. I no longer resented my friends with two parents, I learned to deal with my father's stubbornness, accepted my brother's drug habit, and most importantly, I accepted myself. In August, as I was getting ready to leave for college, I met with Maria in Barnes and Noble, our first meeting as friends, not doctor/patient. She lauded my progress and my ability to come out of a horrific situation with my health intact. She gave me a small stuffed bunny for luck and remembrance, with the comment that she thought rabbits feet were trite, and that is why a whole bunny. I laughed, and so did she. I was sad when I left Barnes and Noble that day, knowing I would no longer have Maria down the street should I need her. However, I had the little bunny, who, might I add, is next to me as I write this.

From the instant I arrived at SUNY Albany, I was unhappy. I didn't want to go to this school, and the fact that I had no other choice made me angry. My saving grace was that my boyfriend of one year had decided to attend the same school. We were assigned to the same building. When we received our housing arrangements, I was thrilled. We would be down the hall!! However, it is our closeness that caused my mental decline and ensuing depression. Before we came to SUNY, our relationship could not have been any better. He left me little notes in my books, critiqued my poetry, and encouraged my creative self. Once we arrived, it was as if he was a different person. He began to put down my ideas, he never wanted to spend time together, and he was just plain mean. When we would get into arguments, he would invariably turn it around to make it my fault, and eventually I began to think it was. I thought the whole situation was my fault; this led me to want to take out my anger on my possessions or myself. I frequently slammed doors and smashed my phone apart, which were all signs of my violent temper. I felt my mental health regressing, as though I had thrown away the previous three years. Friends told me to just leave him, but as we all know, nobody listens to their friends when they're in love. The situation got worse, and so did I. I went from a healthy 130 pounds, to a sickly 103 in a matter of 2 months. My hair was flat, my skin was sallow; I didn't look good. I couldn't turn to my father, for he had started drinking again after being sober for nearly 10 years. This was a huge factor in my declining health. I didn't want to be at home, I didn't want to be at school; I felt alone in the world. I kept a journal and in it I wrote, "If I had the guts I would have killed myself about 3 minutes ago. I just want to fucking hurt myself so bad and if I had a fucking knife sharp enough I would. NOTHING is going okay in my life. I hate myself. I hate this school. I hate my father. I don't feel comfortable in my own home. What does that say? I was doing SO well until I came here. I was done with therapy. Now I feel I could use 3 more years. I just want to end it all. I feel as though I'm in a deep state of depression. The majority of the time I just want to run away from myself and everything I have. I hate it and I hate me. I wish I had a mother to call right now, I wish she never left so I didn't have all this shit. I just want to fucking die."

The day after that passage was written I finally called Maria. I had been denying to myself for months that I was depressed. After feeling such strong urges to kill myself, I knew something was wrong. She asked me if I needed to be hospitalized, and I quickly said no, as it was finals time and I could not afford to leave. Once the semester was over, I returned home to the familiarity of Maria's living room. We decided together that medication was my best option. However, since she was not a psychiatrist, we had to go to the local hospital and speak with her colleague.

The day we decided to go to the hospital, we awoke early and went to the diner down the street for some breakfast. She told me what to expect inside the mental health ward. I had my own visions. After seeing movies such as One Flew Over the Cuckoo's Nest and Girl, Interrupted, I was frightened. When we got there, I had to be admitted to the emergency room. From there they took me up to the fourth floor, which is the floor for temporary stays. I sat in the waiting room, surrounded by "crazies," who looked no different from you *or I. Granted, I saw them mumbling to themselves or yelling loudly to make sure the nurse knew that they were there. One man, as my therapist told me, was a regular. He would come in, especially in the winter, claiming he wanted to kill himself. He was homeless and was looking for a warm place to stay for a few nights at a time. Sitting there, waiting, I felt my problems were insignificant in comparison.*

When I finally saw the doctor, about an hour later, I was nervous and uncomfortable. It was not the person Maria wanted me to see, and after my 5-minute exam, he decided I didn't need medication. Maria was infuriated. She told me that we would come back when her friend and colleague would be there.

A few days later, I found myself going through the same intimidating locked doors at the hospital. Our wait was shorter, and after seeing the psychiatrist, I was given a prescription for Wellbutrin. This drug, for me, was the miracle drug. After several weeks of building up the chemical in my body, I began to feel some relief. My thoughts weren't as jumbled, I could smile again; I took joy in little things. I had dinner with my aunt over that break, and she gave me a fantastic piece of advice. I wrote about in my journal: "She said when you're depressed, do one nice thing for yourself every day. I did that today by hanging my stained glass clock, and having the satisfaction of knowing, every time I look at it, that I made it. That's a good feeling. One good thing today, and tomorrow and next week could just mean the difference between life and death."

I followed that advice, and a strict medicinal regiment, and was feeling healthy again in a month's time. I went back to Maria, who was key in my recovery. They say that which does not kill you makes you stronger; I could not agree more. Although I have had several battles with depression since then, I have been able to handle them with a clearer head, having been through it already. Depression is a disease; one that I believe cannot be cured, but only treated.

Becky read the essay aloud in a composed, soft-spoken voice. I had not read the essay before, and I felt emotionally in control as she was reading it, but as soon as I began to praise it, I could hear my voice crack. Suddenly I found myself crying—the only time during the semester when that happened. Becky's loss of her mother reminded me of my wife's death twenty months earlier, as well as my daughters' grief over their mother's death. I could identify with Becky's father "annoying habit" of talking about his wife's recent death to friends and strangers alike—something I myself did. At the time, I was writing a memoir of my wife, and I was often talking about her to my students. Was this annoying to Becky? She mentioned in the essay that there were days following her mother's death when she couldn't stop crying, though she dreaded to see her father in tears. Was she unnerved when she saw me cry in class? It did not appear so, for she maintained her composure throughout our discussion of her essay.

Becky writes about her younger self with a keen, often satirical eye. She uses humor effectively when she parodies the name of her first therapist, whom she found insincere. The statement that she was afraid to hear what her father was going through at the time reminds us that sometimes we are unable to empathize with another person for fear of being emotionally overwhelmed. She knows that recovery is not a linear process but a movement filled with advances and retreats. Sometimes it is hard to remember how wrenching the past can be. Her first diary entry recalls vividly her state of mind when she was depressed and suicidal, just as her essay for the class reveals the progress she has made as a result of psychotherapy and medication. She does not mention emotional contagion by name, but her reference to the films *One Flew Over the Cuckoo's Nest* and *Girl, Interrupted* implies that she became infected by their frightening portrayals of psychiatric hospitals. She makes little effort to hide the fear she experienced in the hospital, but she also goes out of her way to reassure readers that she has recovered from depression, a recovery that has withstood the test of time despite occasional setbacks.

Tears, like words, can lead to emotional contagion, and during the next few days, when I had a second conference with my students, I asked them how they felt when they saw me cry in response to Becky's essay. No one had seen a professor cry before, particularly a male professor, but they all felt that my tears were understandable in light of the sadness in the essay. They felt closer to me, more connected, even protective of me. Some said that my tears made it acceptable for them to cry. They knew from the comments about my wife's death that I understood the grief arising from the loss of a loved one. My tears were probably a more telling confirmation of the power of Becky's essay than were my words. All of the students could see that I was actively engaged with her essay. During the moment of my tears, our relationship changed from the asymmetrical teacher-student relationship to one of equality: we were two human beings who were both grieving the deaths of loved ones. Marsha Linehan, a cognitive-behavioral psychologist, would call this moment in therapy one of "radical genuineness," in which a therapist relates with his or her "genuine self" to a patient" (378). My tears were proof of the intersubjective nature of teaching, where the teacher's subjectivity encounters the student's subjectivity, each influencing and being influenced by the other.

After the semester ended, Becky told me that she thought about cutting herself when she was depressed but decided against it. The other essays included here all explore the link between depression and cutting.

Francesca: "Writing about It Now Is Making My Skin Burn"

I began writing this essay after we heard the essay about being in love with cutting in class. Originally I had not intended on finishing this essay, I found it difficult to write on depression. Although I have dealt with my own depression and that of other immediate family members, I felt as though I were whining. I decided to complete the following essay.

The essay we heard in class about cutting fascinated me. Maybe because I never considered cutting as something that you could fall in love with, but I do know that it is something that one can easily become infatuated by. For a brief time I would cut myself on a regular basis. I was anorexic, and for some reason slitting my arm satisfied this hunger inside of me. Most often I would draw a bath and make it really hot; almost scalding. I'd grab a pink lady Bic and strategically pick the spot where I would cut myself; three-quarter sleeves were in style that year, so I was unable to cut my wrists. I'd angle the blade against my skin until I could feel a twinge of pain, I'd then begin to run it back and forth against my arm. Writing about it now is making my skin burn.

I'd saw at my arm to the point that I was both amused and numb, not only to the pain but the emotion as well. I'd lie in the hot water and not wash the blood off of my arm; I would just let it slide down my arm and let it stay where it felt comfortable. Typically the water around me would turn a tint of orange; I wouldn't let enough blood leave my arm for the water to completely turn pink. I would then stare at the sea foam colored tile in my bathroom, and be completely content with myself, often times with a smile across my face. Between the heat from the tub, and my latest cutting project, I would be completely [de-stressed]. Oftentimes I felt as though I just had a deep tissue massage. Usually I would end up falling asleep in the hot water. When I'd wake up, most of the blood would be dried, and had turned a copper color; I would miss the red color, but knew that my now pruned fingers couldn't "responsibly" handle a razor. I'd clean up my arm, take a shower, to get the orange tint off of my skin, and often would have to scrub the bathtub which would be stained with the same orange tint. Normally I'd be exhausted by the experience and would climb into bed, still in my towel, and go to sleep.

I'm not sure what drove me to cutting; eating disorders themselves are a form of self-mutilation. I still have scars as a reminder of my ignorance, selfishness, and utter delusion. I feel bad for the person who was in love with cutting because that meant that she was in love with her own physical and mental destruction. Once a former therapist told me that people who are ill, whether it be with an eating disorder or depression, enjoyed their destruction because it was their own. I sympathize for anyone who believes that self-destruction is the answer to their problems, for only treatment can truly aid in putting problems to rest.

This is how I responded to hearing about cutting, something that I am ashamed of doing in my past. I guess when people are sick, they are unable to see what they are doing to themselves; I was unable to see what I was doing to myself while I was depressed and anorexic. Being emerged in depression is extremely difficult, not only for the obvious reasons of being upset and what not, but the feeling of being alone. I recall wallowing in my own depression, and not allowing anyone to penetrate this wall that I had subconsciously built around myself. My friends attempted to comfort me, but I felt as though they had ulterior motives. I guess there is a reason why depression, eating disorders, and self-mutilation are referred to as forms of mental illness.

The contrast between Francesca's moral disapproval of her past cutting history and the sensuous, almost erotic description of lying in a bathtub of hot water after cutting herself is palpable. So too is the way in which these distant memories evoke a sudden physical sensation. That her skin begins to "burn" when she writes about self-cutting reveals the power of the contagion effect. She recalls these experiences not in Wordsworthian emotion recollected in tranquility but in shame and, perhaps, unruly desire.

Lea: "That Moment Defined My Weapon of Choice"

When you started reading the essay about that person's addiction and love for self-mutilation, I felt my whole body tense up. I didn't realize I was holding my breath until you reached the end and I let out a huge sigh of relief. The graphic descriptions of the way the person cut him- or herself made my skin crawl; I never had a good tolerance for gore. I became nervous by the sheer honesty of the story. I think I have a fear of the truth. This person was so truthful in the essay, allowing all of his or her vulnerability to sit on a page in black and white. I loved and envied this person's honesty and it made me want to be honest with myself. Although I never dealt with self-mutilation to the degree that the person we heard about did, I have experienced the same feelings of despair and hopelessness. All I wanted to feel was confidence and happiness, but it always seemed just beyond my reach.

It all started for me when I was about 14 years old. I was a dancer and had danced with the same group of girls for seven years. We all knew each other well, but like all groups, cliques formed. I was always on the outside. I'm sure if you asked any of these girls if they thought I was an outcast, they would say no. But I was. Far from the best dancer, I couldn't compete with the girls that had perfect pirouettes or legs that stretched on for days. I was friendly with most of the girls, but didn't share the same interests outside of dance. While they listened to rap, I liked rock. Most of them were cheerleaders or members of their high school kick lines, while I played lacrosse and ran track. They wore girly outfits. I loved jeans and tee shirts. Normal adolescent insecurities ran through my mind, as I wondered if the other girls would ever fully accept me. And then I got what I thought was my chance to prove that I could be "one of them."

At one particular dance competition, we were all in the dressing room, putting on our costumes and preparing for our performance, when I heard one of the girls cry out, "OW! What the hell did you just do to me?" A few others and I ran over and saw the one girl had taken the cap of a water bottle and twisted it into the other girl's upper arm. "See," the other girl said, showing her own tricep. "I've got one, too." Before I could understand what had come over me, I stuck out my upper arm and said, "Do one on me." I felt a deep dig and a painful sting, as the sharp edges of the cap scratched into my skin. It hurt, but I watched as a smile of approval formed on my mutilator's face. And that moment defined my weapon of choice.

I've made circle scars on different parts of my body. I had one on the inside of each ankle, on my upper thighs, the back of my wrists—anywhere that I could easily conceal. Even though I never showed anyone the rings that decorated my skin, it made me feel better, in some weird way. It was like I kept reassuring myself that people liked me. That behavior stopped after I finished dancing two years later. I think this story was like a warmup to what I really thought about after hearing the self-mutilation story from class.

If it hasn't become obvious up to this point, I'll state it in plain English: my insecurities could eat me alive. I think I'm a fairly attractive person; I get good grades and have been lucky enough to fall in love with a great man. But I have an amazing sense of insecurity and it won't let me go. I think it started between 6th and 7th grade. I began to admire girls in the "popular" group and made friends with people who had older siblings. I felt like being associated with them made me cool, too. However, I quickly learned that these people were not true friends, as I never completely found a niche among that group. Feeling low about myself and trying to see what made the other girls different from me, I analyzed the different qualities that I thought people liked in my popular friends. They were all so skinny. I wanted to be skinny like them. I wanted older guys to grab me by the waist and remark about how my ribs jutted out. And that's when a different kind of self-mutilation started.

Lea's essay is noteworthy for several reasons. Like Maryann and Paige, she became infected by the idea of self-mutilation. (Francesca never tells us how she first learned about cutting.) Her language suggests that she was unable to resist a force that suddenly and mysteriously overwhelmed her body's defenses, rendering her vulnerable to physical harm. "Before I could understand what had come over me, I stuck out my upper arm and said, 'Do one on me.'" According to Favazza, Lea is typical of self-cutters in that her action is spontaneous and untypical in that she knows precisely when she began harming her body. "For the majority of self-mutilators this behavior is impulsive and has obscure origins. Indeed, when 250 chronic self-mutilators were asked, 'What influenced you first to harm yourself?' 91 percent answered that it just happened. The response can be understood as a reflection of the cultural embeddedness of self-mutilation in the profound, elemental experience of healing, personal salvation, and social amity" (189). Lea's essay also demonstrates the connection between cutting and low self-esteem. Using a water bottle cap as a "weapon of choice" is but one of the many ways in which the female body becomes an object of violence—a target for both men and women alike. It is striking to see how many female students write about violence against their bodies. Hearing the anonymous essay on cutting made Lea's body "tense up." This was the same reaction reported to me when I told a colleague in another department that Patty and I were writing a book about cutting. "I felt like someone had punched me in the stomach," my colleague exclaimed, and she then proceeded to tell me about her daughter, who had cut herself in high school. Indeed, many times when I discussed this book with colleagues, friends, and students, I learned about other people who cut themselves, most of whom are female. It is almost as if cutting has become a female rite of passage.

Hypercriticism of the body appears more common in women's writings than in men's. This helps to explain the coexistence of self-cutting and eating disorders in many women, reflective, in Favazza's words, of the body under siege. "A most intriguing recent finding is that as many as 50 percent of female chronic self-mutilators have a history of anorexia nervosa or bulimia. In some cases the eating disorder precedes self-mutilation while in others the reverse is true" (206). Hypercriticism of the female body recalls the provocative observation made by novelist and art critic John Berger:

> The social presence of a woman is different in kind from that of a man. A man's presence is dependent upon the promise of power which he embodies. . . . A man's presence suggests what he is capable of doing to you or for you. . . . By contrast, a woman's presence expresses her own attitude to herself, and defines what can and cannot be done to her. . . . A woman must continually watch herself. She is almost continually accompanied by her own image of herself. From earliest childhood she has been taught and persuaded to survey herself continually. . . . She has to survey everything she is and everything she does because how she appears to others, and ultimately how she appears to men, is of crucial importance for what is normally thought of as the success of her life. Her own sense of being in herself is supplanted by a sense of being appreciated as herself by another. . . . Men look at women. Women watch themselves being looked at. This determines not only most relations between men and women but also the relation of women to themselves. The surveyor of woman in herself is male: the surveyed female. Thus she turns herself into an object—and most particularly an object of vision: a sight. (45–47)

Violence against the female body can be seen in the next two student essays, turned in the last week of the semester. Rosemary writes poignantly about her feeling of helplessness as she witnesses her sister's ongoing depression.

Rosemary: "It Is Terrible to See Someone You Love Degenerate before Your Eyes

My younger sister Lois is a 5'10" piece of artwork. She has sparkling blue eyes and silky, long blond hair that would make even the most confident woman jealous. She is eighteen years old and still has golden, babylike skin. If every human being had a theme song to define his or her persona, hers would be "Heartbreaker" by Pat Benatar. But, she's oblivious to her beauty; Lois is suicidal and manic-depressive.

It didn't always used to be this way. She used to be one of the most enthusiastic people I knew. I remember Christmas morning of 1993. The smell of pine permeated the house and freshly fallen snow blanketed the grass outside. I woke up to the delighted sounds of my siblings, thrilled at the overflow of presents under the Christmas tree. "Look at this!" I bragged, holding a new toy in my small arms. "No way!" exclaimed Lois, "Santa brought you the pink Porsche to match Barbie's dream house! Can I use it, please?" she begged. "Not until I'm done with it. You have plenty of new toys, too," I said. Secretly, I was thrilled that she wanted something I owned.

Lois always wanted to be around me. She would get excited when I'd invite her to go anywhere with my friends and me. If she ever asked to join us on an outing to which I said no, she would look at me with sad, suffering eyes that would make me regret my decision instantly. She never questioned my authority. We had our share of fights during childhood: who had the better nail polish color, which Disney movie we should watch, and who would be "it" in a game of freeze tag.

My relationship with Lois was solid until I reached the age of eighteen; she was fifteen. Until this point, we were inseparable. Conversation was never awkward or mundane; we talked about everything from sex to Star Wars. We have three older siblings, yet I knew that Lois liked being around me the most. We could engage in a full conversation with a single glance. It was great to have that kind of relationship with a family member.

During summer vacation of 2004, Lois was brutally raped. It took a full year before she would talk about it. She had a couple of drinks at a house party and was physically unable to fight off her attacker. When she told me, my heart sank. My sorrow turned to rage. A part of me blamed her for making the poor choice of choosing to drink with one of her girl friends and a house full of strangers. She put herself into a bad situation, but that does not justify a rape. If she knew the beast that did this to her, I would be in jail for homicide. I am a composed woman but if in my life, I ever encounter her attacker, he will be sorry he crossed my path. I can't think about the rape for more than a minute before I break down. The pain he has caused my sister and my family is unforgivable.

Flash forward to the year 2005. Lois has been struggling with weight issues but in the last year, her anorexia and bulimia grew worse. She lost control over one aspect of her life, so she takes pleasure in her alarming eating patterns. I didn't know it at the time, but the rape factored into her consumption routine. She lost 50 pounds off her 5'10" frame, now standing at a frightening weight of 110 pounds. She mutilates herself not only by starvation and binging and purging, but also by cutting and burning various parts of her body. I don't understand it. She smokes weed every day, but sadly I see this as the least of her worries right now. My mother has sent her to doctors, therapists, and treatment centers; nothing is helping her. One night during summer holiday, I was relaxing in the living room after a long day of work. My mother was folding laundry in a nearby bedroom. Lois quietly stepped downstairs from her bedroom, two empty bottles of Tylenol in hand. With tears streaming down her face she whispered, "Mom, I've just taken these pills but it's a mistake; I'm not ready to die." She was rushed to the hospital, where her stomach was pumped. I sat in the waiting room for three hours in a daze. Did this just happen? A neighbor works in the emergency unit of this hospital and was shocked when she saw why Lois was brought in. I tried to tell her, but I couldn't speak. That's when the tears began to flow. My neighbor was in denial about Lois's suicidal nature.

My family started to lock up the kitchen and bathroom cabinets so Lois wouldn't be tempted to binge and purge or cut. My mother and I took turns monitoring her while she was in the shower, her favorite place to vomit. I realized this was an invasion of privacy, but I didn't want my sister to die. I felt sick staring at her naked and fragile body. We threw away or locked up any items considered dangerous, but it was easy to confiscate a nail file or a pair of scissors; all it took was one sharp edge.

A few months ago, Lois moved out of my mother's house and in with some friends. She has no desire to go to college right now and works sixty hours a week at a fast food shop. She is so smart, and it pains me to see her destroying her future. Depression is a dangerous illness because of its ability to ruin a life that you've worked so hard to build. There used to be a time when Lois was carefree. I miss that Lois and know she will never come back. I want her to see how beautiful life is again; I want her to know that she can overcome these obstacles. I talk to her every week and try my best to keep her motivated. Some days are better than others; she relapses and throws up her food or cuts herself. I know she is fighting a difficult battle. I'm grateful that her friends are just as supportive as her family. I don't know how to help and that is what hurts the most. It is terrible to see someone you love degenerate before your eyes and feel as helpless as he or she does. How can you help someone that doesn't want to be helped? You can't. I would give her all the pink Porsches in the world if it would make her better.

Rosemary read her essay aloud, and my first comment focused on its tight structure, noting that she ends with the affectionate reference to the pink Porsche, on which she begins the paper. Nearly flawless technically, the writing evokes both nostalgia for the past and heartbreak over the present. Whereas most of Rosemary's classmates write about their own depression, she describes her sister's mood disorder, thus giving us the viewpoint of the witness to suffering. She knows she invades her sister's privacy by watching her shower, but she is willing to risk this if it means saving a life. In such a grim situation, she concludes that she is now willing to give anything for her sister's recovery.

Isabelle: "Cutting Was My Way of Making My Depression Real"

"Girls only try to kill themselves to get attention." I had been sitting in my friend's room, enjoying yet another intense debate. None of us seemed to agree on anything, but that only made the deliberation more challenging. Somehow, the topic had turned to depression and suicide. Ed made a comment suggesting that females only attempt suicide to gain attention. I've never lost control to that extent. I rose from my chair screaming until my face became an angry shade of red.

Ted and Ken both tried to comfort me, and censure Ed for saying something so ignorant. Too frustrated to remain in the room, I left. I slammed my door and sat in my bedroom alone, contemplating my past. I had suicidal thoughts from an early age. I was seeing the school psychologist in seventh grade with frequency. After months of skipping class to talk to her, I confided that I believed suicide would solve my problems.

One day after school, I sat crying on the floor of my kitchen. I could see my reflection in the blade of the knife as I held it to my wrist. I slid it across my skin. Beads of blood began to form, and I threw the knife to the ground in fear. That was as close as I came to committing suicide. I thought about suicide all of the time. I'd sit in my room, and stare at a hook hanging down from the ceiling. I wondered if I could find a rope strong enough to support my weight. I tried to hang myself a few times without success. I shrugged it off, and remarked with frustration that if my parents owned a gun I could have gotten it over with by then.

The school psychologist called my mother at work. She told my mother about my visits to her office, and that I was having suicidal thoughts. I knew about the phone call and felt a sense of relief. I thought that if my mother knew about my depression, maybe I could get help outside of school, and I wouldn't have to feel alone.

That evening, after dinner and pleasant conversation, I cornered my mother in her bedroom and asked her if she had received a call from the school. "Yes." I asked her if she had anything to say to me. "She told me that you wanted to kill yourself. That's just stupid." I ran to my room, cried, and decided that my mother could benefit from a parenting course. Nothing changed, and my depression faded into a general loneliness during high school. I wasn't happy, but I wasn't trying to kill myself either.

Freshman year of college was difficult for me. I had many acquaintances, but no true friends. I felt left out and alone. I didn't believe that I was liked. My depression became so difficult for me that I visited the University Counseling Center. I was given a prescription for Zoloft. I didn't begin cutting right away.

I told a friend that I liked him. Surprised by my own courage, I waited for him to tell me that he liked me as well. He didn't. He said nothing, and agreed to think about my revelation. A week later he hadn't responded. We didn't speak at all over Winter Break. A few weeks after our return from intersession, I was beginning to lose faith. I was naive and hadn't yet understood that his silence was his way of letting me down gently.

After a long talk with two girls who lived down the hall, I sat in my room. All of the lights were off; the only objects I could see were those illuminated by the glow of my computer screen. I wrote in my online journal. I cried and typed, slamming my fingers in to the keys in an attempt to take my pain and frustration out on them. What could I do to make this pain go away? I don't recall actively remembering the article I had read on cutting. The issue of Seventeen *was at least three years old, but I had never forgotten the chilling tales it recounted.*

Suddenly, as though my hands were out of my control, I grabbed my box cutter. Slowly I dragged the blade across my forearm. When blood formed, I couldn't resist another cut. The next cuts were not as precise as the first. I was out of control, slashing away at my arm until the sight of my own blood dripping on to the floor jarred me out of my trance. I grabbed a towel and thanked god that I would be visiting my psychologist the next day. I didn't understand what I had just done.

My cutting went on for months. Every time I felt inferior, or like I wasn't good enough, I cut. I signed up for housing on behalf of my chosen suitemates. I chose the dorm that we had agreed on, but everyone else had been delegated into a different building. They blamed me for separating them from our friends with my good lottery number. I cut.

Eventually, a friend found me in the bathroom with a knife. My roommate was in our room, and I had no privacy to cut there. My friend took a Ziploc bag and filled it with my knives, scissors, and razor blades. Ted took them and kept them in his room. I still have scars on my forearms. They're barely visible, but I can see them when I shower. The lines on my arm turn bright red.

In retrospect, I believe that I did cut to get attention. It was not intentional. I didn't know why my low self-esteem caused me to reach for my box cutters. Perhaps after reading the magazine article on cutting, I believed subconsciously that cutting is what people do when they are depressed. Cutting legitimized my depression.

During my childhood, my mother never believed me when I told her that I was sick. I coughed until I couldn't breathe for three weeks before she brought me to the doctor. I had whooping cough. My stomach had hurt since elementary school, and I wasn't taken to a doctor until I was 18. I was diagnosed with Ulcerative Colitis.

Whenever I feel unwell, I don't think that anyone will believe that

I am truly sick. I've refused to go to doctors because I didn't trust that they would believe that I was ill. I thought of my depression in the same terms. No one would believe that I was depressed unless I could prove it with my cutting.

Cutting was my way of making my depression real. Even now I question the reality of my depression. I think that I acted the way I did for attention. I've stopped believing in myself and my feelings. The cutting didn't make the depression real for me. Neither did the drugs, or the therapy. I feel like an imposter writing about my depression, because everything we've read about depression indicates that it should be more intense than my past.

The reality is that I did cut. The pain that I felt was real enough. Maybe, I would be more of an imposter if I maintained that my cutting came from a purely depressed and hopeless place.

Isabelle gave me permission at first to read her essay anonymously to the class, but she then changed her mind. She disclosed in an early autobiographical paragraph that she had cut herself in high school, yet she provided no details. Now she does. She begins the essay by disagreeing angrily with a friend's assertion that "Girls only try to kill themselves to get attention," but she then concludes by admitting that she cut herself for precisely this reason, though there were other reasons as well. She is almost certainly aware of this contradiction. Another contradiction is that she begins by declaring that she enjoys intense debates but soon becomes infuriated by her friend's offensive generalization.

Unlike Maryann's response to intervention, Isabelle welcomes the school psychologist's telephone call home, though she is disappointed by her mother's apparent unconcern. The daughter's inability to talk with her mother recalls Louise Kaplan's observation that "one of the reasons a delicate cutter is unable to communicate her anxiety and rage and longing in words is that she has learned never to bother her parents with unpleasant thoughts or feelings" (385). The most understated sentence in the essay occurs when she observes wryly, in understated language, that her mother "could benefit from a parenting course." Isabelle implies that the impulse to cut herself arose from a magazine article she had read three years earlier. Like Maryann, with whom she has much in common, she was infected by the idea of cutting herself. She doesn't describe herself "falling in love" with cutting, as Maryann does, but she seems to cut herself for the same reasons, experiencing the same psychological relief. She implies that she would not have cut herself had she received the attention and support she needed. She felt so insecure that she even wonders whether she was depressed at the time—something which Maryann and Paige never question about themselves.

Three men wrote essays about cutting themselves while depressed, two of whom allowed me to read their essays anonymously. (The third essay was turned in too late for me to read anonymously.)

Aaron: "The Culmination of My Worst Night of Depression"

The scissors glistened in the moonlight as I gripped them in my right hand. Tears slid down my face as I opened them and cut myself across the palm of my left hand. Blood trickled from the cut and landed on the off-white sheets of my bed. This episode was the culmination of my worst night of depression ever.

My freshman year of college was rough. I didn't know many people. I had a few friends from high school that came here, but none lived in my dorm. As I tried to become comfortable living with my roommate and suitemates, it seemed as if we wouldn't get along. They were much different than I. They drank, smoked, and stayed out all night. I was focused on my academics. My idea of going out on a Friday night was going to the movies with my friends. The thought of going to a bar never crossed my mind. Night after night, I would sit in my room alone either doing homework or watching TV. My parents would tell me during our weekly phone conversations to be myself and I would make friends. I didn't have the heart to tell them that being myself wasn't working. I was willing to do whatever it took to become friends with the people that I lived with.

I began to seclude myself from everyone in my suite. I would go to and from class and not talk to anybody. My door would always be closed, and I would spend hour after hour in my room or in the library. I couldn't understand why my roommate and suitemates didn't want to be friends with me. I was miserable in my suite. I found myself going home every other weekend just so I could be around friends from home. I literally started to dread every moment that I spent in my suite. For awhile, I thought that maybe I had done something to upset them and they didn't want to be around me. Then, one day, I was approached by one of my suitemates. He knocked on my door and asked if he could talk to me. He asked me if I had problems with anybody in the suite. I said that I didn't but felt as though everyone else had a problem with me. He told me that nobody else had a problem with me and that they were all wondering why I never spent time with them.

After that talk, I started to socialize with the people with whom I lived. I found myself doing things that I had never done before. I never drank before I entered college, now I found myself drinking at least 3–4 times a week. If we didn't go out to the bars, we were funneling beer in our suite. I was so happy these guys wanted to be friends with me that I didn't care about anything else. My grades started to suffer and I was failing 2 of my classes. As long as I've been in school, I've never gotten less than a C in a class so getting any grade below that was unacceptable to me and my parents. However, I found myself not caring. The guys that I lived with and I were enjoying our freshman year of college to the fullest and everything else just seemed irrelevant. Then came the night that changed everything.

My suitemates were selling mushrooms from our suite, something that I didn't find out until I started hanging out with them. At all hours of the night, random people would come into the suite to buy mushrooms and enhance the night that was ahead of them. Even though I found myself drinking on a regular basis, drugs were something that I swore to myself that I would never mess around with. However, as time went on, I found myself becoming curious about mushrooms.

One night I walked into my suite to find our friends Carly and Frannie sitting in the corner of my bathroom with a blanket on their head. They were both known for their excessive drinking so I figured that they had just passed out in the bathroom. Then I heard them talking about seeing colors while laughing hysterically. Mind you, all of the lights in the bathroom were off so this led me to believe that something was going on. I walked into the bathroom and turned on the light. Carly peeked out from under the blanket and told me to turn off the light cause they couldn't see the colors anymore. I stared at them confused and bewildered and shut the lights off as I walked toward my bedroom. I walked into my room and asked my roommate what was going on with my friends. He told me that they were on mushrooms and tripping and to just let them be. Not being familiar with the drug, I became like a 5-year-old child and started asking every question that came to mind. The prospect of hallucinating and seeing different colors made me curious beyond measure. I had to try it. He warned me that I shouldn't take them by myself because it was possible to have a bad trip. He said that people have killed themselves while having a bad trip before so I should always be with someone.

A couple of weeks later, I convinced Carly and Frannie to eat the mushrooms with me so I wouldn't have to trip by myself. I bought a 1/8 from my suitemate for $30 and crushed them up into a bowl of pasta. After consuming the pasta, I felt nothing. It wasn't until an hour later that the feeling kicked in. I found myself becoming somewhat light-headed. I was watching the movie Animal House *and the movie seemed to be a lot funnier than usual. I found myself laughing hysterically at the entire movie even during the noncomical scenes. After the movie was over, I walked to Carly and Frannie's room across the hall. They were both sitting on their bed talking. I couldn't make out their conversation at first, but as I got closer I heard them talking about sitting in their oceans. I walked in and sat on Carly's bed and was told to get out of her ocean because the* *sharks would eat me. I fell on the floor laughing uncontrollably. An hour or so later, I got the urge to go back to my room and lie down. I walked into my bedroom and kept the lights off. For some reason, I felt happy being in the dark.*

My roommate walked in and saw me with the scissors in my hand. He ran to my bed and pulled the scissors out of my hand and saw the blood. He started screaming to my suitemates that I had cut myself and to grab some towels. A frenzy broke out in my room. The guys that I lived with ran in and out of my room with towels and bandages to try to mend my wound. Ultimately they thought it would be best to take me to the hospital to have them look at it. I spent the night in Albany Medical Center and returned home the next morning. My cut hadn't been deep enough for stitches so they had bandaged me up and let me leave. When I got back to my room, I apologized to my roommate and suitemates for the ordeal that I put them through and they told me that it was cool.

Even though everything seemed to go back to normal in the suite, I knew that everything wasn't normal. My underlying depression of not fitting in and the drop of my grades had caused me to have a bad trip and physically harm myself. I hadn't seen the colors that I had desperately wanted to see. Except for the excessive laughing, the mushrooms caused me nothing but regret. I knew that I had to make some changes in my lifestyle. The excessive drinking had to stop and I knew even despite my curiosity, there would be no more encounters with any drugs, ever. I eventually did pull my grades up and I took my parents' advice about being myself. I realized that the guys that I lived with really weren't people that I wanted to surround myself with. My parents always told me to surround myself with people who will enhance me and I finally understood why.

Aaron appears to be a "one-time cutter." He doesn't tell us how he learned about cutting, why he felt the need to cut himself, whether cutting provided him with psychic relief, or whether he was consciously aware of what he was doing. The most compelling sentence for me is the first one, in which we see the scissors glistening in the moonlight. The scissors reflects not only the moon but also the desperation that compelled him to consume an illicit substance. The nocturnal light proves illusory in the end, as he discovers, and he concludes the essay by acknowledging his parents' good advice, which he dutifully conveys to his readers. Significantly, though Aaron's story differs from those of Maryann and Paige, his experimentation with hallucinogenic mushrooms recalls a similar scene in the novel *Crosses*.

Many college freshmen as well as upperclassmen would identify with Aaron's cautionary tale. Desire for peer acceptance is intense, especially when one feels loneliness as a result of living away from home for the first time. Forty percent of college students drop out during their freshman year, largely because they don't know how to adapt to a strange new environment. This can also be seen in Greg's story.

Greg: "How Could I Stop the Pain without Stopping the Beating of My Heart?"

Depression is much more than the blues; it is more than normal, everyday ups and downs. There are various forms or types of depression. Some people experience only one episode of depression in their whole life, but many have several recurrences. I am grateful to say that I have had only one instance in which I have been greatly affected by this.

During my freshman year at the University at Albany, I found myself overwhelmed with what was going on in my life. There were very few reasons to hold my head high. I knew that the road would contain a few bumps but I was not prepared for such a difficult ride.

Entering SUNY Albany as a seventeen-year-old freshman, I felt as if I ruled the world. Life seemed to be worth living. All the hard work during high school had paid off. Living on my own was a reality and I finally had reason to smile. Things couldn't get any better, or at least that's what I had thought. Much as it has always been, good times never last too long.

Throughout high school, I always found a way to get by in all of my classes doing the minimum work that was asked from me. Being a procrastinator always seemed to suit me best and as I entered college I felt as if I would be able to continue this routine and all will work out in the end; I was wrong.

At the end of my first semester I was shocked to receive my final grades. "How could this happen to me? Could it be possible that all of my teachers incorrectly entered my grades?" Immediately, I looked through all of my exams and realized that I was the one who was to blame.

"Thank god the grades were not mailed home" is all I thought. Staring at the computer screen which revealed my final grades, I imagined the reaction of my family when they found out the news. "We sent you away to college to be a failure? Why are you in college?"

I wanted to tell the computer that it was wrong and convince it that my grades should be higher than what it showed. My heart pumped violently and my eyes watered with the fear of my parent's shame in mind. "How can I let them down? What am I doing with my life?" I pinched myself many times hoping that I could awake from this horrible hallucination. Sadly enough, I was not asleep and my arm was filled with tiny red markings from all of the pinching.

After receiving the bad news of my final grades, I picked up the phone and called my ex-girlfriend in order to receive some comfort and shed some light on this already dim situation; she answered the phone upon the first ring. It was almost as if she knew what had happened; I knew more bad news would come my way. I spoke with very few words before she began weeping. Confused, I remember asking what felt like thousands of questions before she decided to share the information that would change the rest of my life. She was pregnant with my child and had no idea what to do.

"I'm too young to be a father," I thought. I never had the heart to tell her about my grades with fear of the tears that would be shed by

both of us. Few words were spoken after she delivered the news, and we both were uncertain of what the future held. "What was there to do?" There is no way I can handle bringing a child into this world if I can't handle college. My head felt as if it were filled to capacity with worries and fears of what the future held.

There was no way that I was going to share the news of my ex-girlfriend being pregnant. "How could I?" There was no one in the world that could make things better, and I felt a feeling of solitude that still feels to be kept in me till this very day. I learned that if you share little information with others, there will be little room for disappointment. Although I knew this was an incorrect way of carrying on with life, I felt as if there was no other option.

For days I kept the news about my academic standing away from my family. Anytime someone would ask about my grades I would respond by saying that they hadn't arrived. I wanted no part of being the family shame. The worst part of it all was that all of my relatives cheered for me as I shared the news that I would be going away for college. "How could I have let so many people down?" I understood that I was the only one to blame in this situation and I knew what must be done in order to do better. I feared the hours of lecturing and scolding that seemed to draw closer by the second.

The day arrived when I finally told my family about how my semester concluded. I printed out my final grades and I handed the paper to my parents. I saw a look on my parent's eyes that sent goose bumps down my skin. But it was not a scary look, it was more like an "I'm ashamed that you share my last name look"; or at least that's how I felt. To my surprise there were no lectures or scolding that followed this. The look of disappointment [that] seemed to burn straight through my body proved to be enough punishment. They both walked away at the same time leaving me to ponder my plans in life.

I have always been the main focus of attention in my family and I wanted nothing more than to give this responsibility away. I had partied too much throughout my freshman year and my grades suffered. I began recalling all of the crucial moments in the semester where my lackadaisical attitude drove me to mediocrity. I wanted a second chance but I felt as if I would never restore my parent's feelings of pride in me.

There were so many obstacles that I was supposed to overcome that I felt hopeless and felt as if my only purpose in life was to disappoint others. I had no clue of which problem I should deal with first; I never decided to solve either one. My depression hit an all time high as I was neglected by the family that was once proud of me for every little accomplish I had. I had let everyone down and no one was more disappointed than I was in myself.

Shortly after, I decided to withdraw myself from everyone. I did not want to grow closer to anyone else. My life felt as if it were on a down-whirl spiral and felt its conclusion was soon to come. I would lock myself in the room the entire day and would only come out to eat. I was ashamed of myself and I didn't want anyone to know; I knew I would be pitied.

I was hurt for days. I ignored my family and they did the same in return. Eye contact was not an option because I knew they would not be able to look at me. My winter vacation was drawing close to its end and I did not want to come back to Albany. I felt incapable of being successful in life and wanted to run away from my current situation.

There came a point where I could not perform even the simplest daily activities like getting out of bed or getting dressed. I felt alone and frustrated; my soul felt destroyed. There was a deafening sound of emptiness and I felt as if I could not stop myself from falling into a deep abyss. "How could I stop the pain without stopping the beating of my heart?" I thought to myself.

I contemplated suicide on multiple occasions. One day, I was alone in the house and I could bare the guilt of being a failure no longer. I stared at a sharp knife that I found in the kitchen and knew that it could all go away with a simple slice of the wrist. I placed the knife beside me on the bed as I grabbed a sheet of paper and wrote my last words. I apologized for being a huge disappointment and hoped that they would understand why I had decided to take my own life. I broke out in tears as I imagined the look on my parents' faces as they stared down at my body on the ground. "How could this be so difficult?" I didn't seem to have stood a chance in life on my own.

As I concluded my letter I held the knife to my neck in an attempt to slice my throat. "Would this make everything better?" Is this my escape from the world?" I was terrified to commit to my own demise and, out of frustration, sliced my arms. "If this could only be that easy" I thought. I raised the music on my radio to its maximum in an attempt to drown out my sorrows; it did not work. I knew that killing myself would not give me a chance to clear my name. I did not want to be pitied and I knew by giving in to suicide I would never be able to explain my actions.

I dropped the knife and my eyes felt exhausted from tearing so much; I could no longer cry. I realized I was alone yet also understood that I was the only person that could make it all better. I thank God everyday for stopping me. I was given a second chance and knew that redemption was soon to come.

Life seemed to be promising very shortly after when I received a call from my ex-girlfriend. She informed me that she took another pregnancy test and it came back negative. I felt overcome with joy and knew that this was God's way of giving me a second chance to restore what was important in my life and focus on what needed to be done in order to brighten my promising future.

I returned to SUNY Albany for my second semester with hopes of accomplishing the high grades I felt I was capable of doing; I did just that. I stayed away from numerous parties and did what I had to do in order to be successful. I returned home after the semester concluded and felt proud to show my parents that they were wrong for thinking little of me. I finally could hold my head high as I walked around.

I once read in a novel by A. B. Curtis, "Depression always ends. Not because of psychotherapy. Not because of psychoanalysis or shock treatments. Depression always ends because it is in the very nature of depression to end. The only question is, how can we get it to end sooner, the way we want it to, instead of later." Fighting off depression was the most difficult task I have encountered. For the first time in my life, I'm happy to be alive and I have reason to live another day.

Several students, including Maryann, referred to the shame they experienced when they cut themselves, but Greg's description is the most intense. His essay is a textbook case study of the role of toxic shame in depression and suicide. Before entering college, he felt as if he "ruled the world," a statement that alerts us to his impending downfall. His pride hints of arrogance, what the ancient Greeks called "hubris." He takes full responsibility for his fall from grace. He then describes the two types of shame discussed by researchers: the "fear of *feeling* ashamed (e.g., the actual aroused emotions and internal feelings)" and the "fear of *being* shamed" (Gilbert 7; emphasis in original). Devastated that he has disappointed his parents, who will be ashamed of him, he then learns that he has apparently fathered a child. The "look of disappointment" that seems to "burn" straight through his body, compelling him to avoid eye contact, conveys the corrosive physical effects of shame, including "gaze aversion, head movements down, and constricted and collapsed posture" (Keltner and Harker 88). The decision to withdraw from his family, and their withdrawal from him, suggests the sociological phenomenon of shunning. His statement that he was unable to establish eye contact demonstrates the wish to hide from others and become invisible. As James MacDonald observes, "The word *shame* is in fact thought to derive from an Indo-European word meaning *hide*, and the idea that shame motivates hiding and concealment is a central defining component of shame for most theorists" (142). This may explain the apparent Freudian slip when he refers to his inability to "bare" (as in "expose") rather than "bear" ("endure") his shame. "He who is ashamed would like to force the world not to look at him, not to notice his exposure," remarks Erik Erikson. "He would like to destroy the eyes of the world. Instead he must wish for his own invisibility" (252–53).

Greg's shame was so crushing that he could not imagine remaining alive. Fortunately, he knew that killing himself would not allow him to clear his name. Shame is the most virulent of emotions, so deadly that it feels as if one is being eaten alive, but social scientists have noticed its prosocial value. "Shame interrupts any unquestioning, unaware sense of oneself," Helen Merrell Lynd writes. "But it is possible that experiences of shame if confronted full in the face may throw an unexpected light on who one is and point the way toward who one may become. Fully faced, shame may become not primarily something to be covered, but a positive experience of revelation" (20). Keenly aware of how he had fallen short of his standards, Greg needed to prove to others and himself that he was worthy. His essay illustrates the need for worthiness, particularly in his acceptance of responsibility for his actions and his decision to change his life. The pride he feels at the end of the essay is not that of arrogance but of earned self-respect.

It is difficult to imagine anything more agonizing than acknowledging shame to one's classmates and teacher. This is precisely what Aaron and Greg proceed to do in their essays. Their decision to remain anonymous and have me read their essays aloud indicates that they are not ready to show their faces, yet they know that others might try to identify the anonymous writers, about which Paige also worried. One must disclose shame carefully and selectively, for it is the riskiest of all emotions to reveal. As Paul Gilbert writes, "It is now known that keeping secrets . . . can be psychologically costly, but revelation is not without its risks—especially if it results in rejection" (20). However much they trusted their classmates, Aaron and Greg were not ready to risk the possibility of rejection. Anonymity allowed them both to reveal and conceal their shame. Because anonymous writers are hiding in plain sight, I keep my eyes focused downward on the page when reading these essays, so that I do not inadvertently glance at the authors. I could see Greg, out of the corner of my eye, with his head bowed, listening intently as I read aloud his own words.

Eric: "Cutting Is Like Killing Yourself and Coming Back"

I apologize in advance for the non-sequitur nature that this essay will probably take on. It's difficult to articulate these thoughts, and far more difficult to organize them.

Depression has been a constant theme in my life for the past couple of years. Until my freshman year of college, I didn't understand depression or how people could be so hopeless that they would consider taking their own lives. The events that have unfolded in my life since then have not only given me an understanding, but they have placed me in such a position. I'm partly thankful that I know what the darkest depths of despair are like, but it is unsettling to have these thoughts and emotions residing in my head.

Depression is impossible to define in the context of science. Sure, it involves a combination of some sort of chemical imbalance and some unfortunate events, but the emotion is too powerful to describe so efficiently. It involves a feeling of complete worthlessness. I have struggled to find my worth, and often come up with nothing to reassure myself. In those moments, I could feel the serotonin rush from my head and energy leaving my body. My brain would race, and I would wonder where I could find the nearest razor or bottle of toxic cleaner. If I have no interest in being part of a system that I've grown to despise and I cannot find an ounce of worth within myself, what am I waiting for?

I'm describing a time, not too long ago, when I constantly thought about suicide. I barely had time to consider one serious problem without another manifesting itself. I consider myself a level-headed person and a good problem-solver. However, when you begin to lose hope in every aspect of your life which was once positive, the thought of a quick escape is tantalizing. Every day I became more disenchanted with the world and with myself, until I could no longer find a reason to live. My biggest apprehension regarding suicide was the immediate effect it would have on the person who discovered me. I was so infatuated with the idea that I conjured up a plan to call 911 before I executed my own demise, in order to spare a friend from having the macabre responsibility later on. I was reminded of a scene in the film Rules of Attraction in which a woman stumbles upon the dead body of an acquaintance who has slit her wrists in a bathtub full of water, which has turned crimson.

Of course, I also considered the long-term impact that my suicide would have on friends and family. My parents, who feel as if I am growing more and more distant, would be heartbroken. They have made several subtle comments to me about suicide; kind words that come across as desperate pleas for me to explain my sorrow before it consumes me completely. My sister is one of my best friends, but our relationship only allows me to reveal so much to her. I know that she, like my parents, would spend the rest of her life wondering what she could have done to help me. My friends would be shocked and dismayed. I'm good at hiding my depression from them, and I'm sure they would be confused and angry. Am I really capable of such a selfish act? No, and that is why I am still here. The thought of my ghost haunting someone I care about makes me more upset than I already have been.

Depression is like your shadow. It is silent and sometimes forgotten, but it's always just behind you, keeping in perfect step with you at all times. Even the most joyous moments feel ephemeral when compared to the seeming permanency of sorrow. Most people would suggest that a depressed person focus on the good things in life, but from experience I can tell you that true depression washes over happy feelings and memories like a tidal wave, leaving a barren wasteland behind.

More than once, I have cut myself and sat and watched the droplets of blood form and fall away. I don't consider myself a "cutter" because I've only done it a few times and I'm not addicted. Still, I completely understand the cathartic effects of cutting. Bleeding is a physical manifestation of the release of pain. This may sound *counterintuitive, as cutting causes some degree of pain itself, but the immediate rush of energy and subtle stinging of the wound gave me a primitive sense of strength and power that quells the far greater pain inside my head. I suppose that cutting is like killing yourself and coming back. I hope for a new perspective or some kind of clarity, but each time I spend five or ten minutes staring at my arm to no avail. When you read the anonymous essay about cutting, I found myself out of breath and extremely disturbed by the words that the writer chose to explain her habit. She seemed to share my sense of worthlessness, not knowing her place in the world or if she even had one. As I've said, this, to me, is the key aspect of depression. Sometimes it feels as if I'm floating in a vacuum; unanchored in a vast, dark expanse.*

My friends are the only stability I have. They make me happy and I have the same effect on them, which gives me some hope that my life is a positive force in some way. For a while, I thought I had found the person who could take away all of my pain. She thought like me, and I wanted to believe that if there was someone who could truly understand me, she could eventually take away my fears and insecurities. Unfortunately, she also became discontent with life and fell further and further down the hole that I was already in. We could no longer help each other and our love fell apart. Again, I was left feeling hopeless. If I couldn't hold on to the best thing that ever happened to me, what was I good for? Our breakup was fairly recent, so I still have to grapple with these thoughts daily.

Much of my depression has subsided lately. I realize now that self-worth is a measure of your own satisfaction with the way you live, and only you can alter it. Spending more time with good friends, being kind, getting better grades; all of these actions can help you feel better about your station in life, and your possibilities for the future. There was a time when I didn't even regard the future because I was certain that my life was going to end soon. Now I am trying to look forward, to the end of a dark chapter in my life.

Eric's inability to define the "darkest depths of despair" of his recent life recalls William Styron's statement in *Darkness Visible* that depression is a "disorder of mood, so mysteriously painful and elusive in the way it becomes known to the self—to the mediating intellect—as to verge close to being beyond description. It thus remains nearly incomprehensible to those who have not experienced it" (7). Like Styron, he then uses metaphorical language to describe his mood disorder. Thus he can feel the serotonin "rush" from his head, the energy "leaving" his body. However debilitating depression may have been for him, writing about it produces the most powerful sentences in his essay, including the feeling that he is "floating in a vacuum," "unanchored in a vast, dark expanse." He reserves his most metaphorical language to describe cutting, which he views in terms of rebirth imagery: "like killing yourself and coming back." It is rebirth without revelation, however, for it brings no new perspective or clarity, only relief.

It is unwise to generalize from only three examples, but Aaron, Greg, and Eric portray cutting differently than do their female classmates. They did not cut themselves on a regular basis, as the women did, nor did they mention an eating disorder or physical self-consciousness. We do not see the hypercriticism of the body that appears in the female students. In John Berger's terms, the three essays display a "male presence" that shows the "promise of power" they are prepared to use against themselves, rather than a "woman's presence" that is "surveying herself."

Aaron, Greg, and Eric describe events that occurred during their freshman year in college, when they were on their own for the first time. Greg refers to writing a suicide note to explain to his parents why he was ending his life; the essay he wrote for me may be viewed as an *anti*suicide note. Like Aaron, Greg, and Eric, many freshmen have difficulty adjusting to college. A week after they submitted their essays, a freshman at the University at Albany hanged himself in his dormitory room. The number of students seeking counseling is increasing. "Student mental health is a rising concern at universities across the country—86 percent of campus counseling centers report they've seen an increase in recent years of students with severe psychological problems—nine out of 10 believe students with significant psychological disorders are a growing concern on campus" (*Albany Times-Union*, 20 December 2005). Personal writing courses may be helpful in identifying students at risk and encouraging them to visit counseling centers. While it's true that a study conducted of

333 colleges found that only 31 of the 161 students who committed suicide during the academic year 2002–2003 sought mental-health treatment on their campuses (*Chronicle of Higher Education*, 16 December 2005), experts are seeking new methods to find those who need help, such as the use of the Internet for anonymous online depression-screening questionnaires. Another possibility is a low-tech one—the use of diaries and essays to identify students at risk. This is particularly true when students have the option to ask their teacher to read their writings anonymously, as I did with most of the cutting essays. Since English teachers are often the first to become aware of a depressed student through self-disclosing writing, they can play an important role in identifying students at risk and encouraging them to seek professional help.

Six students wrote about cutting themselves, exactly 25 percent of the class. This figure is higher than I would have expected, higher, even, than the 17 percent found in the study by Whitlock, Eckenrode, and Silverman. Interestingly, the figure is close to the "eight" Maryann predicted about the number of cutters in her own class. How do we explain this high incidence? One possible explanation is that my students are not representative of those who attend a large public university. Do I draw students who are more depressed than those who enroll in other college courses? I asked my students this question during our conferences, and many told me that they did not know anything about the course or the instructor when they registered for it. Thus, I have no reason to believe that my students are significantly different from others. Five students wrote about being suicidal: Becky, Morgan (the student experiencing writer's block whom I mentioned in a previous chapter), Isabelle, Greg, and Eric—a figure slightly over 20 percent, which is consistent with the percentage of high school students who seriously consider suicide each year.

"Affected, Not Infected"

Is writing about depression depressing to the writer? Is it depressing to hear these essays read aloud? Will students be infected by such writing and reading? I did not ask these questions of Maryann and Paige's classmates, but I did the following semester during the final week of the semester. I gave the students an in-class assignment and asked them to respond to it after hearing the essays written by their classmates

Becky and Rosemary and by the two anonymous authors, Aaron and Greg:

> Today you will be hearing several essays submitted this week by members of our class focusing on depression, cutting, and suicide. These are wrenching topics to write on and often painful essays to hear. You may find yourself becoming infected by the dark emotions in these writings. As you know, I am writing (with a former graduate student) a book called *Cutting and the Pedagogy of Self-Disclosure.* After you hear these essays today, would you please write a paragraph indicating whether you believe you have become infected by these essays—or by other writings you have heard this semester. If so, what if anything could I have done differently to prevent you from becoming at risk? Did you become at risk as a result of any of your own writings? If you have become at risk as a result of writing or hearing an essay, do you regret having written or heard it? Please be as truthful as possible, and don't sign your name to this paragraph. It will count as one page toward the required forty. I plan to use your anonymous responses in our book. Thank you.

Twenty-two of the twenty-three students present in class turned in paragraphs. No one felt that he or she had become infected in the sense of being contaminated or burdened by dark emotions. The following statement reflects all but two of the responses: "At no time during this course have I felt myself becoming at risk. The essays that I have heard from my classmates have touched me, but have not sparked an interest in self-mutilation." These students felt that they were "affected, not infected" by their classmates' writings. The two students who believed they were infected used the word positively. One wrote, "I have become infected by the essays in this semester, but I wouldn't have it any other way. I've been able to communicate with fellow students and professors. Even though many of these essays are written on touchy subjects, the course is led in a way that allows a student to leave the classroom if he or she feels uncomfortable. 'Becoming at risk' is not necessarily bad; students are encouraged to write about some of the most important issues they will ever face in life. Hearing about other students' experiences promotes prevention and awareness. The hardest essays I had to write were some of the most helpful works." The other student felt infected largely in the same way. "While in this class I do sometimes feel infected by the essays; the topics we have dealt with throughout the semester have been very heavy. It would be hard not to be infected. Yet, as soon as I leave the class I feel as I did before I entered. I don't think being 'infected' by the essays is entirely bad. I feel that writing and hearing about these topics is therapeutic." No one regretted writing or hearing an essay.

I did not use the word "therapeutic" in the questions I asked the students to write on, nor had I discussed the inoculation theory at any time in the semester, but many implied that the course had strengthened them. "Writing is like therapy as far as I am concerned; it forces one to confront their 'demons' and in a way helps to relieve them." Observed another, "for me, writing is therapeutic and simply putting my thoughts and feelings down on paper helps relieve the sense of anxiety I feel." Another implied that writing is a way to unburden oneself from heavy emotions. "This class has allowed me to rid myself of some loneliness and anguish, as I realize that my 23 classmates each have their own stories and horrific trauma." Another wrote that the essays "shocked and astonished me; this is a good thing, though. At first glance I would never have assumed that the students in the class had such powerful stories to tell. After hearing these stories, I retell them to my parents and friends because I am so enamored of them. My own writing has been therapeutic. It has been the first time that I am disclosing personal information to people, and it felt great." And Greg, the author of the anonymous essay on suicide (one can infer his identity from the context of the paragraph), wrote:

> After hearing my essay read anonymously today I feel no regret in writing it. It felt therapeutic as you read it aloud. I felt as if I were reliving the moment and remember all of the shameful thoughts which overcame me. I no longer hold the feeling of suicide and understand that although this was a focal part in my life it was even more important that I overcame this obstacle. You have helped me deal with this situation more than I ever could have imagined. By opening up to our class, you allowed me to do the same. I am no longer shameful and understand that we all encounter obstacles in our life. I do not feel as if I am infected by these essays and am satisfied to have shared my experience with others. I would like to thank everyone for respecting and understanding my situation.

All the students implied that writing was helpful to them. Those who wrote about depression took comfort in knowing they were not alone.

Indeed, this was perhaps the greatest benefit of hearing essays on depression: the knowledge that many could identify because of their own experiences:

> *Though some papers have reminded me of my depression, none have put me at risk of self-mutilation again. Writing my own paper simply made me realize how troubled I used to be, and still am. The writings in this class have made me revisit the idea of entering therapy, as they've released issues and sadness that I've repressed. Writing the paper was therapeutic. While people have known the facts of my depression, I've never shared my feelings and thoughts about it until recently. Hearing the papers gave me comfort that may have helped me during my depression: others went through similar problems and feelings. If anything, this topic has shown me that I'm not alone.*

Another student who wrote about depression and suicide noted that "even though plenty of statistics" exist on these topics, "they do not have the same effects as a personal disclosure." Still another student observed that "when you're in the throes of depression, you think you're the only one who knows what you're going through; this class has taught me otherwise." And another wrote that "a lot of times we feel as if we are the only ones that are going through tough situations. These essays allow us to see that we are not alone and in turn potentially have the power to help us through our own situations."

Those students who have never experienced clinical depression were able to appreciate how fortunate they are. "As I was listening to the essays, I became upset. I was not upset with the content, but with myself. How could I become upset over a bad hair day? Or waking up 15 minutes late today? I do not feel at risk from these essays; I feel aware. I am aware that I have a wonderful life and should feel ecstatic that I do not suffer from depression. I have no other words for how I am feeling at this moment." Students who had cut themselves did not express a craving to begin cutting again; those who had never cut themselves or engaged in other types of addictive or self-destructive behavior had no interest in beginning. "If anything, hearing these essays has only confirmed the fact that I have no desire to partake of drugs or cutting."

Nearly all the students commented on feeling close to their class-mates, attached to them, inspired by their stories of suffering, growth, and maturation. They demonstrated what Dominick LaCapra calls em-pathic attunement, "being responsive to the traumatic suffering of others, notably of victims, [but without] the appropriation of their experiences" (41). "I am proud of my classmates for their willingness to divulge some of the most wrenching and emotionally charged topics in their lives. I feel closer to my classmates. I feel that taking this course has brought me closer to them. I do not fear depression or suicide, because I know with the thoughts I share, many others feel the same way. I look to my classmates as to how they dealt with problems unique to their own lives, and try to follow their courage. After hearing today's essays, I do not feel like going home and cutting myself, but I feel like writing to relieve the pain that inflicts my life. I am proud of every essay I hear for the strength that it displays and the example that it leads." Another felt that the most disturbing essays were also the most insightful. "Those of us who have experienced traumatic events in our lives are often forced to grow up faster than others. Therefore, these are the people who have the wisest words of advice. My peers' essays are learning experiences, not a disease you become infected by, like the plague."

The Write Stuff

I suspect that the empathic classroom was the main reason no one felt contaminated by an essay. The classroom became a safe container, hold-ing and detoxifying shameful emotions. Depression was no longer an ill-ness that happened to other people; students now realized how many of their classmates suffered from mood disorders. It is nearly impossible for students to read aloud essays on depression or suicide without their voices trembling. I could feel my own voice hesitating as I read aloud the anonymous essays, and they could see me crying after Becky finished reading her essay. I felt moved but not contaminated by these writings, and my students felt the same way. They began to understand how a depressed person feels—and how helpless a loved one feels in the pres-ence of a depressed relative or friend. One can read and hear pain in the essays on depression, cutting, and suicide. Consequently, no one felt the temptation to resume or begin self-destructive behavior. No one made a cutting comment like the one Isabelle's mother made upon hearing her daughter was suicidal: "That's just stupid." Indeed, no one made a judgmental comment about a classmate's essay. No matter how harrowing, each essay sought to find a solution to a conflict. The bleakest writings ended on a note of hopefulness, or at least a desire to move toward health and well-being.

The in-class paragraphs suggest that students can learn much from each other that they usually do not learn from their teacher. They learn that many of their classmates have struggled with serious problems, an insight that was not apparent at the beginning of the semester. They learn about the importance of destigmatizing mental illness and the value of psychotherapy and medication. They learn about the constructive and destructive ways in which classmates have responded to illness and adversity. They learn about the many reasons that motivate students to cut themselves or contemplate suicide, and they learn what helped these people regain control of their lives. They learn that sometimes their problems are worse than their classmates and that at other times their problems pale in comparison to others'. They learn that shame can be both a negative and positive force, making them wish to hide but also motivating them to restore their good name. They learn that reading and writing can be as helpful as therapy in heightening self-awareness and relieving anxiety. And they also learn the value of balancing two seemingly incompatible needs, the wish for self-acceptance and the desire for self-change.

The students were strangers to each other when the course began in late August, but by December they knew more about each other than they did about classmates in other courses. Sometimes they disclosed experiences they had not revealed to their parents or best friends. My experience with students who write about cutting is identical with Michelle Payne's with students who write about sexual abuse and eating disorders: "As I talked with students, a few of them told me they would rather their classmates knew about their experience than their friends at home or their family because their words would be less dangerous within the classroom" (16). The knowledge students acquired about each other arose from their writings and readings. Each class reaffirmed the importance of writing, of finding the right word to express complex thoughts and feelings. They discovered, if they had not already known, that writing is inherently affirmative, reminding us how we felt when we were happy or sad, hopeful or despairing, accepting or questioning. To cite but one example, Becky can reread her diary to recall how she felt when she wished to die, and should she become depressed again, she can reread the essay she wrote for our class, when she was in control of her life again. She and her classmates wrote survival stories, healing narratives in which they described overcoming illness and adversity. The talking cure and the writing cure are parallel endeavors, both leading to self-empowerment. Writing is, to use Becky's therapist's example, a kind of "worst case scenario," allowing us to imagine what to do in the face of catastrophe; writing also enables us to "do one nice thing" for ourselves every day, giving us the satisfaction of accomplishing something worthwhile. Wielding a pen instead of a knife is a way to make something real without leaving a permanent scar on the writer's body. Such writing—and reading—may lead to contamination, but more likely it will lead to inoculation, preparing us for the expected and unexpected challenges of the future.

"I Was Committing a Crime against My Body, against Women"

"Cutters are everywhere," Patty concludes in her section, and we end the book with Anna's writings to show how students can write healing narratives on self-injury. Anna was a member of Jeff's Love and Loss course taught in the spring of 2006. Most of the texts on the reading list equated loss with death, but the final book, *Empathic Teaching*, explored other types of loss: the loss of one's physical or psychological health, the breakup of a relationship, the crushing of one's self-esteem, or the fragmentation of one's family. The seventh and final essay asked students to discuss three of Jeff's former undergraduates in the book who had suffered a major loss in their lives. After writing about students who had suffered from depression, Anna added a postscript in which she revealed her own experience with mood disorders:

I have a history with both depression and empathy, and I wish to examine the two topics in relation to and in light of my history. The word "empathy" has a significant meaning in my life. If I played the word association game with "empathy," my mental response would consist of razor blades and therapists. I cannot remember the first time I heard the word spoken, but I do remember the meaning that Merriam-Webster provided me. It is a wordy definition, but it boils down to being able to understand what another person is going through without directly experiencing it for oneself. I have looked it up, without exaggeration, close to one hundred times. I know what it means, but perhaps one day I will stumble across a version of the dictionary that provides me with an illustration. Maybe it will look like a hug.

When I was thirteen years old, I bought a box of razors from

CVS. *They were not attached to plastic handles; they were exposed as if they were made for my purpose. I did not expect the clerk to sell them to me. I swore that my intentions were written across my forehead, visible through my parted bangs. I had never mutilated my body before, but I acted as though I was a professional. I cleaned my skin with rubbing alcohol before I carved into the outside of my right arm: E M P A T H Y. My teachers spotted it before my parents did. When I was forced to show my mother, she asked me what it meant.*

When I talked to my therapist, years later, about the first time I ever cut myself, he acted as though he [had] solved a puzzle that was so obvious; he was amazed that no one had seen the connection. "You practically spelled it out for them." There was no "practically" about it. I did, in fact, spell it out. He asked me if I thought I was empathic. I told him I was not certain. I told him a story of how, returning home from third grade, I came across a squirrel that had been hit by a car. I sat by it, at the side of the road, crying in hysterics as blood bubbled out of the split in its throat. I can say that I felt the squirrel's pain, or at least I could see the horror and sadness of it. I told him how an adult came over to me, told me he would take it to the vet, and for me to continue home. I knew he was not going to take it to the vet, but I left anyway. My therapist asked me, if I were to return to that event as the adult, would I be able to kill the squirrel. I could not answer; I could only cry. I knew that no matter what, I could not kill the squirrel.

I found something in Gabriella's essay that I could understand. I have been battling depression since I was thirteen. When I was thirteen years old, I hid in my bedroom and unplugged the power cord from my radio. I wrapped it around my neck and pulled each end as hard as I could. I woke up with a headache. I told my therapist about this event, ten years after it happened. He called it a "childhood suicide attempt," and I believe this is what provoked me to pay attention to the comment Gabriella made about just wanting to be kids again. Her sister and I were very much kids.

Angie's essay strikes me because of the value she places on outside support. She questions where she would be if she did not have such loving support from her family. I have a better relationship with my parents now than I had when I was growing up. I would say that I am close to my mother. We speak on the phone every day, and I visit my parents at least once or twice a week. I also have a loving husband who strives to make every day a perfect day, always asking what he can do to make things better. Because of how much they love me, because of how much they try, I cannot depend on them to make me happy. I see the irony in this. It does not escape me. Perhaps I should explain it. They love me. Why would I ever subject them, purposely, to my uncontrollable moods? Why would I let them believe that they can fix it all? Who needs that kind of pressure? My biggest fear is that they will grow to internalize my unstable moods, much in the way that Chloe internalized her mother's moods. Not only do I suffer from a mood disorder, but I have also dated someone with a mood disorder. I know how terrible it feels to believe that one word, one look, one hug should be able to change everything. It cannot.

So I am left with questions. Where does empathy stop? Is it merely an act of "bearing witness?" How can one bear witness without wanting to help, to offer advice, to diminish suffering? What draws the line between my third grade self, understanding and relating to the pain that squirrel was feeling, and the adult who took matters into his own hands? Who was right? Who was empathic? I keep seeking a definition, but all I am finding are words.

Jeff was intrigued by Anna's response to the suffering squirrel, which reminded him of one of his favorite quotes, from George Eliot's novel *Middlemarch*: "If we had a keen vision and feeling of all ordinary human life, it would be like hearing the grass grow or the squirrel's heart beat, and we should die of that roar which lies on the other side of silence. As it is, the quickest of us walks about well wadded with stupidity" (189). Anna's disclosure of self-cutting compelled Jeff to tell her after the semester ended that he and Patty were writing a book on the subject, and he asked her whether she would be willing to read their manuscript. She agreed. Upon Jeff's request, she then wrote the following essay in which she discusses the origins of her cutting, her responses to reading the manuscript and learning about other students who wrote about the experience, and the value of writing as a method of self-discovery and self-healing. There are many similarities between Patty's and Anna's stories, including a conflicted mother-daughter relationship, acute self-consciousness toward her changing body during puberty, adolescent depression, suicidal ideation, and social isolation, all of which led ultimately to cutting, which the latter describes as a "crime against my body, against women." Both imply that cutting provided them with much-needed psychological and, in Anna's case, physical relief. Both attempted to conceal their cutting from everyone, though Anna's teachers and parents later found out. There is also a major difference: whereas Patty stopped cutting herself when she was in high school and can hardly remember the person who harmed her body, Anna has stopped cutting only recently and regards her recovery as ongoing.

Like Patty, Anna cut herself without knowing why, and most of what she has learned about self-mutilation comes from reading. Also like Patty, she acknowledges the dangers of emotional contagion. She remarks near the end of her essay that she could easily fit the category of a reader "at risk" for contagion. Her writing represents a test case to see whether reading a book on cutting reawakens a former cutter's desire to return to self-mutilation. The answer for Anna is, happily, in the negative, a finding Jeff and Patty hope will be true for other readers as well:

> As I made my way through the first few chapters of your book, I couldn't help but feel as though I was flipping through my secret and private school of medical files. Reading about all of the problems encountered with inaccurate diagnoses, all those psychological terms for disorders, all those titles for crazies struck me with a terrible familiarity. I have been treated for nearly all of them: depression, post-traumatic stress disorder, borderline personality disorder, bipolar disorder. It made me wonder if therapists simply use a medical version of the barnyard speak and say.
>
> What caught my attention about so many of the essays and so

many of the interpretations was the recurring theme of the cutter learning the behavior from a peer, a television show, or a movie. I do not remember how I first learned of cutting. Trying to dig up such a memory would be as pointless as attempting to recall how I learned that sticking up my middle finger is offensive; I feel I have always known. Some people develop problems with alcohol or drugs by means of peer pressure. The behavior starts out as something friends are doing, something that might be cool before it spins out of control for an unlucky practitioner. Others are born with a gene of addiction; it's almost hereditary and biological. Maybe cutting is the same.

I believe that cutters share another similarity with people addicted to other harmful forms of self-medication: the process of quitting is life long. A cutter remembers the first cut the way an alcoholic remembers that first drink. And it is always romantic before it is dangerous. And it is always difficult to come to terms with. And who knows if six days from now, six weeks from now, or six years from now, something could happen that would make it all sensible again. The ladder's rung may break under pressure. A slip may be inevitable. For me, this process of healing, both figuratively and actually, happens one day at a time. Instead of tallying up the disappointments on my arms or legs, I'm letting the days go by unscarred. Day by day, I've racked up seven months. Cutting is almost in my past. The scars on my arms have been covered and the ones on my legs have faded to mere traces of lines, mostly indistinguishable. I was born with a strawberry birthmark on my right thigh. But the time I was thirteen, it had disappeared completely. Not even a trace remains, and I hope someday to say the same of my scars.

When I attempt to understand the motivation behind that first cut, I find myself first questioning the depression that inspired it. The connection between depression and self-mutilation is apparent, and I suppose it makes the most sense to uncover the story at the beginning. As I read more and more essays of personal battles with depression, I cannot help but wonder why I can't recall a single event that transformed me from a typical child into a markedly despondent adolescent, teenager, or young adult. Neither one of my parents suffered an untimely death. They are both still alive. I did not suffer through a divorce. My parents are happily married. I was not forced to attend college in an unfamiliar city. I was born and raised in Albany. I have lived with depression for so long that it is impossible to remember living without it. It is the birthmark that did not fade away.

I do not remember much from my childhood years. I remember that it was difficult to make friends at school or in the neighborhood. I remember that I spent most of my out-of-school time in the public library or riding my bike in solitude. I would pretend that it was not a bike, but a horse, and that my streets were not lined with economy priced apartments, but rows of apple trees and tulips. Other kids played freeze tag, hide and seek, or war, but I relied on my imagination as a sole comrade. I do not know if this sort of environment triggered depression or if depression kept me from playing with other children. I felt as different from my peers back then as I have at any other time in my life.

For children, life seems to change when they turn twelve or thirteen. Expectations are changing. Bodies are changing. Even schools change. I was taken out of public grade school and placed in a Catholic middle school. I was also diagnosed with scoliosis and fitted with a brace that I was instructed to wear twenty-three hours a day, removing it only to shower. I never kept up with the doctor's orders. The last thing I needed was a noticeable and patent difference between the other kids and me. The skirt I was required to wear to school would not fit comfortably around the fiberglass contraption, and no matter how many different ways I tried tucking in my shirt, the brace was always visible, mocking me with its prominence. Around this time is when I became self-conscious of my body. I hated that I was not as tall or as thin as other girls. I hated that my bangs insisted on a middle part. And most of all, I hated that my spine, my very center, was crooked. I hated that I had to be the one to inherit this from my mother, and I hated that my case was so much more severe than hers. With what I know now, I suppose it was just a matter of time before I unleashed my anger on what I believed was causing my grief: my body. At the time, I did not understand that I was mutilating myself. I did not understand that I was committing a crime against my body, against women. I was looking for proof, and I found so much more.

I was thirteen years old, and like so many women before me, I used a razor. But unlike other girls my age, I was not practicing the art of smooth and silky legs. I bought the razors from the CVS drugstore in my neighborhood. My first surprise came when I realized I could purchase razors that were not attached to plastic handles. Before searching the aisle, I was prepared to break apart the plastic protective case, using a pair of nail clippers, and pull apart the connected metal strip. I was delighted when I found a ten pack of loose razors. It seemed dangerous to me that a store would sell such an item. I wondered what other people were buying them for and concluded that it certainly was not for anything good, certainly not for shaving. My second surprise came when I purchased the razors without hassle, without questioning. I had expected I would have to explain that my father sent me to the store to pick these up for him. I did not have to explain anything. I simply had to pay.

I brought all the supplies I imagined I would need into my bedroom, and I sat with my back against the door, preventing a surprise intrusion. I cleaned the skin on my right arm with rubbing alcohol and, for safe measure, I also moistened the edge of the first razor. I did not start with a small line. I did not conduct a "test strip." It did not occur to me simply to draw a line. I scratched it out in long, thin letters: E M P A T H Y. The blood did not become visible until I was working on the A, and then, bead by bead, the letters lit up, connected like a strand of Christmas lights. I took my time with *the rest of the letters, stopping frequently to admire my work. I was dazed. I was amazed. I bled, just like everyone else. It was the proof I needed to see, the affirmation that I was made of flesh and crooked bone. What I did not expect, what I did not know I would find, was the relief. My mind seemed to stop spinning as I focused on the ways the blood changed from tiny beads to threatening drops. Physical relief followed my psychological relief. I felt as though my whole body was part of a tremendous exhale. This is where it began.*

Unlike some other cutters, I did not seek out or want any recognition or attention for what I had done. I wore sweaters at school and long shirts at home. I was careful never to push up my sleeves while the cuts were healing. I was not careful enough, however, and before the cuts had time to sufficiently drop their scabs, a teacher noticed the edge of "E" sticking out of my sleeve. My parents were called. When asked to explain myself, I tried to convey that I simply liked the word, and that I was curious about cuts. My parents did not push the matter, and they did not try to get me help. I would not have been a willing participant in therapy, even if my parents could have afforded it.

In the years that followed, I was simply more conscious about where I cut myself; the insides of my arms, the tops of my thighs, the bends in my elbows, my stomach: they were all fair game. I made sure to cut my forearms only in the winter, and I made sure not to make the same mistake again. I would keep my sleeves pulled down and limit my cuts. I no longer needed words; a few lines would do just fine, and the lines were easier to blame on a friend's cat or the wire binding of a notebook. It was not a constant or nightly ritual, but I turned to cutting the way a casual Catholic may turn to prayer. When all else failed, I would invoke the help of this higher power.

It was not until two years ago that I had a visit with my first therapist. My general doctor had started me on antidepressants. I had come to him for help, feeling as though I could not take any more, feeling as though I was slipping, looking for something to grasp on to. I confessed to him that I had been cutting myself. The first medication I was given was Cymbalta. My doctor told me that it could take a few weeks before I felt the full benefits of the drug, and to hang in there until then. I would see him in six weeks, and we would evaluate my progress. I did not make it six weeks. The drug was not working, not the way it was supposed to. I kept cutting. I even attempted to put cigarettes out on my wrists. My thoughts became more and more nonsensical and increasingly terrible until my urge for self-destruction reached its climax.

One night, my husband and I went to Home Depot. He was driving. I decided not to go in with him. He left the engine running, allowing me to stay warm despite the snow and wind outside. I sat in the passenger seat and focused on a black pickup truck parked a lane over. I imagined myself climbing into the driver's seat next to me, putting the car in drive, and just smashing, as hard and as fast as the car could go, right into the front of that truck. I was convinced I would do it out of curiosity, not out of any desire to die. I was curious to see if the airbags would employ. I was curious to see if the owner of the black truck would come running over, screaming about the mess I made. My husband came back before I unbuckled my seat belt. I did not reveal my thoughts to him.

Later that same night, I went to visit my friend at work. She was bartending, and it was a slow night. She wanted company. I thought nothing of taking the Valium that was left over from a series of visits to the dentist. I took a single dose of twenty mg (a dose, I later discovered, adequate for a patient entering surgery), and I drank a bottle of Tequila Rose, and had a series of shots. I did not tell my friend that I had taken the Valium. I did not tell my husband before I left him at our apartment. I simply wanted to relax. And when my friend was closing the bar, I did not tell her I was leaving. I simply began to walk. My husband found me on a side street by our house, propped up on someone's front steps, covered in wet snow. I did not answer him when he talked to me. He was afraid I was dying. He called an ambulance. I have a slight memory of someone in the ambulance asking me what I had, and I confessed to it all. He asked if I wanted to die, and I said no. I knew what would happen if I said "yes," even in the state I was in. I knew that I would be hospitalized. I knew that I would not be able to start school. The beginning of the semester was two days away. When I woke up, attached to tubes and monitors, I realized that the antidepressant was not working. I knew I needed something else. My doctor agreed. He stopped my medication and found me a therapist.

This was my first attempt at therapy, and I suppose I had a lifetime of stories to tell him. I probably would not have brought up the cutting if he had not asked. After all, I felt I was there because I kept trying to kill myself. But when we talked about my teen years, it was difficult not to bring up self-injury. It was only after we discussed the many different ways I had tried to hurt myself that I realized they were all connected; they were all dangerous.

Until my first visit with a therapist, I never spent much time analyzing why I chose the word "empathy" to carve into my arm. My therapist seemed to believe that I was marking myself with what I needed. He believed it was a cry for help, a cry for understanding, spelled out in clear letters. When we first discussed that possible motivation, it made sense. My therapist was convinced that my parents influenced much of my negative behavior and helped spread the seeds for the problems that continued to blossom in my teens and early adult years. While I do not completely disagree with the influence parents have, I cannot blame my problems on the way I was raised. My brothers and sister seem just fine.

I have always been emotional. I have always been sensitive. It's too easy for me to cry during movies, and sometimes even during commercials looking to raise funds for starving children or kids with leukemia. The first time I watched E.T., the television had to be turned off. I was a sobbing mess. Whenever it was time for me to go to sleep, I made sure all my stuffed animals had a spot on my twin size bed. I was certain that if one fell on the floor, it would feel isolated and alone, cast off from the rest of us. My mom told me I was born with a big heart, a big beautiful heart, and she was worried it would keep me in pain for most of my life.

I have not learned to distance myself from other people's pain. I have learned, instead, how to distance myself from other people. I have only a few close friends, and I tend to be mostly antisocial. I believe it's because the friends I do have are close to my heart, and when they ache, I also ache. I can hold only so much. I do not know how to listen, how to be available, without becoming concerned, without wanting to help fix [it] or just make it all better.

I believe that empathy is an extremely powerful concept. I have not yet learned how to harness that power and keep it under control. If I let myself feel something, be it my own emotion or what someone else is going through, it seems as though I feel it with every molecule of my body. Sometimes it's an overwhelmingly beautiful experience, but other times it can be overwhelmingly exhausting. If I knew where to draw the line, where compassion ends and emotional vulnerability begins, I cannot say I would heed it.

So while there may be some truth to what my first therapist said, while he may have been onto something when he decided I was seeking empathy from my parents, I like to think of the expression as a modified version of someone wearing a heart on his or her sleeve. I carved empathy into my arm.

My therapist discussed different theories of cutting, and I tried different medications. Some were just as scary as Cymbalta. One turned me narcoleptic, and I would fall asleep while smoking cigarettes. The blanket on my couch still bears the burn holes. One pill made my hands shake. Another made me stutter. They all made me gain weight. Ultimately, none seemed to work out. I lost hope. I stuck with therapy for as long as I could. But I eventually grew sick of listening to myself, and I grew sick of watching my therapist's *poker face. I became angry with him. I grew sick of the expensive co-pay and all the prescriptions that were lining the shelves of my bathroom. I had neither the patience nor the paychecks to support therapy. I decided to lie. I told him that the new medication was working and that life was wonderful. I told him that I could not think of anything that was missing, and that I did not even feel like the same girl who first introduced herself to him. He bought it all, with a self-assured grin, and told me he would make appointments with me on an "as needed basis."*

So now what? I do not feel let down. I did at first, but the more I replay the events in my head, the less upset I am. There is no wonder drug, not for me at least. I believe that there are benefits to therapy. I became aware of some of my own triggers and some of my own tell-tale signs that I could be heading toward an unpleasant place. I know when to seek help. I am not angry at my former therapist anymore. He helped me through the roughest patch, and now I suppose I am walking the path he cleared for me, or at least trying to. It's all day to day. And it's been seven months.

When I was offered the opportunity to read Cutting and the Pedagogy of Self-Disclosure, *I was excited. I had never read any factual work on cutting, and I had certainly never read any essays written about personal experience with cutting. I had watched films like* Girl, Interrupted *and* Secretary. *I even saw the* Beverly Hills 90210 *episode that featured a girl who turned to cutting to feel better about life. There was something that all these works were missing, something that I could not put my finger on.*

The missing piece was made abundantly clear in Cutting and the Pedagogy of Self-Disclosure. *Berman and Wallace address the issue of cutting with a seriousness that these other works only stumbled toward. The other works, even though they attempted to disclose the dangers of self-mutilation, never made it clear. What was so wrong about an attractive woman who bangs her wrists, ends up in a mental hospital, yet has a life-defining moment of realiza-*

tion? What's wrong with another attractive woman who finds the love of her life through cooperative abuse? What's wrong with yet another attractive guest who is visible only because of her cutting? Perhaps the focus was all wrong in these pieces. Perhaps there is not enough attention placed on the real dangers that accompany self-mutilation. Perhaps, because each piece was so cleanly wrapped up, any girl, any person under the power of suggestion would feel compelled to repeat what s/he witnessed.

Berman and Wallace have successfully applied a warning label to their work. There is a chance that readers may feel inspired by what they read, but the work does not glamorize or romanticize cutting, no matter how lovely the description of that "first cut." I read the entire manuscript, and at no point did I feel the need to delve back into the dark world of self-mutilation. Perhaps I could easily fit the category of readers at risk. If this is the case, it means so much more that I did not feel the need to cut myself because of what I read. What I also find important in the book is the information about cutting, motivations behind cutting, and the inner turmoil to which so many cutters confess. Maybe someone will read it and not be inspired to cut, but instead become painfully aware of what the scratches on a friend's arm really mean. Cutting, for myself and for many others, is a step on a dark road that has a potentially very dark end.

I believe in the power of the contagion effect. I have read enough examples that prove it to be true and dangerous. The question, in my opinion, is not whether or not something is addressed. The question is whether or not it is addressed with the seriousness it deserves. In my opinion, Cutting and the Pedagogy of Self-Disclosure is successful in its approach to the topic of cutting. I found that cutting was treated seriously and without the glamor that so often is applied to it.

Until my class with Jeff, I had never attempted to write about cutting. I never wrote a story or a journal entry about it, and I *certainly had never written an essay about it. In many of the class-room responses, when students were asked to discuss what it was like to write on a personal example of love and loss, many claimed that words seemed to pour from them. Pages are filled at breakneck speed. The essays tend to be cathartic and painfully honest. I agree with this.*

I never mentioned cutting in any of the earlier assigned essays. My only reference to cutting appeared on the last essay, which I knew would not be returned until after the end of the semester. There was safety in this, even though Jeff reads essays anonymously and only with permission. Each student would pay a visit to Jeff's office to pick up the essay. There were questions I asked in my paper, and I was curious to see how Jeff would address them. Talking to Jeff in his office seemed much safer than asking the questions in class, perhaps because it was one of the larger English courses I have taken.

When asked to elaborate on my first cutting experience, I was surprised at how many pages I had filled. These were thoughts, important thoughts, that had never found their way to paper and perhaps never would have. There is an art to essay writing, and when that art is applied to memories and experiences, sometimes the revelations are shocking. Sometimes it hurts to see my feelings, ideas, and emotions put in black and white, but most of the time it helps. It's as though I am going through my desk, cleaning out old drawers and coming across pictures or letters I have not seen in years. Like some nostalgia, it is a good hurt.

APPENDIX

English 447: The Historical Imagination
English 581: Models of History in Literary Criticism
Summer 2003
Jeffrey Berman
Call number: 2075/2080 Monday, Wednesday 6:00–9:30 p.m.
Required Books:

Freud	*Fragment of an Analysis of a Case of Hysteria (Dora)*
Chopin	*The Awakening*
Plath	*The Bell Jar*
Nabokov	*Lolita*
Thomas	*The White Hotel*
Berman	*Surviving Literary Suicide*

June 23	Introduction
June 25	*Dora*
June 30	*Dora*; chap. 1 in *Surviving Literary Suicide*
July 2	*The Awakening*
July 7	*The Awakening*; chap.2 in *S.L.S.*
July 9	*The Bell Jar*
July 14	*The Bell Jar*; chap. 5 in *S.L.S.*
July 16	*Lolita*
July 21	*Lolita*
July 23	*The White Hotel*
July 28	*The White Hotel*; chap. 8 in *S.L.S.*
July 30	Final Exam

Description: "The Historical Imagination" investigates the relationship between history and literature and the meaning of the concept of literary history. This summer we will focus on "The Age of Freud." We will read stories that explore the relationship between history and hysteria: the complex ways in which history, culture, and psychology contribute to mental illness. These stories simultaneously reflect and challenge historical, cultural, and psychological assumptions of mental illness. We will also discuss the genre of the psychiatric (or, in the case of *Lolita*, the antipsychiatric) novel. I will emphasize psychoanalytic and feminist approaches to literature, but you may use other approaches.

Requirements for undergraduates are a ten-page essay (typed, double-spaced), five reader-response diaries, and a final exam; requirements for graduate students are a fifteen-page essay, five reader-response diaries, a class presentation, and a final exam. Your essay should be on one or at most two books on the reading list and is due no later than the second class on which we discuss the book(s). (An exception is the essay on *Dora*, which is due on July 2). Thus, an essay on *The Awakening* is due on July 7; an essay on *The Bell Jar* is due on July 14; an essay on *Lolita* is due on July 21; and an essay on *The White Hotel* is due on July 28. A paper on *Surviving Literary Suicide* is due on July 28. A paper on two books is due on the second class on which we discuss the second text. (Essays on *The Awakening* or *The Bell Jar* should reveal that you have read my discussions of these novels in *Surviving Literary Suicide*.) Late papers will not be accepted.

Important: regardless of the book(s) you write on, I want you to agree with two statements that I made in class (or in *Surviving Literary Suicide*) and to disagree with two other statements I made in class (or in *Surviving Literary Suicide*). This will demonstrate to me that you have been listening attentively in class.

The reader-response diaries should focus on how you felt about each of the books in the course; they should be written on five of the six books, including *Surviving Literary Suicide*. You don't need to write a diary on the book on which you are writing your formal essay. If your formal essay focuses on two books, then you need to write a diary on only one of the two. The diaries should be 2 pages long, typed, double-spaced. They are due at the same time the formal essay is due. (See the above schedule for the due date of the formal essay). The diary on *Surviving Literary Suicide* is due on July 28; at that time, you will need to turn in the other four diaries, all of which I will have presumably read. The diaries should focus on your responses to the books. Each diary needs to convince me that you have read that work carefully. The diary can also refer to our class discussions of that particular story: what you liked and disliked about our discussion. I would like to read about four diaries aloud (always anonymously) before returning them to you the next class, but if you do not want me to read your diary aloud, simply write the word "no" at the top of the diary. I will not be grading each diary as I receive it, but on July 28 I will collect all the diaries and assign a grade to them. I will not grade your diaries on the degree of self-disclosure, nor on whether I read any of them aloud; rather, I will grade the diaries on their insights and quality of writing. I will return the diaries to you on July 30, the date of the final exam. The formal essay is worth 50 percent of the final grade, the reader-response diaries 25 percent and the final exam 25 percent.

Attendance is crucial. If you miss more than two classes, you will not receive credit for the course. I will take attendance every class: please call or email me in advance if you must miss a class. Office: HU 348; office phone: 442-4084; home phone: 355-4760 email address: jberman@albany.edu.

Office Hours: Monday, Wednesday: 12:00–12:30; 5:30–6:00.

Reading Empathically

Any course that encourages personal writing and self-disclosure runs the risk of heightening students' vulnerability. The more one self-discloses, the more one acknowledges painful and shameful feelings and experiences that generally remain hidden from view. Writing about these feelings and experiences is an act of courage and trust, and it requires a classroom situation in which all of us strive to read as empathically as possible.

Empathy is a translation of the German word *Einfuhlung*, which was used at the end of the nineteenth century to signify a reader's "feeling into" or projection into a text. To empathize means to enter into another person's point of view in order to understand his or her inner life. Empathy is similar to sympathy but implies a more active and intense process. Empathy is a merging with another person without the loss of one's own identity. Empathy thus implies an awareness of both self and other.

Empathy is an important concept in psychotherapy, for it allows a therapist to understand a patient. I believe that empathy is no less important in education, for it enables teachers and students to understand and learn from each other. Empathy helps us to intuit each other's *feelings*, which tend to be ignored or dismissed in classroom discussions of literature or writing.

When responding to an essay, let's try to discuss what we like about it and offer constructive suggestions for improvement. There is an art to empathic reading, listening, and speaking, and I hope that we can all develop this ability. Let's not criticize the author's feelings or value judgments. At the same time, we should be able to disagree with an essay's conclusions: we do not all feel or think the same way. If you find an essay to be moving, try to suggest why. If you say that you "like" an essay, I will ask you to tell us specifically what you like about it. The more specific you are in your comments, the more helpful you will be to the writer.

Since even the best essays are seldom written perfectly, I will always ask you to find a word or a sentence that can be strengthened through revision. The mark of the good writer is the willingness to revise.

Remember that on certain topics you have the option to remain anonymous when it is your turn to bring copies of your essay to class. (I will tell you in advance when you can exercise this option.) If you do exercise this option, please write "Anonymous" at the top of the essay and indicate whether you wish me to read it aloud. (There will be no class discussion of essays that I read anonymously.) I hope that you will use this option only when you feel it is necessary.

WORKS CITED

Ainsworth, M. D. S. "John Bowlby (1907–1990): Obituary." *American Psychologist* 47 (1992).

Anderson, Charles, and Marian MacCurdy. *Writing and Healing: Toward an Informed Practice.* Urbana, Ill.: NCTE, 2000.

Baker, Carlos. *Ernest Hemingway: A Life Story.* New York: Bantam, 1970.

Bass, Thomas. *Vietnamerica.* New York: Soho, 1996.

Berger, John. *Ways of Seeing.* New York: Penguin, 1977.

Berman, Jeffrey. *Diaries to an English Professor.* Amherst: University of Massachusetts Press, 1994.

———. *Dying to Teach: A Memoir of Love, Loss, and Learning.* Albany: State University of New York Press, 2007.

———. *Empathic Teaching: Education for Life.* Amherst: University of Massachusetts Press, 2004.

———. "'The Grief That Does Not Speak': Suicide, Mourning, and Psychoanalytic Training." In *Self-Analysis in Literary Study: Exploring Hidden Agendas,* edited by Daniel Rancour-Laferriere, 35–54. New York: New York University Press, 1994.

———. *Narcissism and the Novel.* New York: New York University Press, 1990.

———. *Risky Writing: Self-Disclosure and Self-Transformation in the Classroom.* Amherst: University of Massachusetts Press, 2001.

———. *Surviving Literary Suicide.* Amherst: University of Massachusetts Press, 1999.

———. *The Talking Cure: Literary Representations of Psychoanalysis.* New York: New York University Press, 1985.

Berryman, John. *The Dream Songs.* New York: Farrar, Straus and Giroux, 1977.

Blum, Virginia. *Flesh Wounds: The Culture of Cosmetic Surgery.* Berkeley: University of California Press, 2003.

Bowlby, John. *Attachment and Loss.* 3 vols. New York: Basic Books, 1969–80.

Bracher, Mark. *Radical Pedagogy: Identity, Generativity, and Social Transformation.* New York: Palgrave Macmillan, 2006.

Brian, Denis. *The True Gen: An Intimate Portrait of Ernest Hemingway by Those Who Knew Him*. New York: Grove Press, 1988.

Broucek, Francis. *Shame and the Self*. New York: Guilford Press, 1991.

Chekhov, Anton. "Gooseberries." In *The Portable Chekhov*, edited by Avraham Yarmolinksy. New York: Viking, 1947.

"Colum Cille Cross Symbolism." www.celtarts.com/colum.htm.

Conterio, Karen, and Wendy Lader. *Bodily Harm*. New York: Hyperion, 1998.

Deletiner, Carole. "Crossing Lines." *College English* 54 (1992): 809–17.

Durkheim, Emile. *Suicide*. Translated by John Spaulding and George Simpson. New York: Free Press, 1968.

Elbow, Peter. "Bringing the Rhetoric of Assent and the Believing Game Together—And into the Classroom." *College English* 67 (2005): 388–99.

Eliot, George. *Middlemarch*. London: Zodiac Press, 1967.

Engelgau, Donna. *Discovery Health Channel*. http://health.discovery.com/ premiers/cutters/article.com. Page no longer available.

Erikson, Erik. *Childhood and Society*. 2nd ed. New York: Norton, 1963.

Farber, Sharon Klayman. *When the Body Is the Target*. Northvale, N.J.: Jason Aronson, 2000.

Favazza, Armando R. *Bodies under Siege: Self-Mutilation in Culture and Psychiatry*. Baltimore: Johns Hopkins University Press, 1987.

Fitzgerald, F. Scott. *The Crack-Up*. New York: New Directions, 1945.

Forrest, Emma. *Thin Skin*. New York: MTV Books/Pocket Books, 2001.

Foucault, Michel. *The History of Sexuality*. Vol. 1, *An Introduction*. Translated by Robert Hurley. New York: Vintage, 1978.

Fulkerson, Richard. "Composition at the Turn of the Twenty-First Century." *College Composition and Communication* 56:4 (June 2005): 654–87.

Freud, Sigmund. *Fragment of an Analysis of a Case of Hysteria*. Vol. 7 of *The Standard Edition of the Complete Psychological Works of Sigmund Freud*. Translated by James Strachey. London: Hogarth Press, 1953.

———. *New Introductory Lectures on Psycho-Analysis*. Vol. 22 of *The Standard Edition of the Complete Psychological Works of Sigmund Freud*. Translated by James Strachey. London: Hogarth Press, 1964.

———. *The Psychopathology of Everyday Life*. Vol. 6 of *The Standard Edition of the Complete Psychological Works of Sigmund Freud*. Translated by James Strachey. London: Hogarth Press, 1960.

Fromm-Reichmann, Frieda. *Principles of Intensive Psychotherapy*. Chicago: University of Chicago Press, 1950.

———. *Psychoanalysis and Psychotherapy*. Edited by Dexter Bullard. Chicago: University of Chicago Press, 1959.

Gaynor, Mitchell. *Sounds of Healing*. New York: Broadway Books, 1999.

Gilbert, Paul. "What Is Shame? Some Core Issues and Controversies." In *Shame: Interpersonal Behavior, Psychopathology, and Culture*, edited by Paul Gilbert and Bernice Andrews, 3–38. New York: Oxford University Press, 1998.

Gilligan, Carol. *In a Different Voice*. Cambridge: Harvard University Press, 1993.

Goffman, Erving. *Stigma: Notes on the Management of Spoiled Identity*. Englewood Cliffs, N.J.: Prentice-Hall, 1963.

Goleman, Daniel. *Emotional Intelligence*. New York: Bantam Books, 1995.

Gould, Madelyn, David Shaffer, and Marjorie Kleinman. "The Impact of Suicide in Television Movies: Replication and Commentary." *Suicide and Life-Threatening Behavior* 18 (1988): 90–99.

Greenberg, Joanne [Hannah Green, pseud.]. *I Never Promised You a Rose Garden*. New York: Signet, 1964.

Hacking, Ian. *The Social Construction of What?* Cambridge: Harvard University Press, 1999.

Hartman, Geoffrey. *Scars of the Spirit: The Struggle against Inauthenticity*. New York: Palgrave Macmillan, 2004.

Hatfield, Elaine, John Cacioppo, and Richard Rapson. *Emotional Contagion*. Cambridge: Cambridge University Press, 1994.

"Highlights of Women's Earnings, 2002." AFL-CIO. www.aflcio.org/issues politics/women/equalpay/highlights. Page no longer available.

Hill, Carolyn Ericksen. *Writing from the Margins: Power and Pedagogy for Teachers of Composition*. New York : Oxford University Press, 1990.

Holmes, Jeremy. *Attachment, Intimacy, Autonomy*. Northvale, N.J.: Jason Aronson, 1996.

Hood, Carra Leah. "Lying in Writing or the Vicissitudes of Testimony." *Composition Forum* 14 (2003): 133–50.

Hyman, Jane Wegscheider. *Women Living with Self-Injury*. Philadelphia: Temple University Press, 1999.

"Interview with Pat McCormick." Front Street Books. www.frontstreetbooks .com/apage/maintcut.html. Page no longer available.

Ivanoff, Andre, Marsha Linehan, and Milton Brown. "Dialectical Behavior Therapy for Impulsive Self-Injurious Behaviors." In *Self-Injurious Behaviors: Assessment and Treatment*, edited by Daphne Simeon and Eric Hollander, 149–74. Washington, D.C.: American Psychiatric Press, 2001.

Jamison, Kay Redfield. *Night Falls Fast: Understanding Suicide*. New York: Knopf, 1999.

Jay, Gregory. "The Subject of Pedagogy: Lessons in Psychoanalysis and Politics." *College English* 49 (1987): 785–800.

Jelinek, Elfriede. *The Piano Teacher*. Translated by Joachim Neugroschel. London: Serpent's Tail, 1999.

Kafka, Franz. *The Penal Colony: Stories and Short Pieces*. Translated by Willa and Edwin Muir. New York: Schocken, 1974.

Kaplan, Louise. *Female Perversions*. New York: Doubleday, 1991.

Kaysen, Susanna. *Girl, Interrupted*. New York: Random House, 1993.

Keltner, Dacher, and LeeAnne Harker. "The Forms and Functions of the Nonverbal Signal of Shame." In *Shame: Interpersonal Behavior, Psychopathology, and Culture*, edited by Paul Gilbert and Bernice Andrews, 78–98. New York: Oxford University Press, 1998.

Kettlewell, Caroline. *Skin Game*. New York: St. Martin's Press, 1999.

Kesey, Ken. *One Flew over the Cuckoo's Nest*. New York: Viking Press, 1962.

Kohut, Heinz. "Forms and Transformations of Narcissism." *Journal of the American Psychoanalytic Association* 14 (1966): 243–72.

Koren, Yehuda, and Eilat Negev. *Lover of Unreason: Assia Wevill, Sylvia Plath's Rival and Ted Hughes' Doomed Love*. New York: Carroll and Graf, 2006.

Krims, Marvin. *The Mind according to Shakespeare*. Westport, CT: Greenwood Press, 2006.

LaCapra, Dominick. *Writing History, Writing Trauma*. Baltimore: Johns Hopkins University Press, 2001.

Levenkron, Steven. *Cutting*. New York: W. W. Norton, 1998.

Leys, Ruth. *Trauma: A Genealogy*. Chicago: University of Chicago Press, 2000.

Linehan, Marsha. "Validation and Psychotherapy." In *Empathy Reconsidered: New Directions in Psychotherapy*, edited by Arthur Bohart and Leslie Greenberg, 353–92. Washington, D.C.: American Psychological Association, 1997.

Lynd, Helen Merrell. *On Shame and the Search for Identity*. New York: Science Editions, 1961.

Macdonald, James. "Disclosing Shame." In *Shame: Interpersonal Behavior, Psychopathology, and Culture*, edited by Paul Gilbert and Bernice Andrews, 141–57. New York: Oxford University Press, 1998.

MacKinnon, Catharine A. *Feminism Unmodified: Discourses on Life and Law*. Cambridge: Harvard University Press, 1987.

Marcia, James. "Empathy and Psychotherapy." In *Empathy and Its Development*, edited by Nancy Eisenberg and Janet Strayer, 81–102. Cambridge: Cambridge University Press, 1987.

Marcus, Jane. "Art and Anger." *Feminist Studies* 4 (1978): 69–98.

McCormick, Patricia. *Cut*. New York: Scholastic, 2000.

Mellow, James. *Hemingway: A Life without Consequences*. Boston: Houghton Mifflin, 1992.

Menninger, Karl. *Man against Himself.* New York: Harcourt, Brace and World, 1938.

Meyers, Jeffrey. *Hemingway: A Biography.* New York: Harper and Row, 1985.

Middlebrook, Diane. *Anne Sexton: A Biography.* Boston: Houghton Mifflin, 1992.

Miller, Alice. *Prisoners of Childhood.* Trans. Ruth Ward. New York: Basic Books, 1981.

Morris, David. *The Culture of Pain.* Berkeley: University of California Press, 1991.

Nabokov, Vladimir. *Lolita.* New York: Vintage, 1989.

Nafisi, Azar. *Reading Lolita in Tehran.* New York: Random House, 2003.

Payne, Michelle. *Bodily Discourses: When Students Write about Abuse and Eating Disorders.* Portsmouth, N.H.: Boynton/Cook, 2000.

Pennebaker, James. *Opening Up.* New York: Guilford Press, 1997.

Pennebaker, James, and M. E. Francis. *Linguistic Inquiry and Word Count: LIWC.* Mahwah, N.J.: Erlbaum, 1999.

Pfeiffer, Kathleen. "Comment and Response." *College English* 55 (1993): 669–71.

Phillips, David. "The Influence of Suggestion on Suicide: Substantive and Theoretical Implications of the Werther Effect." *American Sociological Review* 39 (1974): 340–54. Rpt. in *Essential Papers on Suicide,* edited by John Maltsberger and Mark Goldblatt, 290–313. New York: New York University Press, 1996.

Phillips, David, and Lundie Carstensen. "The Effect of Suicide Stories on Various Demographic Groups, 1968–1985." *Suicide and Life-Threatening Behavior* 18 (1988): 100–114.

Pickering, George. *Creative Malady.* New York: Delta, 1976.

Pipher, Mary. *Reviving Ophelia: Saving the Selves of Adolescent Girls.* New York: Ballantine Books, 1994.

Plath, Sylvia. *Collected Poems.* Edited by Ted Hughes. New York: HarperPerennial, 1992.

Rancour-Laferriere, Daniel, editor. *Self-Analysis in Literary Study: Exploring Hidden Agendas.* New York: New York University Press, 1994.

Reik, Theodor. *Listening with the Third Ear.* New York: Farrar, Straus, 1949.

Rogers, Carl. *Freedom to Learn.* Columbus, Ohio: Charles E. Merrill, 1969.

———. *A Way of Being.* Boston: Houghton Mifflin, 1980.

Salinger, J. D. *The Catcher in the Rye.* New York: Bantam, 1986.

"Scar Tissue." The Red Hot Chili Peppers. *Californication.* Warner Brothers, 1999.

Sexton, Anne. *The Complete Poems.* Boston: Houghton Mifflin, 1981.

Showalter, Elaine. *Teaching Literature.* Malden, Mass.: Blackwell, 2003.

Skorczewski, Dawn. *Teaching One Moment at a Time.* Amherst: University of Massachusetts Press, 2005.

Solomon, Andrew. *The Noonday Demon: An Atlas of Depression.* New York: Touchstone, 2001.

Stefl, Ronni S. "Self-Injurious Behavior: Examination of Causation and Treatment." http://aet.cup.edu/~edp656/stefl/sib.htm (accessed 19 Feb. 2004).

Steinhauer, Harry. Introduction to *The Sufferings of Young Werther,* by Johann Wolfgang von Goethe. Edited and translated by Harry Steinhauer. New York: Bantam Dual-Language Book, 1962.

Stoehr, Shelley. *Crosses.* Lincoln, Neb.: iUniverse, 1991.

Strong, Marilee. *A Bright Red Scream.* New York: Viking Penguin Putnam, 1998.

Styron, William. *Darkness Visible.* New York: Random House, 1990.

Tannen. Deborah. *The Argument Culture.* New York: Random House, 1998.

Tedeschi, Richard, Crystal Park, and Lawrence Calhoun, editors. *Posttraumatic Growth: Positive Changes in the Aftermath of Crisis.* Mahway, N.J.: Lawrence Erlbaum, 1998.

Todd, Sharon. *Learning from the Other.* Albany: State University of New York Press, 2003.

Turner, Scott. "Blood Tests Can Identify Children with Strep-Related Behavior Disorder." *Brown University News Bureau* 8 (1997): 1–3.

Turner, V. J. *Secret Scars: Uncovering and Understanding the Addiction of Self-Injury.* Center City, Minn.: Hazelden, 2002.

Turp, Maggie. *Hidden Self-Harm: Narratives from Psychotherapy.* London: Jessica Kingsley, 2003.

"Understanding the Female Consumer: A North American Perspective." Comp. Brock University. *Marketing in a Global Economy Proceedings.* 2000: 180–92. Yahoo. Keyword: female consumers.

Valentis, Mary, and Anne Devane. *Female Rage.* New York: Carol Southern Books, 1994.

Vonnegut, Kurt. *A Man without a Country.* New York: Seven Stories Press, 2005.

Whitlock, Janis, John Eckenrode, and Daniel Silverman. "Self-Injurious Behaviors in a College Population." *Pediatrics* 117 (June 2006): 1939–48.

Wilde, Oscar. *The Picture of Dorian Gray.* Edited by Isabel Murray. Oxford: Oxford University Press, 1974; rpt., 1982.

Winkler, Martin. "Prevalence of Cutting, Self-Mutilation and Self-Harm among Teenagers." http://web4health.info/en/answers/border-selfharm-prev.htm.

Wurtzel, Elizabeth. *Prozac Nation.* Boston: Houghton Mifflin, 1994.

"Young Adults' Consumption Behavior." Datamonitor Global Information Systems. www.the-infoshop.com/study/dc13290_y_adults_behavior.html.

Young, Allan. "Bodily Memory and Traumatic Memory." In *Tense Past: Cultural Essays in Trauma and Memory,* edited by Paul Antze and Michael Lambek, 89–102. New York: Routledge, 1996.

INDEX